FRACTURED LIGHT

BOOK ONE IN THE FRACTURED LIGHT TRILOGY

NICK COOK

VOICE FROM THE CLOUDS

ABOUT THE AUTHOR

Somewhere back in the mists of time, Nick was born in the great sprawling metropolis of London. He grew up in a family where art was always a huge influence. Tapping into this, Nick finished college with a fine art degree tucked into his back pocket. Faced with the prospect of actually trying to make a living from his talents, he plunged into the emerging video game industry back in the eighties. It was the start of a long career and he produced graphics for many of the top-selling games on the early home computers, including *Aliens* and *Enduro Racer*. Those pioneering games may look crude now, but back then they were considered to be cutting edge. As the industry exploded into the one we know today, Nick's career went supernova. He worked on titles such as *X-Com*, and set up two studios, which produced

Warzone 2100 and the *Conflict: Desert Storm* series. He has around forty published titles to his name.

As great as the video game industry is, a little voice kept nagging inside Nick's head, and at the end of 2006 he was finally ready to pursue his other passion as a full-time career: writing. Many years later, he completed his first trilogy, *Cloud Riders*. And the rest, as they say, is history.

Nick has many interests, from space exploration and astronomy to travelling the world. He has flown light aircraft and microlights, an experience he used as research for *Cloud Riders*. He's always loved to cook, but then you'd expect it with his surname. His writing in many ways reflects his own curiosity about the world around him. He loves to let his imagination run riot to pose the question: *What if?*

ALSO BY NICK COOK

Prequel to the Multiverse Chronicles

The Earth Song Series (The Multiverse Chronicles)

The Fractured Light Trilogy (The Multiverse Chronicles)

THE SIGNAL

Before you begin **Earth Song**, you can download the novella **The Signal**, the prequel to the **Multiverse Chronicles**, for **free.** The story features Lauren Stelleck from **Earth Song**, a radio telescope operator at Jodrell Bank who's dropped into an extraordinary first contact situation. To get your free copy right now, sign up to Nick Cook's free newsletter here:

https://www.subscribepage.com/s6z3s9_copy

For Frank Herbert, Isaac Asimov and Arthur C. Clarke, for fuelling the furnace of my imagination and my lifelong love affair with science and science fiction.

'Reality is merely an illusion, albeit a very persistent one.'
Albert Einstein

CHAPTER ONE

MAYBE IF I'D known how that night would impact my life and the lives of everyone I knew – not to mention the fate of the entire world – I would have turned round and headed straight back to college. Maybe I would have kept my head down, got on with my studies, and tried my best to avoid any involvement. Or maybe, and much more likely, I would have done exactly what I did...

The winter rain had already soaked through my jeans, making the cold wet denim stick to my legs. I trudged home from my late-night study session at college along the quiet side street, feet sending ripples out across the flooded pavement. Christmas tree lights reflected on the windows of several of the houses as I passed them. Everyone else seemed to have taken the warnings seriously and were already tucked up safely inside their homes from the disaster that might have their name on it.

Of course, the Stoneham Stalker as he – presumably it was a he – was becoming known might also have something to do with the lack of people out and about. However, I, the odd one out like always, had my whole attention focused skywards on the rolling clouds and hint of stars in the breaks in between.

And I'd been counting the days down to tonight for weeks, despite my growing sense of foreboding.

The news reports had been filled with hardly anything else: Varuna, the rogue Indian weather satellite that had gone out of control and was headed for an uncontrolled crash-landing somewhere over England tonight. The erratic flight of the satellite hadn't helped the panic either, with the authorities, and even NASA, having no idea of exactly when or where the satellite would make eventual landfall. The emergency services had already been mobilised by the new prime minister, Alexander Langton, a man who'd seized power in a coup that made a political thriller look like a Disney movie complete with fluffy animals. But he'd made all the right reassuring noises over the last week, saying that statistically the satellite would probably crash harmlessly somewhere in an unpopulated part of the countryside.

Thanks to the disaster-movie-type reporting by the tabloids – including the now infamous 'We Are All Going to Die!' headline – people's apocalypse paranoia had been well and truly fuelled. Supermarket shelves had been stripped bare, even including Christmas crackers and the mixed nuts that normally no one bothered with. Now everyone was holding their breath for the metal hammer about to be dropped by the sky gods on to their heads.

It seemed even I wasn't immune. For the last five days, I'd had the same recurring dream about the satellite rushing towards me. As my flesh had been boiled away by the impact blast I'd woken in a cold sweat. Those twenty-four-hour news channels with their constant analysis about the potential huge loss of life had a lot to answer for.

Despite that, and unlike most of the population, my uncle

Allan and I could both see past the mass hysteria, and rather than prep for the end of the world we had made other plans for tonight.

I quickened my pace for Celestial Skies, the telescope shop that Allan owned and ran, and which we lived over in our cramped flat. We'd already agreed to head up to Ravens Hill, with its unrestricted views of the sky, to try to spot the satellite burning up on its return later tonight. This was going to be a once-in-a-lifetime opportunity and I wasn't going to miss the chance of a brief glimpse of the crashing satellite, however awful the weather.

A tell-tale hacking cough snagged my ears and my attention snapped back to the dreary, rain-soaked world around me.

Gavin. I'd recognise his asthma cigarette-fuelled cough anywhere.

I pulled my hoody up over my head, a vague attempt at a thin disguise. I could certainly do without any fresh agro from him. Maybe I'd get lucky and he wouldn't notice me. After all, melting into the background was something I'd had enough practice in. But as I approached the corner my heart began to race and adrenalin made my blood sing. Under the glow of the streetlight ahead I saw a curl of cigarette smoke rise from the broadest and tallest of the group.

The unmistakable profile of Gavin.

Then I spotted Chloe hanging back from the group, sitting on a brick wall sheltering from the rain under a tree. She had her red Beat headphones on, denim jacket wrapped round her, face glowing like a ghost's from the illumination of her trademark laptop that was balanced on her lap. The cool college geek who could hack her grades and who'd once been my best friend... And as much I tried to convince myself otherwise there was still a Chloe-shaped hole in my life.

Chloe watched Gavin over the top of her laptop screen with

the narrow-eyed expression of a wary cat, her gaze flicking past him towards the kid in the middle of the group, who must have been all of twelve.

Gavin was famed for this sort of thing – hooking youngsters in to do his dirty work. The rumour going around town was that his gang had been responsible for the mini crime wave that had hit Stoneham over the last year, with Gavin pulling all the strings.

The group had knotted itself around a monstrous white BMW four-by-four that shouted new and expensive. The gang kept glancing up and down the street. It didn't take a genius to work out what was about to happen next.

My mind raced ahead. If Gavin spotted me doubling back the way I'd come, he'd know he'd psyched me. And weakness of any kind was something he fed on. Nope, that wasn't an option. I stepped out, tension spreading across my shoulders. But Gavin and his gang were so intent on what they were doing none of them even cast a glance in my direction. Not wanting to press my luck, I got ready to cross the street to skirt past the group. Gavin pushed a hammer into the boy's hand and shoved him towards the car. The way the boy looked at him pinched at me, his face uncertain; a line was about to be crossed that would change the rest of his life for ever...

Don't, Jake...

I glanced back along the street. There was no one else. Who'd stop this if I walked past and pretended I hadn't seen anything? That was what most people would do. I didn't even know the boy, so why was I even thinking about doing something so insane?

Just don't...

And then Chloe was on her feet, headphones off, shaking her head at Gavin, hand cradled protectively over the boy's shoulder. No one ever did this...ever. Disagreeing with Gavin was something you just didn't do, even if you were his girlfriend.

The speed of Gavin's reaction was shocking: the uncaged fury of a wild animal released and all focused on Chloe. He slapped her so hard across the side of the face that it sent her laptop flying from her hand and skittering away over the puddle-soaked pavements, its screen going dark. And I knew, everyone knew, that laptop was Chloe's whole world.

But Chloe didn't back away; she didn't even waste a glance at her broken laptop. Instead she narrowed her cat-like gaze on Gavin. The boy stared between them as if they were his parents having a fight. He glanced down at the hammer in his hand gleaming under the lamplight. The street theatre was building to its grand finale.

A chink of light appeared in one of the windows opposite, but the curtain settled again. Probably a cat fussing with them.

Gavin's mouth had become a tight line and he pulled the boy away from Chloe and shoved him towards the car.

'Stop!' I shouted, surprising even myself.

Gavin noticed me for the first time and a slow thin smile filled his face, like a wolf spotting its prey. I could handle his hate for me, was well used to it, but it was the unreadable look that Chloe gave me that pierced my emotional armour like nothing else could.

My heart accelerated way beyond max, but I was committed.

'Let him go, Gavin,' I called out.

'Well, miracles of miracles – Jake Stevens, the mute, can actually speak,' Gavin replied.

Around him his gang laughed like a pack of hyenas sharing a particularly bad joke.

But the boy's eyes hung on to mine, his face pleading. I'd no choice. Not really.

As if I was on some sort of autopilot, I started to speed up. I was less than ten paces away when Gavin bent down and whispered into the lad's ear. The boy's expression hollowed out and he drew the hammer back.

Chloe tried to reach the boy but one of the gang blocked her way, a blond razor-cut guy, all smirks and swagger.

I was running, but the young lad was already swinging the hammer forward. Time seemed to slow as it smashed into the BMW's window, shattering it into a rainstorm of glass. The alarm's cry barked out into the night and the hazard lights started to flash.

I reached the boy and pulled him round to look at me, no longer caring about the consequences. 'Why?'

He gestured towards Gavin, face pale. 'He said he'd break my arm if I didn't.'

I swivelled round to pierce Gavin with my stare, but his gang had already surrounded me. Chloe's mouth twisted as she watched me with those crystal blue eyes that always seemed to judge. I stood before them, picked out by the stage-like spotlight of the lamp post.

Gavin sneered. 'You shouldn't be sticking your nose into my business, Stevens, not if you don't want to have it carved off.'

My shoulders rose, fists clenching. The familiar knot of anxiety pulsed inside me.

The curtain in the window opposite was pulled back, revealing an old grey-haired lady watching me with spectacled eyes, a phone in her hand. At that same moment a police car sped round the bend and headed towards us, siren off, but lights strobing, turning the street nightclub-blue.

Gavin leant in close, finger poking me on the chest, his hot breath on my face. 'Next time, Stevens, next time.' He nodded to the rest of his gang and a moment later they were off running down the street.

Chloe, someone who never usually maintained eye contact,

stared at me for the longest moment, feet rooted to the pavement, her expression unreadable.

'Chloe?' I said.

'Come on, you silly bitch,' Gavin shouted back at her.

She blinked at me and chewed her lip. Then with a slight headshake, she was away and running after the others.

What had happened to the girl I'd once known...the girl who'd shoved pencils up her nose to make me laugh and danced with me in the puddles?

I stood with the young lad, us both staring after them as the sound of the approaching police car grew behind our backs. I grabbed the hammer the boy was still holding.

'Get out of here and do yourself a favour – have nothing more to do with Gavin and his crew from now on. OK?'

His eyes beaded with tears. 'I will. Thanks, Jake.'

I felt the usual surge of surprise that a stranger knew my name, but then, of course, everyone in Stoneham did, for all the wrong reasons. And with that the boy was gone too, racing away.

Distant laughter and whoops from Gavin and the others echoed between the buildings.

I dropped the hammer behind my back as the police car screeched to halt. Two uniformed police officers leapt out and the taller policeman's eyes narrowed at mine.

'But it wasn't me,' I said, knowing just how lame that must have sounded.

The other officer stared at the hammer at my feet and then at the broken glass on the pavement by the BMW. 'Of course it wasn't, lad.'

Before I could move he pulled my hands behind my back and steel-cold cuffs clamped round my wrists.

The other policeman crouched down to examine the hammer. 'Tut, tut, tut.'

I didn't resist as the tall officer shoved me into the back of the car. I wouldn't have believed me either.

I still felt an echo of the heat in my blood from when Chloe had squared up to Gavin and he'd hit her. Even though we hadn't spoken in years, of course I still cared about her. But that wasn't the reason I'd stepped in tonight. There'd been something about that haunted look in the boy's eyes that had snared me. Walking past was never going to happen.

That lost and frightened boy reminded me of myself at that age.

I gazed at my own reflection in the window and saw a confused eighteen-year-old teenager frowning back. I slumped back into the seat and listened to the rain drumming down on to the car's roof as we pulled away.

CHAPTER TWO

I SAT in a white-walled room with a small barred window and a battered desk in the middle. The faint scent of locker-room sweat added a really homely feel to the place. *Nice.*

The tall police officer who'd arrested me fiddled with the buttons on a recording device on the desk.

I'd had enough time in the patrol car to work out how I was going to play this – the only way I could – to plead ignorance and keep Gavin and the others out of it. Anything else would mean my life would be as good as over in Stoneham.

A woman's voice drifted through from outside. 'It's just been confirmed by his wife: Jason Stone never returned home from work tonight.'

'But that's the third person to go missing this month,' a man's voice replied. It was followed by a long sigh. 'All right, let's give it the standard twenty-four hours and hope the guy has just run off with his secretary before everyone starts panicking.'

'OK, sir.'

Another disappearance. That was only going to throw fuel on the fire of the Stoneham Stalker rumour. The door swung open and a guy walked in with grey hair and a matching beard. Although it had been six years, and he'd darker hair back then and had been clean-shaven, I still recognised Inspector Clarke immediately – the officer who'd broken the news of Dad's death to me.

I slumped into the seat as Clarke took off his jacket and hung it over the back of his chair before he sat down.

My gaze skated over the hammer in the clear plastic bag.

He fixed me with his piercing steel-grey eyes. 'Hello, Jake, long time no see. Just a shame it's not under better circumstances, hey?'

I gave him a faint nod.

'Just so you know, we have contacted your uncle, Allan Stevens, and he's on his way.'

'Right...' I cringed inside. Allan was no longer my legal guardian since I'd turned eighteen, but he was still a father figure to me. He was one of the few who'd stood by me as the rest had either drifted or, as in Chloe's case, been pushed away.

I glanced at Clarke. 'Shouldn't I have a solicitor in here or something?'

'No, this is just going to be a friendly chat, nothing more at this stage.'

The policeman frowned at Clarke and dropped his hand away from the recording machine. It looked like they weren't on the same page about how to deal with this delinquent, but I guessed the inspector got the casting vote.

My neck muscles loosened a fraction. 'OK...'

The inspector pointed to the hammer. 'Would you care to explain this to us, Jake?'

I focused hard on the chipped white wall beyond him. 'It isn't mine. It was just lying on the pavement.' Pretending ignorance might be an awful defence but it was all that I could come up with.

'Yeah, right,' the tall policeman said. 'So if we checked it for prints we wouldn't find yours plastered all over it?'

'Yes, you would. I saw it lying in the street and picked it up. I was going to drop it off at the police station. Then I panicked and dropped it when you guys turned up.'

'How very community-spirited of you.' The policeman rolled his eyes at Clarke before he leant forward. 'So you're seriously trying to tell us that you didn't use this to break into that vehicle you were loitering beside?'

'I wasn't loitering, just walking past on my way back from college.'

Clarke sat forward and steepled his fingers together. 'And you didn't see Gavin Knotley hanging around the area?'

I managed to keep the shock off my face. How could Clarke have known he'd been there? 'I didn't see anyone.'

'That's not what our witness said.'

The old woman. She must've spotted Gavin and the others under the streetlight and seen what had really happened. And she knew his name because Gavin was something of a local celebrity, but for all the wrong reasons – just like me.

Clarke tapped his pen on a notepad. 'Tell me what really happened, Jake, and why you would want to take the rap for something you didn't do?'

I knew he knew I was lying, could see straight through me, but I tried to make my lie sound convincing. 'I'm telling you the truth, Inspector.'

The tall policeman muttered under his breath, 'Oh, give me strength.'

But Clarke gave me a look that had more than a hint of kindness to it. 'Look, Jake, give us some credit here.'

'Inspector, you have this all wrong. I just found the hammer in the street.'

He gave me a long look that I did my best to hold.

'OK, if that's how you want to play it...' Clarke drummed the pencil on the table. 'Here's my problem, Jake, and, believe it or not, it isn't with you. You see, there's been a whole spate of recent car break-ins across town, and garages too – all easy targets. And we have plenty of soft evidence for who's responsible, but nothing solid enough to get a conviction. However, if someone were to give us information that led to an arrest...'

So there it was. They knew Gavin was behind the mini Stoneham crime wave and wanted me to drop him in it. I turned the thought over. It would be one way to get Gavin out of my life. For a second I was tempted. But I also knew it could never really be an option. If Gavin thought, even for a moment, that I'd talked, then he'd make my life a bigger nightmare than it already was. No, it wasn't worth the risk. Keep my head down like usual and it would all be OK.

I sat back. 'Sorry, Inspector. I really don't know anything about that.'

'But let's pretend for a moment that you do, Jake. The thing that I don't understand is why you would try to protect him. Especially when the two of you have had all that history together.'

History...that was one way of putting it. A screwed-up tangled mess of mutual hatred would be a more accurate description.

'So why, Jake?'

I peered over the edge of a metaphorical cliff, seriously tempted.

Clarke took a deep breath and his face relaxed into the same understanding look that my tutor always gave me.

'This is a small town, Jake, and I hear things. Gavin's father was a caretaker at that university research building and was killed in the same explosion as your father.'

The old pain pulsed inside my chest. It was like the inspector was deliberately picking at the scab of that awful day that had changed my life for ever.

Clarke pressed his fingertips together. 'Sometimes, Jake, people aren't fair and they need someone to blame.'

This was so not where I'd expected this conversation to go. The rain intensified on the window. Rivulets of water ran over the glass like golden snakes lit by the streetlights outside.

'Look, Jake, I'm on your side. Anyone with half a brain is.'

I wished I could believe that, but the hostile stares didn't always just come from Gavin. I'd learnt long ago to look at the pavement as I walked through town. Unfortunately for me, it seemed like everyone held the son of the professor responsible for the explosion that his experiment into dark energy had unleashed. A single awful mistake that had killed so many local people.

Clarke's eyes bored into mine like a hypnotist's. 'You need to tell me what happened... Tell me the truth, Jake.'

I felt myself teetering on the edge, ready to give him what he wanted. I stuck my fingernails into my palm and locked my gaze on to the small window with a view of the darkened office block opposite. My silence thickened the air.

There was a knock, the door opened and a policewoman popped her head in.

'Jake's uncle is here.'

Clarke closed his notebook and relief surged through me. 'It would seem we're all done here, so show him in please.' His searchlight gaze narrowed on me for a second. 'Think on what I've said, Jake.'

I raised my shoulders in a vague shrug as the door opened.

Allan stood there leaning on his stick, his old green Burberry jacket beaded with rain.

'Seriously, Jake?' he asked.

I shrugged. 'Honestly, I didn't do it, Allan.'

Allan's look was like a laser as he searched my face. Then his gaze relaxed as if he'd spotted a grain of truth somewhere and he slowly nodded. 'I didn't think any of this sounded like something you would do.'

'It wasn't.' Allan was hard on me sometimes, pushing me to do even better with my grades, but he believed in me too.

'Come on, Jake, let's get you home,' he said with a scowl towards Clarke.

I avoided Clarke's gaze and followed my uncle out of the door.

———

The windscreen wipers thumped backwards and forwards, as Allan continued the lecture that had begun the moment we'd climbed into his ancient Volvo estate, its light-blue paintwork decorated with pimples of rust.

'You do realise you're lucky the inspector didn't charge you,' Allan said.

'I know...'

'How do you think this would have gone down with the Oxford University admissions board if he had?'

'Not well.'

'To say the least.' Allan blew out his cheeks. 'So why get involved rather than just ring the police?'

Because of the boy; because of Chloe; because something inside me cracked. I shrugged.

'So you're sure you didn't see who was responsible?'

'No...'

Allan actually rolled his eyes. 'I might not be your dad, but I understand you well enough to realise when you're holding something back from me.'

Of course he did.

He let out a long sigh. 'I realise I can never replace Martin, but please know how much you mean to me, lad.'

The mention of my dad's name made me stiffen. I found myself reaching for my watch, an old habit I used to anchor myself. It was a diver's watch that had belonged to Mum. 'I know, Allan, and you me.'

'And that you can tell me anything...'

'Of course I do.' Not that I could...or would.

'And for someone who didn't think of themselves as academic, look how far you've come.'

He wasn't wrong. The transformation of Jake Stevens over the last six years – from an academic lost cause to class swot – had surprised everyone, even me. But then again, school, followed by college, had become my whole world – certainly the only thing that had made sense as my life imploded around me. It was also partly based on a guilt trip. When Dad had been alive I'd shirked my schoolwork and had disappeared down the rabbit hole of computer gaming whenever I could. Even though Dad had never said it I knew he'd been disappointed in me. And I'd been trying to make that up to him ever since his death.

Allan dragged his top lip over his teeth. 'I'm not sure exactly what happened with you tonight, Jake, but I hope you know that I'm on your side and always have been.' He glanced at me. 'And it's not always been easy for me either since Martin...'

I spotted the same deep pain in his eyes that I often saw in mine. 'But you're doing OK, aren't you?'

'As well as anyone can be who lost a very close younger brother. But the real question is: what about you? You're a complicated lad, Jake, but then after everything you've been through that's hardly surprising.'

Yet another person to pick at that scab today... This time a stone lodged in my throat.

'Just try not to trip yourself up when you are so close to realising your dreams.'

To run away from Stoneham to Oxford University and never come back. Nothing was going to get in the way of that strategy.

Allan gave me a sideways glance and his face softened. 'All right, Jake, enough lectures for one day.'

I forced myself to look at my uncle, but could only manage a nod.

Beyond his head a flare of light in the sky was glowing through the clouds. It pulsed again, this time brighter.

I sat up straighter. 'Pull over.'

Allan's eyes tightened on the road as he braked. 'Did I hit something?'

'No. I think I just spotted a flash above the cloud line.'

'Oh hell, I'd forgotten all about Varuna with everything that's happened.'

'That makes two of us.'

The car had barely come to a standstill when I leapt out into the middle of the deserted country back road. Allan got out more slowly, using his stick to support the leg with his bad arthritic knee.

I pointed towards the patch of sky where I'd spotted the burst of light. 'It came from that direction.'

For a moment there was nothing, but then it came again, a brief burning spiderweb of light blazing through the cracks between the thick cloud cover. The air caught in my throat, the sheer awe of what was happening starting to sink in. This was way bigger than anything I could have ever imagined. I took out my phone and snapped a shot.

'At the rate that thing's shifting, it will be over the coast in less than a few minutes,' Allan said.

'So much for it crashing over land,' I replied. 'All those people who stocked up with food are going to feel really stupid...' My words faded away as the streaking satellite started to curve back in a large arc, a dazzling white ball through the cloud cover, trailed by golden flames. 'How can it be possible for it to change direction like that?'

'Maybe its directional attitude jets are misfiring.'

The satellite continued to turn, tracing a glowing ribbon of light above the cloud until it seemed almost aimed straight at us.

'Allan?'

'Relax, Jake, you know the maths. The chances of it hitting us are one in several billion.'

The point of light burst through the clouds, becoming a burning blue meteor and shedding pieces in a stream that trailed behind it as a growing swarm of fiery debris. The constellation of objects began to arc towards the ground, spinning shards of metal that would hit the ground at hundreds of miles per hour. And if anyone was underneath them as they hit...

A boom thundered from the sky and a slap of air punched into my body, rocking me back on my feet.

Allan clapped. 'Sonic boom! Will you look at that son of a bitch go?'

I laughed. 'This is beyond incredible.'

The plummeting hunk of metal ate up the remaining distance in a shockingly tiny amount of time, but I guessed it was still going to pass several miles over our heads.

Allan winked at me. 'See, told you.'

I was about to reply when Varuna seemed to buck around in the sky like someone had begun shaking it. A jet flame blossomed into life at its rear and it swung round in a large arc until it was almost travelling in the direction it had come from.

My mouth became dry and I put my hands on top of my head. 'About those odds. I think they just narrowed.'

Allan scowled. 'OK, I have to admit this is looking a bit more worrying.'

It shot past the three-hundred-metre-high TV mast on top of the Mendips just a couple of miles away. Once again Varuna altered its course but this time directly towards us, closing in like a homing missile.

The sound of whistling air grew to a banshee roar. My dream whirled through my mind... A dream or a premonition?

With one glance at each other, we turned and I helped Allan back towards the car.

The branches of bare winter trees lining the hedgerows started to bend and twist as the ground under our feet began to tremble.

We were still metres from the car when a huge fist of wind punched into my back and sent me sprawling. Allan slid over the verge and came to a stop next to me, face down. We both instinctively covered our heads with our hands. The temperature rose from winter cold to a hot summer's day in a second, as brilliant light burned the night away around us. The ground drummed beneath my body as the thundering roar numbed my ears and the metallic taste of blood filled my mouth – I'd bitten down on my lip.

We were going to die in a billion-to-one freak accident. And somehow part of my subconscious had known and tried to warn me about this exact moment through that damned dream. But I hadn't listened and had rationalised it away like I did with everything. Now I was going to pay the ultimate price for my blinkered thinking.

Allan's hand clamped round mine. No time for any goodbyes.

But I had to see, had to witness my last moment before my life was scrubbed from the face of the planet.

I rolled over on to my back to see a burned hunk of metal with twisted spines speeding towards us...and then the orange flame burst from its rear once more. The furnace heat washed

over us for a heartbeat as the satellite lurched up with a shriek
that split the sky and soared directly over our heads.

The man-made meteor streaked beyond us, past one field,
two, almost as if someone was in control and trying to save us.

A pure blaze of light lit up the sky, turning night into day as
the shockwave hit. The ground bucked beneath our feet and
branches tore from the trees and tumbled away in a hurricane of
wind. The Volvo bounced on its shocks like a fairground ride
gone badly wrong.

The air was sucked from my lungs as the fallen metal angel
roared its death at the world.

I didn't move, didn't do anything, just lay there watching the
billows of smoke in the sky. Then, so slowly, reality crept back in.

I was shaking, a bright stain of vomit on the ground before
me. I felt Allan's hand rubbing my back and I sucked in a lungful
of breath.

'Are you OK?' he asked.

My heart rate slowed and I drew in another large breath. It
was the sweetest air I'd ever tasted, despite the stench of my own
sick. 'Just surprised to be alive.'

I retrieved Allan's stick and helped him get shakily back to his
feet. We stared across the field towards the column of smoke
glowing orange, the impact point in a field just out of sight
beyond a gradual rising hill. Sparks rolled up like fireflies into
the sky.

My mobile warbled and on autopilot I took it out of my
pocket and gazed at the screen. The text was from IIIIIIII.
What sort of phone number was that? *7%5$@....dying...%!¢#*, the
text said.

What? Who was sending me weird garbled messages?

'We should ring the authorities,' Allan said, still staring at the
crash site. He took out his mobile and scowled at the screen.

'You too?' I asked.

'What?'

I showed him my phone. 'It looks like some sort of scrambled message.'

'I didn't get anything like that, but I've got no mobile signal. I expect the satellite sent out an electronic pulse as it crashed that messed with the networks, which is probably why you received that gibberish.'

Allan turned his attention towards Stoneham at the bottom of the bowl of hills beneath us, a couple of miles away. 'Oh hell, will you look at that!'

I followed his gaze. The whole town was in total darkness, not a light to be seen. An astronomer's dream in any other circumstance.

'The electronic pulse must have overloaded the power grid too. But maybe your mobile network is still running,' Allan said. 'Try ringing the emergency services to tell them what's happened.'

'I'm on it.' I tapped 999 and hit dial.

Call failed flashed up on the screen. Then I spotted the lack of reception bars on the top corner of the screen. 'My network's down too.'

Almost in answer, my mobile pinged again with another message. ^)()*!%...*find...urgent*...%^+!

'How come you're still getting messages then?' Allan asked, staring at my mobile.

'Maybe my mobile is glitching out?'

'Hardly surprising with what just happened.'

I gestured towards the column of fire and smoke rising into the sky. As I watched I felt drawn towards it as if I needed to be there to witness it with my own eyes.

'We should go and check it out,' I said.

'No. As much as I'd love to have a nose, there could still be unspent rocket propellant on-board Varuna. We were lucky enough to live through that crash. Let's not push our luck any further and risk getting barbecued for our troubles.'

I knew Allan was making sense but I could almost hear the satellite calling to me. I stared at the scrambled message again. No one ever messaged me apart from Allan, and he was standing right next to me. *A random buffer of data...a message meant for someone else?* I wondered. Still, it seemed like a sign. Just like the dream had been. I'd ignored that, but maybe that was a mistake I shouldn't repeat?

Allan sat in the car and tried the ignition. The engine turned over but didn't catch.

He pulled a lever under the dash, got out and popped open the bonnet to stare at the engine, scratching his chin. 'Hmmmm...'

'How's it looking?'

'Not sure, but we can't call the recovery services with both our mobiles out. I'll try fiddling with the engine and see if I can coax it back into life.'

I pointed towards the burning crash site. 'And what about that? We need to tell someone, don't we?'

'The whole town must have been woken by the shockwave from the impact. It'll only be a matter of time before the authorities turn up to deal with it.'

'But we know exactly where it came down.'

Allan gestured to the fire. 'And you think they won't be able to spot that from miles away?'

'But it may have burned itself out by the time they get here.'

'True...' He sighed. 'I guess we could head back into town on foot to try to get a signal from another mast that hasn't been affected. But if I leave my car here it would be a sitting duck. Knowing my luck, the next time we see it, it'll be crashed into a ditch.'

He wasn't exaggerating either. At least three cars had ended up that way over the last six months. It might well have been Gavin upping his game.

I gestured to a footpath sign to Stoneham that pointed towards a stile in the hedge. 'I could go ahead. It should take less than an hour to get home on foot. I can head over to the local garage and get someone to come out for you. If our landline is still working, I'll ring the police about the satellite.'

'I guess that's as good a plan as any.'

I gazed at my uncle. I could have lost him tonight. I pulled him into a tight hug.

Allan awkwardly patted my back as I pulled away. 'What was that uncharacteristic show of affection for?'

'Maybe my way of an apology for all the stuff with the police earlier.'

He smiled. 'Already forgotten, Jake. Just please don't make a habit of it, hey?'

'Got it.'

'Glad to hear it. Now get yourself off home and call the cavalry.'

I snapped a salute. 'You can rely on me, sir.'

He snorted and returned his attention to the engine. I started to walk towards the stile.

'And, Jake...'

'Yes?'

'Don't get any ideas about taking any detours to the crash site.'

'Do I look like an idiot?'

'Of course not, but I couldn't live with myself if something happened to you.'

'I hear you, Allan...' And in that moment I really meant it. With a final wave I clambered away over the stile.

I used my mobile's torch to light the way and began to cut

across the ploughed field. The ground was muddy underfoot and soon my trainers were caked with earth.

The wreckage burned in silence just two fields over to my left.

The flames were already noticeably smaller.

I reached the next stile. Here the footpath forked, one signed for Stoneham, the other for the nearby village of Hopworth. I was pretty sure the latter path went straight through the field where the satellite had crashed.

I looked at the sign to Hopworth for the longest time. No, I'd promised Allan. A deal was a deal.

I started down the path towards Stoneham.

And then my phone pinged again.

&*^%... Do...not...&?!&...leave...me...%$#!

It couldn't be... I stared towards the flickering flames. But what if someone had been hurt by the impact, a farmer in a tractor or something, and they were trapped in a burning cab. Maybe they'd tried to send a message to the emergency services, but with the scrambled networks it was me who'd received the message instead. I knew it seemed crazy, but I couldn't just ignore it.

Then I was running, faster than I ever had down the path signposted to Hopworth. Straight towards the burning orange glow beyond the hedgerows on top of the hill ahead of me.

CHAPTER THREE

I CLAMBERED over the final gate into a field, its grey barley stalks a wintry stubble. I barely noticed them, my attention focused on the black column of smoke rising into the sky that had been growing steadily as I approached. At its base flickered a few dying flames from pieces of warped metal shards. The satellite must have torn itself apart in its last moments as it gouged out a hundred-metre-long gash through the field.

I cast a wary eye over the wreckage for anything that might explode, but there was nothing larger than dinner-plate-sized bits of debris. If there had been any pressurised cylinders containing rocket propellant they'd already been blown apart and consumed by fire. The crash site looked as safe as a smouldering pile of space wreckage could look. But someone might be still buried alive in there somewhere...

'Hello?' I called out.

No shout came back, yet I had the weirdest feeling I was being watched. I glanced up at the sky, half expecting to see a police helicopter zooming down towards me, but it was clear of anything but clouds. Maybe a fox had crept out for a look at the metal thing that had just destroyed the field?

I took another cautious step down the slope, feeling the residual heat of the blast radiating through the soles of my trainers. The furrowed path steepened until I was having to hang on to the ploughed walls to stop myself slipping. If anything remained of the crashed craft, it was obscured by the billowing smoke ahead of me...and maybe the survivor would be too. But why would anyone have been out in a lonely field in the middle of the night?

I cupped my hands to my mouth. 'Is there anyone here?

Suddenly sonic booms rattled the air and snapped my attention towards the horizon. Two fighter jets were closing in fast, swooping down towards the crash site. I recognised the swept-back delta wing silhouettes at once from the air shows I'd been to with Dad – these were Typhoon fighter jets. They must have been scrambled to locate the crashed satellite.

My phone chimed. *GH#4G...Hurry...YUV#2* My gaze returned to the wreckage. Who was sending these messages?

Even if I couldn't see them, maybe someone in there could see me, just couldn't call out for some reason. But when the satellite had blasted past a hundred metres over our heads, the shockwave had felt almost powerful enough to stop my heart. Surely anyone near the point of impact would have been killed outright?

None of this stacked up, but I'd worry about that later because my instincts were screaming at me to keep going.

The smoke billowed with a change in the wind and started to roll towards me. Within moments I was in the middle of an eye-stinging grey cloud, coughing my guts out.

A banshee roar heralded the two fighters' arrival overhead. They briefly scattered the smoke plume before the fumes billowed back in. At least the authorities knew where to look, but it would still probably take them a while to get feet on the ground. No, it was down to me, at least for the moment, and every second might make a difference to the chances of that trapped person surviving.

'Do you need help?' I shouted into the gloom. No reply came back, not even a groan of pain.

I pulled up my jumper as a makeshift face mask and stepped carefully among the spear-like pieces of metal sticking up from the ground.

I heard the Typhoons throttling back, their jets lessening to a lower roar. I guessed they were probably circling the crash site and radioing back to base for instructions.

The debris field grew in size as I pressed forward into the stinging smoke. I made my way past pieces of twisted pipework, sheared machine panels, melted solar arrays and lumps bent beyond recognition of what they'd once been. Sweat ran down my back as the temperature increased. I passed one piece painted with an Indian flag, the country that had originally launched Varuna. The satellite had been designed to monitor ice cap melting and had been named after the goddess of the oceans.

The charred banks of earth on either side of me steepened to almost vertical walls. Ahead the smoke thinned for a moment and I spotted a crater glowing with faint aqua light.

My skin prickled. I slowed my pace, my heart feeling like it was pumping a million litres of blood per second. I edged towards the lip of the crater, ready to leap backwards and run for my life given the slightest excuse.

What was I expecting to see exactly? A grey alien hand holding a blaster aimed at my head?

I gathered every atom of courage and forced myself to peer over the edge... I almost laughed out loud.

A blue LED, the source of the faint light, shone out like a beacon from a printed circuit board. It was surrounded by petals of metal that looked like the broken remains of a computer system rack that would have run the satellite. Off to one side was a mangled dish linked to the circuit board by wires – presumably the communication system the satellite had used to relay information back to Earth. Was that what had affected the mobile network in the Varuna's dying moments, jamming up the radio frequencies with a burst of static? But what about the words in the scrambled messages? The dying brain-dump of a machine?

I felt myself shiver despite the heat.

The blue LED started to fade and it was like watching an animal dying. I felt a tug of sadness for the fallen satellite. One moment it had been soaring high above the blue marble of Earth, the next it had been reduced to this broken hunk of useless metal lying in a muddy field in England. Talk about a momentous comedown.

I found myself instinctively reaching out for the circuit board as if I was trying to calm the dying sky creature in its last moments. My fingertips brushed across it—

A nerve-burning electric shock blazed through me as a white spark leapt from the circuit board and into my hand. My fingers involuntarily clamped on to the board and I fell backwards with the thing still clutched in my hand. The shock of energy swept through my body, jamming my jaw together.

The next few seconds felt like a lifetime. I finally snatched in a breath as the shock ended and the pain started to recede. Bloody hell, that had hurt.

My phone pinged and I pulled it out of my pocket.

G€2H!...Jake Stevens...run...J#L1

I stared at the screen. What the hell was going on here?

The jets of the Typhoons changed pitch.

R<H2...Run...or you...will die...H\L7

The rational part of my brain froze, but my animal instinct took over as I sprang back to my feet. It was like I could smell the heightened danger in the smoke-filled air around me. I ran, trying to throw the circuit board from my hand, but my fingers refused to obey.

What the hell?

Adrenalin powered my limbs as I sped away. I reached the end of the furrow and in three strides burst clear of the smoke. With one hand on the top bar of the gate, I vaulted over it in a single leap, like this was a track event and I was going for gold.

The Typhoons' growl grew steadily louder as I sprinted away across the next field. I spotted the fighter jets speeding along the valley and rising up towards the crash site, keeping low as if they didn't want to be seen. Their flight was focused – menacing – like hunters coming in for the kill.

A ball of hot fear pulsed inside my chest.

Lungs burning, I increased my pace and hurtled away over the ploughed, uneven field. Within moments I'd reached the stile in the next hedgerow and I was over it, running down the hill on the other side. I heard a whoosh and glanced back to see two bright points of orange appear under the fighter jets' wings, speeding towards the crash site.

Missiles? Seriously?

I shielded my eyes from the brilliant flash. Two whumping sounds and a howling wind threw me face down on to the damp grass. But this shockwave was nowhere near as powerful as the one from the satellite crash. As I got back to my feet, my ears rang like I had them pressed against a surround-sound woofer. Two fresh mushroom clouds rolled up into the night sky.

My mind rebooted. Why had the Typhoons opened fire on the crashed remains of a satellite?

Another ping. A fresh message blazed on my mobile: *&Keep running!*

Who the hell was watching me? I stared at the circuit board still in my hand, and at last my fingers loosened their vice-like grip on it. For a moment I was tempted to throw it away. But I also wanted answers. This was all I had.

Already the two jets were circling back for a second low pass. I guessed to check out their handiwork.

I played enough computer games, watched enough movies, to realise this whole situation screamed specials ops – the pilot's orders to take out the target with extreme prejudice. The sort of mission kept hidden from the general public.

I saw a flick of light spill across several fields ahead of me and spotted the headlights of several vehicles speeding along a track.

The feet on the ground were about to arrive in force and I was in the middle of the field, exposed. There was also the question: had the Typhoon pilots spotted me with the sort of thermal-imaging tech they'd be equipped with? And if so, what would happen to me if I got caught? The last message suddenly made utter sense.

I half slid, half ran down the sodden hillside, ducking into the base of the hedgerow as three black Range Rovers rounded the corner, gunning their engines. They sped up the hill towards the crash site, their four-wheel-drive systems working overtime to give them traction in the mud.

I pressed myself into the shadows of the hedge, thorny spikes piercing my hooded top and stabbing into the skin of my arms beneath. The black vehicles raced past and I caught a glimpse of the logos on their sides, which read 'Genesis Security Systems'. A memory stirred in the back of my mind, though I couldn't pinpoint it.

And then the vehicles were past me, heading straight towards the crash site, red tail lights blazing into the night.

My fingers ran over the bump of the circuit board in my pocket.

If they find me with this...

The ten minutes that it took me to reach the path junction to

Stoneham felt like an hour after creeping the whole way under the cover of the hedgerows and jumping at the slightest sound.

For a moment I stood still, catching my breath and giving myself a chance to think.

The right-hand path led back to Allan and the broken Volvo. He must have at least heard the missile impacts, but he wouldn't have seen what had happened. Allan would probably have thought the explosions were propellant tanks going up on the satellite – just like he'd warned me. I made a half step on to the path that would take me back to him.

No, the less that Allan knew about any of this the better. I didn't want him dragged into my mess. The run-in with the police had been bad enough and I was pretty sure *that* would look like a stroll in the park if these Genesis guys learnt I'd taken the circuit board. Maybe they'd just make me *disappear* like the jets had with the satellite?

My mind wheeled. This was all so messed up, and all I'd wanted to do was help someone.

I took the circuit board from my pocket and gazed at it. Part of me still wanted to drop that broken piece of junk in the field right there and walk away from whatever this was. But the bigger part of me, the part that was the son of a famous quantum physicist, the same part that had always been taught to question everything I thought I knew about the universe, was also desperate for answers. No, I needed to find out what had happened here.

I pocketed the circuit board and turned away from the path that led to Allan. To my surprise I felt an inner tension release, as though my subconscious had decided I was doing the right thing – for what that was worth, even if I got caught by the authorities.

The two Typhoons banked away from the crash site and shot into the sky, though much slower than when they'd arrived, their mission now achieved. I estimated Allan still wouldn't be able to see them since they were heading back towards Hopworth.

I pulled my hoody up over my head and huddled into my jacket as I set off down the path that curved away towards Stoneham.

I trudged along the pitch-dark high street and turned on to a small shop-lined road that led up the hill towards Celestial Skies. People stood outside their homes, their gazes fixed on the column of smoke visible on the horizon, conversations dropped in whispered awe. I could already imagine the headline. 'Stoneham Survives Near Miss With Crashing Satellite'.

I tried to process what had happened. In the space of one night my life had been thrown into chaos. As the adrenalin ebbed away I felt a knot of anxiety growing inside, all too familiar from the last six years.

Ahead of me, Celestial Skies stood in darkness, no twinkling LED Christmas lights that I'd draped over the telescopes to lighten the gloom.

I'd wanted to check here in case Allan had managed to get the car started, but there was no sign of his Volvo.

I was about to turn round and head for the garage when a strange smell pulled at my nose. I paused on the step and stared out into the night along the street, breathing in the scent of wet tarmac. But under that familiar scent was something else, like earth – no, decay... Had someone forgotten to put the rubbish out?

The smell thickened and I clamped my hand over my mouth as the stench stuck in the back of my throat. A flicker of movement broke the shadows to my left. I leapt back. For a mad moment it seemed as if all the shadows around the shop entrance shifted like oil on water. My chest tightened. I took a step back and screwed up my eyes. But when I looked again the entrance was empty and the rain pattered on to the pavement. The air felt fresh and light. The world was back to its ordinary self.

I breathed through my nose, trying to slow my racing heartbeat.

Then I heard the note of a familiar car engine and Allan's Volvo came round the corner. He gave me a wave with a wide smile through the windscreen. He was OK... He was really OK. My shoulders dropped.

But what about that thing with the shadows I'd just seen? I told myself that it could have been a panic attack, like the ones I'd suffered after Dad's death. But had I been wound that tightly that I'd begun to see things? It would hardly be surprising after all that had happened today.

Allan parked up and, with a lurch of the car on its handbrake, climbed out. 'You've only just got back, Jake?'

I threw out the first excuse that came into my mind. 'I managed to get lost in the dark.'

'And you a local lad too – shame on you.'

'But how did you get the car going?' I asked.

'I kept trying the ignition. Luckily enough it suddenly just started working again.' He gestured towards the column of smoke hanging over the town. 'But did you see those satellite fuel tanks go up after those fighter jets arrived?'

So he'd seen the jets but not the missile explosions. I felt myself relax another fraction inside. 'Yeah, a regular firework display with a military flyover thrown in.'

'Exciting times,' Allan said as I unlocked the shop door.

More than I hope you ever know, I thought to myself.

I ran my hand over the circuit board in my pocket. Did I have a clue right here to what had just happened? In another world I would have been straight over to Chloe's to ask for her help. She'd built loads of custom PCs in her time and knew her way around pieces of silicon like no one else. Unfortunately picking her brains wasn't an option. Like everything else in my life these days, if I wanted answers I would have to run solo.

Allan found a battery lantern under the counter and turned it on to light the shop. I paused a moment and looked out into the darkness filling the doorway. Once again I had the weirdest feeling I was being watched.

Get a grip, Jake.

With a silent headshake to myself, I closed the door behind me, shutting out the world and the strange brand of madness it had served up tonight. What I needed more than anything was sleep – and lots of it. Then I would make a start on figuring out all this craziness with a clearer head in the morning.

CHAPTER FOUR

I WOKE UP AND STRETCHED. I hadn't so much slept as passed into oblivion at some point in the small hours.

I tuned into the background burble of the news leaking through the wall from the living room. At least that meant the power had come back on during the night.

I grabbed my mobile from my bedside table and began thumbing through to my messages. The most recent text was an old one from Allan asking me to pick up a loaf of bread on my way back from college. Where were the texts from that unknown number, especially the one that had saved my life? I didn't remember deleting them.

I pressed my head back into the pillow.

None of this made any sense – the way the satellite avoided hitting us in its last dying moments and the strange garbled messages, not to mention the grand finale of the two Typhoons arriving and blowing up what was left at the crash site. A good night's sleep seemed to have only heightened the growing mystery in my mind.

I swung my legs from the bed and pulled back the curtains.

Pearls of condensation ran down the inside of the glass and turned the frosted rooftop view into an abstract image of smeared light.

I smudged a clear patch in the glass with my hand and gazed towards where the satellite had come down beyond Stoneham.

My heart quickened at the sight of a military helicopter, an Apache gunship by the look of it, circling a faint tendril of smoke that drifted up into the sky. Though I couldn't see the crash site itself beyond the hills that ringed the town, Stoneham's very own earthen circular fort.

I pressed my forehead against the cool of the glass. What were the military doing up there? My gaze flicked across to the circuit board. The blue LED was still off. Maybe the board had shorted itself after it had shocked me?

One thing was for certain: I needed coffee to have a fighting chance of figuring any of this out. I'd follow that with some googling to see what more I could discover about the rogue Varuna satellite. Based on the way it had been destroyed by those jets I was starting to think it wasn't a weather satellite at all...

With a yawn, and scratching the back of my head, I shuffled out of my bedroom into the galley kitchen where Allan had already put on a pot of coffee for me. I helped myself to a large mugful and headed into the living room.

Allan was sitting in his thread-worn armchair that was permanently moulded to the shape of his butt. A steaming mug of tea was balanced on one armrest, a plate holding a bacon sandwich on the other. Every wall around the room was crammed with a chaos of books about astronomy and space, and plenty of sci-fi fiction too. Models of old rockets filled every available surface and a lump of a genuine nickel meteorite, cut in two and polished, had been mounted on a wall plaque. In the corner of the room stood a large illuminated star globe, and next to it a brass antique telescope angled towards the attic-room window. This was Allan's version of a man cave and I loved it entirely.

Allan normally only listened to Radio 4, but he was watching the TV. The picture immediately caught my eye – aerial footage of Stoneham and the smoking crash site beyond.

Allan picked up his tea and gestured with the mug towards the screen. 'Apparently news crews have descended on to our town like the proverbial plague of locusts, looking for eyewitness accounts. The prime minister is also going to talk about our satellite crash any minute.'

For the second time in six years Stoneham was about to be put on the map again, but at least this time no one had died. At least as far as I knew...

'You're not going to say anything to them, are you, Allan?'

'No way. I don't want to be bothered with that travelling circus and have my ugly mug plastered all over the news. Besides which, there are plenty of people in town who saw it come down, so they don't need to hear from us. Our little secret, hey?'

'Sounds good to me.' I dropped into the other free armchair, which was angled towards the coal-fired stove that bathed the room with cosy orange light. On my chair's arm sat a plate with a bacon sandwich waiting for me. I knew without even checking that it would have just the right amount of ketchup oozing from the granary bread Allan knew I loved. He must have gone out first thing to the baker's round the corner to get it. For someone who pretended to be an old grump he had a solid heart of twenty-two-carat gold beneath the surface.

I gestured with my chin towards the attic window. 'Did you see the Apache over the crash site?'

'Of course I did. I've been watching it through the telescope and according to Sid—'

'Sid?'

'Only our milkman of over twenty years and counting.

Anyway, Sid tried to drive past the crash site this morning but the military have barricaded all the roads anywhere near it. The soldier who stopped Sid made him head back the way he'd come. You should have heard Sid grumbling about the five-mile detour he had to take to get to Stoneham to do his rounds.'

My glance flicked to the dividing wall to my bedroom. Despite the comforting warmth from the fire, a cold feeling of dread ran through me. What exactly had I got myself mixed up in?

Alexander Langton, our new prime minster – blond-haired, sharp-eyed and with an equally sharp grey suit to match – appeared on the screen. The guy was standing behind a lectern outside 10 Downing Street, as bursts of light illuminated his face and camera shutters clicked.

'PM makes statement about Stoneham satellite crash,' rolled across the bottom of the screen.

'Here we go,' Allan said, taking a bite of his bacon sandwich.

Langton's gaze lifted from his notes. 'I can now confirm that around 12.30 a.m. last night, the Indian Varuna satellite made landfall near the town of Stoneham in Somerset. However, I am delighted to confirm that it crashed in a deserted field and that no one was harmed. Our military has been deployed and at this very moment is recovering the remains of the satellite so that it can be handed over to the Indian government as soon as possible.'

'I doubt there's a lot left of it to hand back,' Allan said.

That was truer than he realised, especially after the military Typhoons had used it for target practice. And that also meant Langton was standing in front of the world and lying through his teeth...but then why was I surprised? He was a politician.

The prime minister's mouth thinned. 'I would urge members of the public not to approach the crash site under any circumstances. Our experts believe that, despite an initial explosion caused by the crash, there is still unspent rocket propellant on-board the craft that could explode at any moment. A bomb disposal squad is currently working with scientists at the site to extract the fuel and make it safe.'

Allan raised his eyebrows at me. 'Told you.'

I hadn't seen any fuel canisters left and certainly not after the Typhoons had finished the job. But what could be so dangerous to call for such extreme measures?

'As soon as we have more information we will let the public know. Thank you.' Langton turned his back to the chorus of journalists' questions and disappeared back through the famous black door of Number 10.

I was already on my feet and heading out of the living room.

'Jake, your bacon sandwich,' Allan called after me.

'I'll eat it in a moment.'

Back in my bedroom, I flipped up the screen of my laptop. After the operating system had eventually woken up, I opened a browser window.

I typed: *Varuna Indian Satellite.*

Thousands of hits immediately came back. I checked the Wikipedia entry at the top first. A short scan later confirmed what I already knew: that Varuna had been the pride of the fledgling Indian space industry. It was their statement to the rest of the world that their country meant business when it came to space exploration.

But what if it really was something else? I tried a fresh search. *Varuna military satellite disguised as a weather probe?*

I got a dozen hits, but nothing matching the military search criteria. But then the Indian government weren't likely to place a classified mission within easy reach of a Google search.

I leant back in my chair and put my hands on my head. This was so much more Chloe's areas of expertise, the sort of thing she could probably find out from her shady hacker friends who lurked in the dark web. But as I didn't have her expertise to call upon, I had to think like her instead.

I felt a vague tingling sensation in my fingers and shook them as I tried to order my thoughts. If Varuna was a spy satellite, maybe it had sensitive information on-board...

My gaze snapped to the circuit board and I noticed a USB port on the side. I rummaged in a drawer that was filled with all my surplus junk, and at last dug out a suitable USB cable, plugging one end into my laptop and the other into the port on the satellite's printed circuit board.

I held a mental breath – one second, two...

The blue light burst back into life on the board. *New device found*, appeared on my laptop's screen.

I mentally punched the air and tried to open the folder. The system busy symbol popped up. Another long moment ticked past...

Downloading in progress.

A bar started to scroll across the screen. What the hell? I hadn't OK'd anything.

My laptop's desktop display started to flicker.

A virus?

I grabbed the cable to yank it out. But then my hand froze, fell back into my lap and I sagged into my chair, vaguely wondering why I had been so panicked a moment before.

Somewhere deep inside me, a dull sense of confusion swirled, the rational part of my brain screaming at me to do something, yet my trance-like state only deepened the more I fought it. I tried to raise my hand but it wouldn't respond.

The progress bar reached the end. *Download complete*, flashed up on my screen, followed by hundreds of scrolling numbers.

I stared at it for the longest moment. I blinked and any sense of calm evaporated, the world rushing back in. What the hell had

I been thinking? My hand, now obeying me again, yanked the USB cable out of the board and my laptop's screen died.

'No!'

'Are you OK?' Allan called from the other room.

My lips felt dry as I pressed the power key on my laptop. Nothing happened. I pushed my seat back from the desk. Knowing my luck, the satellite board would have been loaded with some sort of virus to stop any information on it falling into enemy hands.

Way to go, Jake.

Allan wandered in. 'Problem?'

'I think my laptop has a virus.'

Allan's gaze skewered mine. 'You haven't been on any dodgy websites, have you?'

'Seriously?'

He raised his hands, palms towards me. 'OK, OK.' He jutted his chin towards the circuit board, its blue light dead. 'What's that from then?'

I grabbed the board and shoved it into my rucksack. 'Nothing, just a college project I'm working on.'

'Looks interesting. Physics experiment?'

'Something like that.'

'It's good to see you taking such an interest in science. Your dad would be proud of you.'

I tried not to visibly wince, but my expression twisted.

Allan's eyes returned to me and he grimaced. 'Sorry...' He gestured towards my laptop, obviously looking for a way to quickly change the subject. 'How are you going to sort that out? A factory reset and reinstall everything?'

A cold feeling grew inside me. 'Oh hell!'

Allan scowled. 'Please tell me you've been backing up your college work?'

'Of course I have. All the important files are backed up

online. But it will still take me days to get my laptop back to how I need it for college.'

'I see...' His gaze flitted away to the window. 'It's a shame you can't ask Chloe for help. I bet she would sort it out in a—'

I held up a hand, stopping him dead. 'I can't go there, you know that, Allan.'

'Can't, or won't?'

I shrugged and, avoiding his piercing gaze, picked up the laptop and stuffed it into the bag along with the circuit board. 'I'll take it to the college IT department and see if they can do anything to help.'

'The same IT department you're so rude about all the time?'

'It's still worth a go.' Not that I really believed that, especially if a military-grade virus had just wiped my system.

With a shake of his head Allan disappeared back through the door.

I stared down at the discarded USB cable on the floor. Why the hell had I watched the circuit download a virus on to my system and done nothing to stop it?

Years ago I'd seen a counsellor – after Dad's death. This was exactly the sort of thing he'd have had a field day with. He'd have probably called it a psychological break caused by stress.

I slowed my breathing. Maybe there was another explanation. What if this was the thing that had stalked me since Dad's death: the sense of panic that at any moment my world would implode whenever I lost control? Maybe I really could put this down to that – a simple panic attack and nothing more, albeit an extreme one. After all, last night I'd pushed myself far outside my normal safe zone, and with that confrontation with Gavin and my near-death experience with the satellite no wonder I'd been affected. I felt lighter as I decided that this had to be it.

What I needed was routine and lots of it – and college work too. The regular numbing rhythm of a normal day would help more than anything else and get my panic monster back inside its cage.

Control – it was all about control.

I'd get on top of this just like I'd eventually done after Dad's death. Everything would be fine... I would be fine. *I will be fine.* I kept repeating my new mantra to myself and headed off to eat my cold bacon sandwich.

CHAPTER FIVE

I THREADED my way between the maze of telescopes and boxes that Allan had packed into the shop for the hectic Christmas period. I paused at the door and glanced up at the photo mounted over it: Mum and Dad, all smiles and happiness, holding up me as a baby up to the eyepiece of a large telescope in the observatory at our old cottage. I reached and touched the photo, another regular habit to try to steady myself. But the usual drumbeat of my anxiety had already powered up as I gripped the door handle. I took an involuntary breath and left the sanctuary of the shop into the dangers of the world beyond.

The frosty air bit into my skin. I pulled my hood up to shield myself from unwanted gazes. The few people hurrying past on their way to work didn't cast me a second glance.

I stepped out on to the cobbled street lined with small galleries displaying bright artwork and gift shops filled with things that no one really needed. Dad had referred to it as the *arty end* of town and Celestial Skies fitted right in.

Further down the hill, the cobbled road was packed with

parked TV vans, large satellite dishes on their roofs, their sides adorned with logos of all the major networks.

There was an unusually long queue coming out of Java's, the best coffee shop in town – according to its blackboard outside. It was also the *only* coffee shop in town and the place where I often caught sight of Chloe. She loved her coffee almost as much as I did, a passion we'd both inherited from our dads. I stole a glance through the window, but there wasn't any sign of her grabbing her usual double latte with a shot of vanilla among the heaving crowd.

A guy with a chiselled face, carrying two cups of coffee, walked out of the shop. He crossed the road round to the back of a black van parked alongside the others. Hands loaded with the cardboard coffee-tray, he knocked on its back doors with his knuckles.

As I drew closer, the van's back door opened wide enough for me to catch a glimpse of the interior. Several seated people stared at a bank of monitor screens filled with maps and flashing markers. As strange as that was, it wasn't that which really caught my attention.

At the very back of the van several bright-orange overalls with breathing kits and oversized helmets hung on racks. Biohazard suits? The guy disappeared inside and closed the door behind him.

What the hell?

I took in the logo on the vehicle's side – Genesis Security – the same guys as the Range Rovers that I'd almost run into last night. There was something familiar about that name, and they certainly weren't just another TV crew. So what then? Undercover agents en route to the crash site to deal with some toxic chemical leak? Maybe that was the real reason the military had quarantined the area...

I stopped dead. What if I'd breathed it in and it had affected my brain chemistry – caused hallucinations, that sort of thing? That would explain a hell of a lot that had happened since.

I caught the driver's face staring at me from the wing mirror.

My phone chirped and I quickly broke eye contact. My heart rate accelerated as I read the message on the screen.

&Hj...Do...not...draw...attention...to...yourself...^&H

I glanced around, half expecting to see someone with their phone out, watching me. But no one was there. I ducked quickly into the doorway of the laundrette and pretended to read a poster about the Christmas pantomime at our local theatre.

Hand trembling, not daring to look towards the van, I started tapping a reply before the message vanished again.

Who are you?

I hit send and *Failed to send* flashed up straightaway. I checked back to my recent messages, but it had already gone. Vanished.

I gripped the face of my watch, trying to pull myself together. There had to be a simple explanation. Perhaps my phone had the virus too and someone was hacking into it? But if that was true, who and why exactly? And it would take some serious tech skills...

Chloe?

Maybe Gavin had put her up to this to freak me out. No – Chloe might have the right skills, but the time and effort needed to coordinate this with the crash of the satellite would be huge, especially just to prank someone. Also, despite everything, she wouldn't do that to me. I knew that much.

The van's engine revved up and it started to move away. I relaxed a fraction. For now it seemed I was in the clear and the Genesis team, refuelled with coffee, were presumably heading to the crash site.

I needed to sit down and try to organise the chaos of my thoughts because nothing was making a lot of sense at the moment. I huddled into my hoody and hurried off down the hill towards college.

I'd almost made it to college when I heard a squeal of tyres from behind me. I spun round, half expecting to see the Genesis van hurtling at me.

Instead Gavin's souped-up bright-red 1970s Mini hurtled round the bend nearly on just two tyres. Chloe was hanging on to a door handle on the ceiling, eyes shut, as Gavin kept casting her sideways glances, all smirks. By the look of Chloe's anxious expression, she was deeply regretting not riding in on her seriously cool electric scooter.

The Mini screamed towards me and Gavin looked away from Chloe long enough to spot me and register a look of surprise. Of course, he probably expected me to be in a police cell after yesterday's stunt. No doubt he, or one of his gang, would be along later to find out why not.

The tiny car roared past me and sped through the gates like they were the finish line of a rally, forcing several people to scatter.

Why the college had ever allowed Gavin in, with his zero qualifications, was still a mystery to me. Just when I'd thought I was free of my chief tormentor Gavin had swaggered along on the first day of college with his arm draped round Chloe like a trophy. Then, much to my horror, I'd learnt Gavin wasn't there just to drop Chloe off – but that he'd signed on to do the mechanic's apprenticeship course. Fantastic!

I ducked in through the entrance as the Mini's tyres squealed to an emergency stop in the disabled bay right outside the entrance. Gavin leapt out and winked at a group of girls walking past, who – unbelievably – smiled back at him. As though he needed any encouragement.

Chloe opened the passenger door and clambered out, her duct-tape-wrapped laptop clutched to her chest like a shield. But Gavin was too busy leering at the bums of the girls walking away to notice Chloe's scowl at him.

That was the thing, right there. Every time I saw them together, a caveman with a smart intelligent woman like Chloe, it felt like someone was messing with the natural order of the cosmos. She could do so much better than him...

Head down, I stealthed my way through the corridors until I reached the physics lab, already filled with the rest of my tutor group. I headed to the back to take up my usual seat away from the rest, catching several snatches of conversations as I passed.

'I heard the satellite killed a cow outright and smeared its guts across the hillside...'

'It sounded like a train crashing into the house when that thing came down last night – the walls shook so badly...'

'Dad says reporters aren't being allowed anywhere near the crash site because there's an alien body there...'

The last one made me smile despite myself. I knew it would only be a matter of time before the UFO conspiracists got going on this.

Eventually, of course, the satellite would become old news and then conversations would drift back to newer hot topics like which wannabe stars would win the latest TV talent contest. That was the way Stoneham rolled and I found everything about it as suffocating as wearing a plastic bag over my head.

I opened my rucksack to grab a book jammed in next to my laptop and the circuit board.

A shadow fell over me. I slowly looked up. Of all the people I expected to see it wasn't Chloe. I felt like a wild animal gripped by the headlights of an oncoming lorry. And Chloe looked as weirded-out as I felt, a million emotions playing out behind her eyes. I noticed the dark-purple bruise across her cheek that had been badly disguised with make-up – no doubt the result of Gavin slapping her last night. What a complete and utter bastard.

Every conversation in the room had stopped dead, and although most people pretended not to look, a few were openly gawping at us. This was not the usual script of 'Chloe and Jake pretending the other one doesn't exist strategy'.

Chloe seemed to focus on a point somewhere over my left shoulder. 'Hey, Jake, about last night...'

Every word from her felt like a detonation going off in my skull.

'I just wanted to thank you for what you did for Joe.'

From somewhere deep inside I found a faint voice. 'Joe?'

'The boy you helped.'

'Ah, right...'

'And I'm sorry you got picked up by the police when you were just trying to help.'

But not sorry enough to stick around to defend me. 'Got it...'

She blinked. 'I did my best to fix things afterwards.'

What does she mean by that?

Chloe moved her head nearer me. She still had the scent of summer meadows that I remembered from a long-lost friendship in a galaxy far, far away.

Her voice dropped to a whisper. 'But Gavin must never find out. He'd kill me if he knew.'

My eyes briefly touched hers and the room began to swirl around us. 'Find out what?'

'That it was me who rang the police and told them you had nothing to do with that car break-in.'

It was like someone had hit the pause button on reality. So it hadn't been the old lady who'd told the police about Gavin. Chloe had stuck her neck out for me. The question was: why?

A torrent of emotions crashed against the wall I kept them locked behind.

I gazed at the desk, not trusting myself to say a single word.

'So we're all square, right?' she said.

I managed a nod without daring to look her in the eye. I did, however, catch the sadness dripping from her every word. Something twisted inside my guts. I glanced up long enough to see Chloe's nostrils flare.

'I'll take that as a yes...' she said.

At that moment the door banged open and Gavin leant in, scanning the room. 'Princess—' He cut off as his eyes locked on to us and everyone went deathly quiet.

Gavin marched across the classroom like he owned the place. 'What are you doing with that prick, Chloe?'

She swung round, eyes hard. 'I can speak to who I want.'

'But him?' Gavin grabbed her by a shoulder.

I was on my feet before I could stop myself. 'Leave her alone, Gavin.'

Gavin growled and pulled back a sledgehammer-sized fist.

Chloe grabbed his arm. 'Don't, Gavin. They'll throw you out of college and then you'll never get your mechanics qualification.'

His grey eyes were slits. I knew Gavin would beat me to a pulp if this boiled over into a fight, and no one would come to my rescue.

Chloe's expression became pleading. 'Please, Gavin. Don't do this.' She caressed his jaw, making him look at her.

The storm broke in his eyes and his face relaxed into a smirk.

'Yeah, princess, you're right; he isn't worth it.'

Then his gaze sharpened on my open bag and his hand flew out. Before I could react, Gavin grabbed the circuit board from inside. 'What's this then – your geek science-fair project?'

'Give it back.' I tried to snatch it, but Gavin held the board out of my reach using his extra six centimetres of height.

'Oh give it to me, nasty Gavin,' he said with a squeaky voice.

There were a few laughs around the room and some students already had their mobiles out. This run-in with Gavin would probably go viral before today was over.

I tried to snatch the circuit board back again but he pulled his arm away and more people laughed. I could hardly breathe.

Chloe's eyes found mine and her expression twisted. 'Stop it, Gavin.' She took the board from his hand, everyone's attention burning my skin.

Gavin's eyes became slits again as he spun on Chloe.

Right at that moment the blue LEDs on the board blinked on. Chloe yelped and jammed her jaw together, before convulsing and crumpling to the ground, eyes widening, the contents of her laptop bag spilling across the floor. A burning smell rose from the board as it fell from her hand. Her eyes fluttered shut.

Everyone stared at her in shocked silence for a moment.

Then one of the other students shook themselves into action and rushed to her side. She pressed her fingers on to Chloe's neck then leant in to place her cheek over Chloe's mouth. A relieved look filled her face. 'She's breathing.'

Gavin grabbed me. 'So what has your bloody toy done to her?'

'I think it might be an electric shock—'

He shoved me so hard across the room that I crashed into some chairs, but managed to stay standing.

Gavin stamped on the circuit board, again and again, sending chips and resistors flying up like computer confetti. He kicked the remains of the board and it skittered away. Then he bent down and laced his arms under Chloe, lifting her as if she weighed nothing.

The room tilted beneath my feet. 'Where are you taking her?'

'To the college nurse to find out just how much I'm going to have to hurt you to make up for what you've done to her.'

One of the girls was already scooping up the contents of Chloe's bag.

As the girl dropped her phone back into her laptop bag, I noticed Chloe's mobile's screen glowing with a message:

JK&E!... Second subject...located... L*P3

I strode towards Chloe, limp in Gavin's arms. 'Chloe, I'm so sorry.'

She murmured and her eyes opened for a moment.

Thank god, at least she was conscious.

'Not as sorry as you're going to be, Stevens,' Gavin said. He kicked the door open with his foot and swept out with Chloe, almost knocking over our tutor who was entering the room at that same moment.

And then every set of eyes returned to me, each one full of blame. I grabbed my bag, picked up the lifeless circuit-board remains and hurried out, everyone's stares blazing into my back. My stomach churned as I headed to the only place that I could catch my breath in: the library.

CHAPTER SIX

As I WALKED into the library Lesley's eyes, framed by her oval glasses, flashed towards me.

'Shouldn't you still be in registration, Jake?' she asked.

I made my hands into a T symbol.

'You've not even made it to first period yet.' She pushed her glasses to the top of her head. 'So what is it this time?'

I raised a shoulder. 'Let's just say it's a worse day than usual.'

'Right. Have you at least had time to register?'

'Nope.'

'OK, I'll let your tutor know that you're here. Do you want to talk about it?'

I paused, seriously tempted. I'd love nothing more than to spill my heart out to Lesley and get the advice of someone who didn't always seem to be judging me. But then if I did that she'd feel duty-bound to tell someone about what she'd heard.

'I'll be OK. I just needed to duck of the spotlight for a moment.'

'Same old?'

'Sort of.'

'OK.' She gave me one of her warm, understanding smiles. 'But if you're looking for something to take your mind off things, maybe I can help you.'

My gaze travelled to the bookshelf behind Lesley where she stacked the new books ready to be catalogued for the library. 'The *Asimov Foundation* series has come in?'

Lesley's smile widened. 'Indeed it has.'

'You are a complete star, Lesley, but maybe another time when I'm in a better headspace.' I didn't think I could get my head around reading right then.

'They'll be here waiting for you behind my desk when you are.'

'Thanks.' I gave her a smile.

'No problem, especially for my favourite student.' She put her hand to her mouth. 'I'm not really meant to admit that, am I?' She grinned and picked up the phone.

I headed over to one of the computer booths screened by a high-sided cubicle – my favourite hiding area in the library. I settled myself in and stared at the blank screen in front of me.

OK, where to start? The circuit board was starting to look as if it might be the key to understanding this. For example: why hadn't Gavin also been electrocuted like Chloe when he'd held the same circuit board seconds before? Then there was that message: *Second subject...located.* It was eerily similar to the messages I'd received. Was that significant too?

I shook out the collection of broken bits of processors, resistors and a few capacitors on to the desk. Where exactly was the power source in this heap of junk?

Something blurred past the window, probably one of the pigeons doing a bombing run on one of the cars. I peered out in the hope I'd see Gavin's Mini covered with a nice dollop of multi-coloured bird crap on it. Instead my attention was drawn to a dark van cruising the street along one side of the college, a small radar-type dish rotating on its roof.

The Genesis Security vehicle. Why weren't they up at the crash site? It was almost as though they were looking for a signal here in Stoneham...

My gaze snapped back to the circuit board remains. At the crash site it had been plugged into some sort of aerial, presumably part of a communication system. And if it had sufficient power to zap me and Chloe, could there be some sort of GPS locator chip hidden on it, maybe even broadcasting right now? It seemed hard to believe that the broken pile of components could still be capable of broadcasting any sort of radio wave, but it also wasn't worth taking the risk. I needed to come up with a way of jamming it just in case.

I forced myself to think. Metal could disrupt radio waves. It was the main reason that mobiles worked so badly at college – it had a ton of hidden metal beamwork in its structure.

I grabbed my lunch from my bag and unwrapped the foil round my sandwiches that Allan always swore was vastly superior to cling film. Not exactly a sheet of lead, but it would have to do. As the van drew closer, I dumped the remains of the circuit board into the foil and rolled them up into a tight ball inside.

My heart thudded in my chest and my hand sought out my watch as the van slid past the college. When it didn't stop, I slumped back into my seat.

'All good?' Lesley called over.

I nodded but avoided eye contact.

OK, so a tracking signal was one thing, but I kept thinking about the biohazard suits I'd seen inside that van. I needed answers more than ever and maybe Genesis Security was the clue to what was really going on in and around Stoneham.

I powered up the PC screen and Genesis Security Solutions

homepage was up a few clicks later. Alexander Langton's face was plastered across the website's masthead.

So our very own prime minister had a nice little business on the side. Interesting. I thought it would be illegal for someone in his position to be running a company too.

Just below his grin, a golden globe rotated with the Genesis Security logo stamped across it. Beneath that was a strap-line: *The world leader in security solutions for every situation.*

Good for them. But the bio-suits? Did their security service extend to dealing with satellite chemical spills? And why would any government want to use a private contractor rather than rely on their own military to sort that kind of mess out? Maybe that came down to the fact that Genesis Security was run by Langton. Could that be it? He was just another dodgy politician on the make, who'd found a way of syphoning public money into his own back pocket?

I clicked back to the Google search page, scanned down the list and read the entry near the bottom of the screen.

Science Park Explosion.

My heart started pounding so hard I was almost surprised Lesley didn't shush me. I opened up a science journal entry on the website.

At the Hopworth Science Park, thirty-six people are believed to have been killed when an experiment into dark energy, run by Professor Martin Stevens, exploded after a catastrophic contain-ment failure. A government enquiry panel interviewed the head of Genesis Security Solutions, the company responsible for over-seeing safety procedures within the research lab. Their chairman, Alexander Langton, informed the committee that Professor Martin Stevens deliberately overrode safety measures that would have shut down the experiment safely. This was also corroborated by Professor Dave Haze, who told the committee that his colleague, believing he was close to making a breakthrough with his research, had pressed on, despite knowing the risks. The committee duly recorded manslaughter by misadventure. The case has now been closed.

The world swam around me. That was why I'd recognised the name Genesis Security. In a rush, the memories of my twelve-year-old self came flooding back... The security guards at Dad's work, the computer experts maintaining the systems in Dad's lab, the engineers he'd worked with... They all had the same gold logo stitched above their white shirt pockets. Genesis Security had been there and Langton had been their chairman. The same man who, along with Dave, had helped to pin the blame on Dad. The same man who was now our prime minister.

I breathed through my nose, clenching my fist round the mouse. My phone chirped, making me jump. The unknown number, bang on time.

DEC.

What was that meant to mean?

Pins and needles swept up my arm. I stifled my groan so Lesley wouldn't hear. I clenched and loosened my fist as a sudden cramp burned through my muscles. The spasm faded to nothing as quickly as it had come. I caught my breath.

OK, I hadn't been holding the circuit board that time so maybe it really was repetitive strain injury.

I tried to reply to the message.

What are you trying to tell me?

DEC tugged at a memory that wouldn't come.

Failed send flashed up on my screen. I googled for DEC but only found the Disasters Emergency Committee. I thought at first it could be linked, but after a bit of digging realised they were irrelevant as they dealt with famines and natural disasters.

'You'll be late for your first lesson if you don't shake a leg, Jake,' Lesley called out.

'I'm on it...' I shouldered my rucksack and, praying to myself I didn't run into Gavin en route, headed off for my maths lesson feeling more confused than ever.

When lunchtime finally arrived, since Chloe hadn't been in any of the classes we'd shared, I checked in with the receptionist. She told me Chloe had gone home with a splitting headache. I immediately felt a mixture of relief – that it wasn't anything worse – and guilt that I'd caused it.

At the end of the day, like usual, I hung back in the library working on my coursework until it was dark outside and most of the other students had left the campus. Not that I'd been able to get much studying done. Endless thoughts spiralled through my head, the main one being: why me? By the time Lesley eventually threw me out and I set off for home I felt mentally exhausted.

In the wintry darkness, it was hard to make out the wreckage itself on the horizon. But the flashing navigation lights hovering in the air told me the Apache gunships were still guarding the site.

If it was possible, the town seemed even more packed with reporters now. What would have usually been a quiet high street on a Thursday evening was thronging with people. Each person I passed seemed to be trying to grab their five minutes of fame, with one of the many microphones pushed into their face.

If they only knew I had the huge story they were after. But I hadn't asked for any of this. Mr Unknown Number had a lot to answer for. And why target Chloe and me? The only thing that linked us was our dads having worked together at the Hopworth Science Park...

My spine sparked with a jolt of electricity. That had to be it – the common denominator in all of this – our dads' research work.

Genesis Security had been at the lab when it exploded and now they were back on the scene again.

So who was Mr Unknown Number? A former employee wanting to whistle-blow about what was really going on? Or maybe a spy from a rival state, one using a sophisticated government virus to unearth the truth, and using the professors' kin to get whatever it was they were after. But if that was it, what about the Varuna satellite itself? How could it be linked to an explosion in my dad's lab and why were Genesis so desperate to get their hands on it?

All I knew for sure was I was completely out of my depth. The only answer was the one I'd been doing my best to avoid.

I turned away from my route home and on to a side road from the high street. I hadn't walked this way in years. As I neared the tall brick building at the end of the road a million dark scenarios sped through my mind. The worst thing was I knew that whatever was hurled my way I deserved all of it. It had been me. I was the one who'd given up on our friendship. And the time had come to talk to Chloe, whatever the cost.

CHAPTER SEVEN

I HEADED beneath the wrought-iron curved sign with flowing script proclaiming the building as 'The Old Brewery' and into a high-walled courtyard. Within it, Porsches, Mercs, BMWs and other expensive cars crammed the parking bays. The glowing windows of the flats in the converted brewery stretched upwards. I could see huge TV sets and designer furniture in many of the apartments, all hinting at the luxury lifestyles within. This place, and the people privileged enough to be able to call it home, dripped with money.

I glanced up to the very top of the building where a large glass balcony extended out from the penthouse – Chloe and Dave's apartment. According to Allan, their flat was worth well over two million. Somewhere along the way, Dave had hit the big time with his research into dark energy, something that my dad had prepared the groundwork for. Standing here it was hard not feel a small stab of jealousy. After all, this could have been my life if Dad hadn't screwed it up so spectacularly.

I headed towards the large glass door with a keypad entry

system beside it. Beyond it was a marble foyer and, off to one side, the polished black doors of a lift and a stairwell.

If I tried buzzing Chloe's flat there was every chance she wouldn't let me in. As I dithered, I heard a muffled ping and a young woman emerged from the lift, eyes on her phone's screen.

As she opened the locked glass door, I grabbed the handle and held it open for her. Her lips thinned at me, eyes lingering on my hooded top, no doubt wondering what someone like me was doing there.

I pointed to my rucksack. 'Delivery for number twenty.' I'd never seen a parcel delivery guy use a backpack before, but she smiled anyway, the suspicion of an 'undesirable' entering the hallowed flats disappearing from her eyes, and headed past me towards a white Maserati parked in the corner bay.

I slipped into the entrance, my stomach clenching. Could I really do this? I cast a glance at the lift, but I might run into another flat owner if I used it, and based on the woman's reaction, I'd prefer to avoid any further unwanted attention. I started the long climb up the five flights of stairs.

So how would I even begin this impossible conversation with Chloe? Any sort of confrontation with her was kryptonite to my comfortably numb life.

At the top of the stairs I approached a solid light-oak door with a video entry system. I raised my finger to the flat's bell, my stomach churning so fast I started to think all Chloe would find when she opened the door was a puddle of vomit. I took a steadying breath and pressed the cold metal button.

Somewhere in the flat beyond I heard the faint chime of a bell. As the seconds ticked past, I had to fight every instinct to turn round and disappear back down the stairwell. But then it was too late because the door was opening and there was Chloe in her PJs staring at me. Her red hair was wrapped in a towel, a few wet strands escaping its folds and hanging down on to her neck like fine curls of flames. But it was the blue bruise, make-up free, that caught my gaze most of all, although she still looked crazy-cute.

Chloe's eyes widened and she took a half step back. 'Jake?'

I stared at her, my thoughts locking up like a traffic jam. What had I been thinking? I started to turn.

'Why are you here?' Chloe asked.

Her question hung in the air for a moment.

'Is this about what happened at college?' she continued.

It was as good a place as any to start. I turned back to face her. 'Yes, in a way it is...'

Chloe crossed her arms. 'You don't need to apologise, Jake. I realised at the time it was an accident.'

'Yes, it was...' Her blue gemstone eyes burrowed into mine.

'Is that it then?' Her eyebrows rose up. 'It's just that Gavin will be over in less than an hour and it's probably best that you're not here when he arrives.'

As in Gavin would tear me apart limb by limb. 'Sorry, I shouldn't have come.'

'What else is it, Jake?'

'What do you mean?'

'You wouldn't have braved coming here unless it was important.'

Psychic like always – or maybe Chloe still knew me far too well, even after all these years of being apart.

'I...' How could I even begin to phrase this? 'I need your help, Chloe.' I stared at her grey furry slippers.

'Help with...?'

'A virus – a virus has taken out my laptop.'

Her eyes widened a fraction and then narrowed again. 'Seriously, Jake. You think because of what happened last night you can come over here to ask me to fix your bloody computer, do you?'

I raised a hand as if it would ward off her words. 'This was a mistake.'

'It was, but...' Chloe took a long breath, nostrils flaring. 'Have you got it with you?'

'What?'

'Your laptop, zombie brain.'

'Right...yes... Of course.'

She stood back, holding the door open.

I hovered on the threshold. 'You're sure?'

'Let's just call it *professional curiosity*, but we'll have to be quick because Gavin will be here soon. I'll have a look at it and afterwards, we can both pretend like this never happened. OK?'

'OK...and thank you.' Head down, I entered the penthouse flat glowing with light behind her.

Something soft pressed into my ankles and a purr drifted up. I glanced down to see Chloe's silver-haired tabby cat Toby winding his way round my legs.

'Seems like he hasn't forgotten you,' Chloe said.

'The last time I saw Toby, he was a kitten.'

Her eyes flashed. 'Exactly.' She shoved open a second door.

Toby led the way, tail up, just the opposite of how I was feeling.

We entered a room with wall-to-wall windows and a breathtaking view of Stoneham stretching into the distance. I automatically hunted out the roof of Celestial Skies. A curl of smoke rose up into the night sky from its chimney pot. Allan had lit a fire and by now he'd be making supper and probably wondering where I was. Then I noticed the pair of binoculars on a tripod by the window, pointed towards the crash site.

'That's an impressive a view,' I said.

'It's not bad.' Chloe gestured towards a huge white leather sofa, which had to be twice as big as my single bed at home.

I sat and Toby immediately leapt on to my lap, headbutting

my chest for attention. It wasn't lost on me that Chloe perched on the sofa as far away from me as possible like I was a bad smell she didn't want to inhale.

I started to dig out my laptop from my bag.

'Do you know what virus it is?' she asked.

'No, just that it took over my system first thing this morning.'

She extended her hand and I got up to pass my laptop to her, disturbing Toby, who jumped down with a tail flick – now as irritated by me as his owner seemed to be.

Chloe opened the screen and the password prompt immediately appeared.

'That's more than it did for me,' I said.

'Maybe it recognises the fingertips of someone who means business.' Her quick smile vanished just as fast as it had appeared.

I gestured for the laptop. 'I'll enter my password for you.'

She gave me the barest headshake and started typing into the password box. A moment later my desktop appeared.

Chloe raised an eyebrow at me. 'Still using your *Spiderpig* password I see.'

Now it was my turn to give a faint smile. I raised a shoulder. 'I guess, but I use that for everything else so it's easy to remember.'

'You, Jake Stevens, are a hacker's dream.'

'Yeah, I know, I know.' The ice-cold tension in the room began to thaw. 'So does this mean my laptop's all clear now?'

She shot me a frown. 'Not if it's what I think it is.'

'You have an idea what this might be?'

'Maybe... You saw a stream of numbers on the screen and then it died, right?'

My pulse leapt. Chloe did know. 'Yes, yes it did. And this virus does what exactly?'

'Still working that part out.' She started tapping again and opened up a black window with a blinking cursor.

'What are you doing?'

'I'm about to check your operating system for footprints of the virus's code.'

She entered a few computer commands. A moment later the window filled with the same scrolling text I'd seen earlier. This time there weren't just numbers, but lines of random text as well. I couldn't make sense of it until I saw the line:

Can you pick up a loaf of bread on your way back from college?

I pointed to the message just as it disappeared off the screen. 'Hang on, that was a text I got from Allan.'

Chloe chewed her lip. 'Yep, this virus seems programmed to go through all your files, contacts, photos, the lot, even to remotely trawl through your phone for information.'

'Well, if the hackers are after my bank account details, they're not going to get rich. I think I've got about twenty quid in the bank. Whatever it's looking for has to be for greater stakes than that.'

'Weirdly, from what I've been able to piece together so far, it doesn't seem to be what they're after. It's more like they are trying to learn as much as possible about you.'

A shiver rippled through me. Who? Genesis Security? 'You seem to know a lot about this virus?'

'There's a good reason for that...' Chloe picked her own damaged laptop off the table and turned its screen towards me.

The first thing I noticed was a piece of tape over the tiny camera above the screen. I pointed to it. 'You're that paranoid about someone spying on you?'

'When you hang out in the hacking community you quickly learn to take precautions. Do you have any idea how easy it is to hack a webcam?'

'No, but I'll make sure I find some duct tape when I get home.'

Chloe snorted. 'You should.'

I spotted the YouTube video she'd been watching. 'Why are you watching taekwondo videos?'

Her expression pinched. 'I need to learn to look after myself...' Her eyes slid away from mine.

A knot of anger pulsed inside me.

'Anyway, that's not what I wanted to show you,' she said. She double-clicked on a monitor-shaped icon and a familiar window appeared with texts and numbers scrolling through it.

I stared at her. 'You've got the virus too?'

'And there is no way that any virus, however sophisticated, should be able to breach my uber-firewall.'

'So where did you get it from then?'

'That's the weird thing, Jake. All my computers are like digital fortresses, with the best virus protection money can buy, and a few extra levels of protection thrown in, thanks to tips from my hacker friends. My best guess is it came loaded on to a random text I got on my phone earlier today. Then it somehow leapt from my phone to my laptop, maybe by hacking its Blue-tooth connection. Who knows, but very impressive.'

'Random text?'

'Yeah, a single word: DEC...'

'You too?' The words were out of my mouth before I could stop myself.

Her gaze locked on to me. 'You received the same message?'

I couldn't unsay the words so I decided I should just tell her. 'Yes, while I was in the library.'

'OK...' She tapped her finger on her lips. 'So that confirms this virus is spread via text messages, which is an original twist.'

Among the random lines of data scrolling across her laptop's screen, a piece of text snagged my attention. *God, I miss our friendship. How did we ever let it get to this?*

Chloe's face flamed as she slammed her laptop shut. 'Just something I'm working on for a character in my Ember sim.'

Every instinct told me that was a lie. So what was it then really – a line from a diary? If so, was she talking about me?

I arranged my expression into something I hoped looked like belief. 'So you're still working on Ember then?'

Her face lit up. 'I've never stopped...and you should see—' She cut off and her features crumpled. 'Sorry, you're not here to talk about that.'

I felt the old familiar pain rising within me.

Just like that line from her computer had said, how did we ever get to this?

I ran my finger over my diver's watch as she crossed to the window, a weight to her walk, and gazed out at Stoneham.

There were so many things I wanted to say, but the small distance between us felt like the width of an ocean. Still, I needed to warn her about my suspicion.

'Chloe, I need to tell you something...'

Her reflection gazed towards me, shoulders rising. 'What, Jake?'

The quicker I told her, the quicker she wouldn't get the wrong idea.

'I think we've both been deliberately targeted by the person who wrote that virus.'

'But why? Who?'

The edge of the abyss that separated us rushed up at me and I got ready to leap across.

'My best guess is it's because of our dads' work.'

Chloe slowly turned to face me. 'You mean because of their research into dark energy?'

'It's the only thing that makes any sense.'

Her mouth thinned. 'OK, but *who* and *why?*'

'I was sort of hoping that your hacker mates might be able to help us out on that. My instinct is some sort of government-sponsored virus.'

'You mean like that one they discovered years ago in the systems running nuclear reactors?'

'Pretty much, I guess.'

Chloe stared at me. 'The code behind the virus is definitely more sophisticated than anything I've ever seen. What you're saying isn't totally bat-shit crazy.'

'So you believe me then?'

'I guess it does kind of fit what I've seen for myself. But why target us, Jake? Why not hack my dad's computer directly if they wanted to learn about his work?'

I shrugged. 'I just know that this all started when I plugged that circuit board into my computer. That's when it downloaded the virus.'

'The same device that zapped me.'

'Yes.'

And I'm guessing that you didn't make it?'

'Nope, I'm useless with a soldering iron.'

'So where did it come from, Jake?'

I pointed towards the binoculars on the tripod.

Chloe gazed at them and then beyond towards the crash site. She spun round to stare at me. 'From the satellite? You've been up there?'

'Yeah, and more. I was there last night with Allan. Varuna nearly came down on our heads.'

'Holy douche nuggets, Jake. And what, you're telling me you found that circuit board among the wreckage?'

'In one.' I grabbed my bag and emptied out the broken remains on to her coffee table.

Chloe started to pick over the broken bits, scowling. 'And Allan let you take it?'

'He doesn't know, Chloe. He also doesn't know that the two Typhoon fighter jets that turned up afterwards took out what remained of Varuna.'

'You're joking, right? This is all one big wind-up?'

'I wish it was, Chloe. But it's true. All of it. And the punch-line is that I started receiving these strange text messages on my mobile just before the crash and ever since. The weirdest part is that the mobile network was down when I first got them.'

'Very strange. All saying "DEC"?'

'Not just that. The first message directed me to the crash satellite. And then the next warned me about the incoming Typhoons, moments before they took out what remained of the satellite. I'd be a pair of smouldering boots on a hillside right now if it wasn't for whoever is behind these messages.'

'You nearly died, seriously?'

'Yes. You're the first person I've told, though.'

She slowly nodded. 'Thank you for trusting me, Jake.'

'I've always trusted you, Chloe.'

For a moment we caught each other's eyes before both glancing away.

My throat tightened as I felt a hole open up in the centre of my being.

Chloe turned back to the window. 'So whoever it is, they're trying to help you at least?'

'I think so, but in a non-direct way. Texts saying "DEC" aren't really all that useful if I don't know what it means.'

'I see your point. But I keep thinking I know that word from somewhere.'

'Me too. I've tried googling it, but came up with nothing.'

'OK, have you got your phone on you?' Chloe asked.

'Yeah, why?'

'Can I have a look?'

'Knock yourself out.' I dug my phone out from my jeans' pocket and handed it to her.

'Come on, follow me,' Chloe said.

'Where are we going?'

'To my bedroom.'

'Right...'

'And you can wipe that look off your face. That's where all my serious computing power is.'

'You really are Miss Super Geek.'

'Wow, I haven't been called that in years. Not since we...' She gave me a small headshake. 'Anyway, it takes one to know one. But we'll have to make this fast. Gavin really will be here at any moment.' She scooped up the circuit board components.

For one glorious moment, I'd started to forget the guy even existed. I felt a tug of sadness. 'Of course.'

I followed her into an enormous room that was bigger than the whole of Allan's flat. But despite the huge bed, this felt nothing like a bedroom. Between the large manga posters that adorned the walls, computer tech had been crammed on to every available surface. I took in at least six computers. Some were just bare circuit boards connected to screens. But there was one computer that really caught my eye. Its circuit boards glowed under neon lights, all mounted inside a clear Perspex case. Tubes of fluid spidered out from a large central processor to something that looked like a fish aquarium pump. Everything about the beast screamed raw computing power.

'That's Deep Thought Two,' Chloe said.

'As in from *The Hitch Hiker's Guide to the Galaxy*?'

'Exactly. See, you're almost as big a geek as me, Jake Stevens.'

'I can only ever hope to walk in your shadow, Chloe Haze.'

She snorted.

Talking to Chloe felt so natural, like slipping into a pair of old, perfectly fitted jeans.

She walked past the supercomputer to an old PC with a yellowing plastic case. When she plugged my phone into that one I felt a mild stab of disappointment.

'You're not using Deep Thought Two then? He looks perfect for something like this.'

'*She* is. But I'm not going to risk getting my beautiful creation fried, especially when that's the system I'm coding Ember on. Plus this old PC isn't connected to the internet. Best not to take any chances.'

'OK.'

'So down to business...' Chloe pressed a button below a bulging monitor screen that looked like it belonged in the Science Museum's history of computing section.

After what had to be at least thirty seconds, a phosphor dot morphed into what I vaguely recognised as a Linux desktop. Chloe checked the cable to my phone and, with a few more keystrokes, the familiar scrolling pattern of text filled the screen.

'It certainly looks like the virus is on your phone, but let's make sure...'

She tapped a few more commands and a series of text messages flashed past. I recognised them instantly as the ones I'd received from the unknown number.

'OK, that confirms the virus is behind the messages,' I said. 'But any chance you can work out who sent them? Who is Mr Unknown Number?'

Chloe bit her lip. 'I should be able to at least see what mobile mast the texts were relayed from. At least then we can work out how they could send you a text without a phone signal. Perhaps they hacked directly into a mast and created their own temporary mobile radio cell network.'

'That so went over my head, Chloe. You really are the right person to be talking to about this.'

She smiled as she bent her head and started typing. Commands flashed past almost faster than I could read them. Her finger memory seemed to be able to move as quickly as her thoughts – a stark contrast to my two-finger typing.

Chloe rocked back on her chair as she started chewing the quick of her thumbnail. 'OK, now that is truly weird.'

'What is?'

'It seems that there aren't any stored IP addresses for those messages.'

'What does that mean?'

'Those messages weren't sent from anywhere, Jake. Don't ask me how, but they seem to have been generated on your phone itself.'

'How can that be possible?'

'I have no idea,' Chloe replied.

A warbling alarm came from Deep Thought.

Chloe rolled her seat over to it. 'Huh?'

'Problem?' I asked.

'That's my code compile alarm.'

'And?'

'And I haven't run any sort of compile on Ember for at least a week.' She moved the mouse and the screen came instantly to life.

Compile complete pulsed on the screen.

Chloe's eyes narrowed as she double-clicked a flame icon on the desktop. At once the screen was filled with a three-dimensional game-world view of a town under a night sky.

In a rush, I realised what I was looking at. It was Stoneham... and a stunningly detailed version of it too. I glanced to the round window in Chloe's room and the maze of rooftops surrounded by the ring of gentle hills. It was identical in every single way to what we were seeing on the screen. In the sim, I spotted the flashing lights of the helicopter in the distance hovering over the crash site.

I whistled. 'That's seriously incredible, Chloe. Putting in that Apache gunship is what I call attention to detail.'

Chloe swung her chair towards mine, eyes wide. 'But I didn't, Jake.'

'What do you mean?'

'I mean I didn't code those helicopters in...or most of this. It's way more detailed than I could have created.' She took hold of a complex-looking mouse with dozens of extra buttons and spun the central wheel. The view zoomed in on the two ultra-realistic models of the helicopters circling the charred pit of the impact crater. It was so detailed I could even see the pilots moving inside the cockpit canopy – and the grass in a nearby field swishing around from the rotor wash. Although, beyond the next rise of hills, the game world seemed to come to an abrupt end.

'You really didn't put these Apaches in?' I asked.

'I wish I could take the credit, Jake. This is mind-blowing.' She mimed her head exploding with her hands. Then she used the mouse to rotate the view back to Stoneham and zoomed to the Old Brewery, to the penthouse, closing in on her own round bedroom window.

We both gasped as we saw ourselves sitting in front of Deep Thought Two's screen.

Chloe turned her head towards the window and the screen version of her did too.

This was so beyond impossible. Someone had to be setting me up. Chloe? Maybe she had a camera in the corner of the room. Gavin would be pissing his pants when this got posted on YouTube the moment I left.

Anger burned up through me. 'Is this your twisted idea of a joke?' I said.

Chloe put her hands on top of her head. 'This isn't my code, Jake. I swear it.'

I took in her pleading expression. Of course she wouldn't do that to me. Gavin, yes. Chloe, never.

'So what are you saying? That someone has hacked your game engine and added these things in?' I said.

'I don't know how. Ember isn't connected to the internet either because I am that paranoid. But in a word, yes. I think you're right.' The skin tightened around her eyes. 'Hang on, what's that?' She pointed at something shimmering over our heads in the virtual version of her bedroom on the screen.

It was so faint that I hadn't noticed it at first: an almost totally transparent crystal hovering in the room.

I glanced up to make sure, but nothing was there. 'Not your work either?'

Another shake of her head. Chloe zoomed in on the crystal to reveal the surface had hundreds of polished faces, each reflecting a different fragmented view of the surrounding room.

Then I spotted the numbers scrolling inside the heart of the crystal. 'Hey, that thing looks just like the—'

Chloe broke off as every computer screen in the room lit up with the same crystal graphic on each screen. Both our phones buzzed at the same time, and when I looked, those displayed the crystal too.

I traded startled looks with Chloe. Just when I thought things couldn't get any stranger a single message appeared on every single screen.

Examine the DEC file.

'Son of a zombie,' Chloe said.

I stared at her, slack-jawed. 'The virus is doing all of this?'

She spread her hands wide. 'It has to be, Jake. Which means the code is way more sophisticated than any government virus could ever hope to be. Technically what just happened is impossible – beyond even the best hackers I know.'

I heard a door opening and closing somewhere in the flat and leapt up, my adrenalin pumping. 'Gavin's here!'

Chloe chewed her lip. 'No, he hasn't got a key.'

'Chloe, where are you?' called out a voice I hadn't heard in six years – Professor Dave Haze, Chloe's dad.

Chloe paled. 'You've got to get out of here, Jake.'

'Why? Dave's not got a problem with me, has he?'

Her expression tightened. 'You just have to make yourself scarce.'

'I've bought you a new laptop to replace your damaged one,' Dave called out.

As footsteps approached the room, Chloe was on her feet, quickly turning off every screen.

'What are you panicking about?'

'You need to go, Jake.'

The door opened just as Chloe managed to blank the last monitor. Dave stood in the doorway, his smile morphing into something similar to a snarl and directed at me.

Dave's gaze snapped back to Chloe. 'What is *he* doing here?'

As I stood to face him, Chloe rushed in between the two of us, her arms extended outwards as though she honestly expected this to turn into a fight.

'He's just going, Dad,' she said.

'I thought we agreed you were never going to see him again. Or do I need to remind you what this lad's father did to all those people? Like father, like son, I've always said.'

I gawped at him. Was he saying what I thought he was?

'I was only helping him sort out a virus on his laptop,' Chloe replied.

'I don't care what you're helping him with, I want him to get the hell out of here,' Dave said. And then his eyes were back on me and filled with darkness.

Spittle beaded his lips, eyes slits, fists clenched. 'Get out of here, Jake, before I do something we both regret.'

This really could turn into a fight, I realised. And Chloe looked as if she'd seen him like this before and knew where it was headed.

I wanted to say something, to stand my ground, to tell him to stop being a dick. But the pleading look I saw in Chloe's face washed away any resolve I had. I grabbed my bag and headed for the door.

'And don't you ever dare step into this flat again, Jake Stevens. You hear me?'

Cold anger swirled around the huge cavern that had opened in my stomach. But I kept walking away – just like I had been doing for the last six years.

My body shaking, I threw open the flat's door and hurtled away down the five flights of stairs and across the courtyard. I caught a movement in the shadows under an archway, but when I glanced over nothing was there. I pulled up my hood and headed out into the darkness beyond the gates, tears smudging my eyes as I strode into the embrace of the night.

CHAPTER EIGHT

HURT AND ANGER rolled through me as Dave's words flared inside my head: *Like father, like son...*

I'd once looked up to him. But I should have known – this was the same man who hadn't even bothered coming to Dad's funeral. At least the rose-tinted glasses had been ripped off my face and I could see the guy as the solid-gold dickhead he really was.

My shoulders hunched forward, I picked my way through the groups gathered around the news crews. I turned off the high street and was heading up the cobbled street towards Celestial Skies when my phone chirped.

Not now – not bloody now.

But this time the text wasn't from Mr Unknown Number.

Hi Jake, Chloe here. I'm so sorry. You didn't deserve any of that. Look, I realise I'm probably the last person you want to talk to right now, but I still desperately need to speak to you. I know exactly where I came across the name DEC before...and so will you too when I tell you. Call me when you can...please. This is important.

I stared at the message, not really knowing what to say, think or even how to respond – so I didn't. I pocketed my phone instead.

I reached the shop, now shining again with enough twinkling lights to give Santa's grotto a run for its money. Had it really only been less than twenty-four hours since the Varuna crash that caused the power cut? Above me, I could see the silhouette of Allan limping about in our flat. I paused on the threshold.

The problem was that in my current mental mess, Allan would know with one look that something was up and start interrogating me. And that was about the last thing I could handle at the moment. I needed some quiet to sort out my headspace.

I turned away from the sanctuary of the shop. Shivering, I stuck my hands into my pockets and set off up the hill towards the park. One by one the glowing shop windows petered out, replaced by terraces of stone houses set back behind their high wrought-iron fences. The gloomy evening seemed to concentrate around them. Every recessed doorway became a pit of darkness, every window a sightless eye.

I passed along the chain-linked metal fence that bordered the park, bent to the ground by kids clambering over it to get in when the gate was locked. The park itself was surrounded on all sides by tall houses, all in darkness, not a lit window to be seen – the owners were probably too busy chasing their five minutes of fame on the high street.

I walked through the gate – still open for the early-evening dog walkers – and cut across the grass. The sounds around me became deadened until I couldn't even hear the traffic any more. It was like the familiar world I knew was slipping away and being replaced by this darker version.

Get a grip, Jake.

The playground ahead of me, which during the day would have been full of young mums and toddlers, was deserted now.

And that was what I needed: somewhere to think and not be interrupted. I crossed to the old swings that Dad had pushed me on when I was little. Around them were numerous cigarette butts and empty crushed beer cans. I wouldn't be surprised if Gavin and his gang were responsible for half of the litter.

My breath steamed. I shivered again. Hell, when had it got this cold? I drew up the zip of my hoody all the way to the top and huddled into it against the sudden Arctic air, which smelled somehow sickly sweet, like someone with cheap aftershave had just walked by.

I began to try to order my thoughts. Why had the virus taken Ember over – and how? And this DEC thing, whatever it was – would that turn out to be the key to unlocking this whole mystery?

I took my phone out and gazed at my screen. All it would take was a phone call to Chloe. And it wasn't lost on me that she'd texted rather than rung, letting it be my decision to take the step. So was this the start of some sort of reconciliation? The gulf between us had always seemed too wide to cross, but maybe that had just been in my head and not Chloe's. But that same emotional barrier I'd constructed to help me cope with all the shit that life had thrown at me had also created the wall that'd kept her out of my life for the last six years. Could I really afford to lower my defences?

My finger was hovering over the call button when I noticed a hint of mist creeping around the edges of the park. A streetlight next to the playground flickered off. If this were a film, any moment now a zombie would shuffle out of the gloom.

A soft sigh came from close by, like a muffled voice. I looked round but nobody was there. But what if they were hiding, waiting to pounce on me? It didn't take a genius to work out who that might be...

I jumped up from the swing and left it swaying behind me. I strode towards the gate at the far end.

The faint tendrils of mist wrapped round me and deepened into fog. The houses around the park became jagged silhouettes pushing up into the sky. Every shrub looked like a potential ambush point. Soon I could only see a few metres ahead of me.

The anxiety monster inside me started to stretch its claws when the chill dropped to way below zero. My skin began to sting as frost rippled out across the grass like someone had hit the deep-freeze button.

My phone chirped but when I looked it wasn't Chloe. Instead the gemstone was on my screen, slowly rotating.

The pressure on my chest increased like someone had me in a bear hug.

Initiate phase two.

Pins and needles burned through my arm, a hundred times more painful than they'd been back in the library. The sensation blazed through the rest of my body, as a bone-grinding headache kicked in too. I staggered forward, my legs folding beneath me, and I sprawled on to the frosted grass. I shook as the agonising fire pulsed through my veins. My vision swam and my view of the world faded to black and white just in time to catch a faint shadow shooting across the path ahead of me.

Part of my mind tried to process what was happening to me – an epileptic fit? The seconds stretched on, but at last the pressure on my chest loosened and the fire faded inside me.

I hauled myself up to my knees and retched, vomit surging up from my stomach and steaming on to the frozen grass. I snatched in several lungfuls of the sickly air and quickly started to feel OK...actually, better than OK – great even. Except for my vision. All I could see was a monochrome world. I raised a hand to rub my eyes and saw the end of my fingers glowing white. I'd heard of something like a migraine attack affecting people's vision, but as extreme as this?

The fog had become so thick it was like having my face pressed into a cloud. But somehow I could see through it a short way, certainly further than I should. A nearby tree stood out white against the surrounding greyness. It reminded me of a photograph negative the arty students at college used for old film cameras. But how could that be possible? And what I could see wasn't quite a negative image. Then I remembered exactly where I'd seen a similar black-and-white view before...

There'd been this TV show where the police had been using thermal cameras mounted on a helicopter to catch some joyriders. A couple of lads had ditched the Audi they'd stolen and tried to hide in someone's back garden. The problem for them was that they glowed like human torches against a dark background through the police helicopter's thermal camera. The helicopter crew had been able to direct officers on the ground straight to their hiding place. But that was a special camera used by the police, so how the hell could I have developed the same kind of heat-sensitive vision? A new message pulsed beneath the gemstone on my mobile still clamped in my hand.

Phase two completed. Subject Awoken.

Subject? Me? Awoken?

I rubbed my temples. OK, was this linked to me getting electrocuted by the circuit board? Had it messed with my perceptions somehow? And if so, would this happen to Chloe next? I had to warn her – and we both needed to get checked out in hospital, and probably have a brain scan.

Dread squeezed my heart. What the hell had happened to me?

I got back to my feet and heard a rustling sound from the path ahead of me.

Gavin and his gang?

I forced myself not to panic and to think this through. There was an alley near here that led away from the park and back to the far end of the high street. I could use that to avoid my potential attackers.

I doubled back, using my new thermal vision as a guide in the murky gloom to work my way towards the entrance to the alley.

I finally reached the passageway and relaxed a fraction as I ducked into its bush-covered darkness. I listened for any sound of pursuit, but could hear only silence, and silence was golden right now.

I edged forward, trailing my hand along the wall. An inner instinct made me glance back over my shoulder. I spotted something shift in the darkness. I stared into the gloom, trying to make it out.

Something is definitely moving in there.

The same putrid smell of rotting rubbish I'd come across outside Celestial Skies flooded my nose again. My skin prickled as dark gas-like vapours carrying black floating particles swirled towards me. The distance seemed to fold in upon itself as the particles converged to form indistinct things – crow-like shapes.

My mind wheeled, my breath smoking in the chill. Maybe this was a migraine and I was hallucinating it all? But then the stench thickened to stomach gagging levels and the shadow creatures surged towards me. Illusion or not, I wasn't about to wait to find out. I whirled round and sprinted away into the fog along the alley.

With every pace, the glow from the high street ahead grew stronger. Stride by stride, I ran back into the world I knew and away from this nightmare version I'd stumbled into.

I was within metres of the end of the alley when something snagged my foot. I sprawled forward on to my chest, pain exploding through my hands and knees as they slammed on to the tarmac.

My breath rasping, I rolled over and pulled at a bramble wrapped round my ankle, knowing that those things would be on top of me any moment. I heaved at my leg and tensed, ready for the creatures to attack, but the moment stretched forward and still nothing came.

I risked a glance back into the alley to see only swirling grey fog, painted amber under the streetlight in the alleyway. So the things had vanished and my vision seemed to have returned to normal.

My mind tilted. I had to be going mad.

'Did you see that? Stevens just materialised out of thin air!' a voice said from close by.

I looked around to see the blond guy with the razor cut pointing at me, open-mouthed. He was standing among a group of guys with their backs to me. One of them was taller than the others and smoking a cigarette. They all turned to look at me.

'You need your eyes testing, mate,' Gavin said in a flat tone to the razor-cut guy.

'I'm telling you...'

Gavin raised his hand and the guy flinched. They all started ambling towards me, shoulders rolling, danger in their eyes.

'Well, well, well, it must be my birthday, because we've been looking for you, Stevens,' Gavin said.

Before I could react, he nodded to his gang. They jumped on to me and pinned my arms to the ground.

'That's it – hold him down,' Gavin said.

My blood thumped in my ears as I struggled to break free. 'If this is about Chloe getting that shock, it was an accident.'

He towered over me. 'This isn't about that...'

I stopped wriggling and stared up at him. 'What then?'

He pulled his lips back over his teeth at me. 'Think you'd make a move on Chloe when I had my back turned, did you?'

'I don't follow?'

'Hear that everyone? He doesn't *follow*.'

His hyena pack cackled.

Gavin squatted behind me. 'Maybe if I help jog your memory.'

He slapped me hard across the face, and my teeth sliced into my lower lip, reopening the wound from the night before. Hot metallic blood trickled into the back of my mouth.

Gavin lowered his face to within centimetres of mine. 'You see I saw you leaving Chloe's flat, Stevens,' he said, his voice now sub-zero.

I thought I'd seen something in the shadows as I was crossing the courtyard. Shit, it must have been Gavin. 'It's not what you think.'

But his eyes became dark slits. 'You two haven't talked in years and suddenly you're waltzing out of her place.'

I spat out some blood. 'You're getting this is all wrong.'

'So why were you there, apart from trying to get into her knickers?'

I glowered up at him. Of course, in his world that was the only reason I'd be at Chloe's. But I couldn't tell him about the satellite. One whiff of the truth and Gavin would be off, spilling it to the reporters in town, almost as fast as he could spit in my face.

'I wanted to apologise to Chloe about what happened at college,' I said.

Gavin's nose flared like a bull's. 'Still not buying it, Stevens. And whose fault was it that Inspector Clarke was waiting for me when I got home from college today?'

I struggled to sit up but his gang kept me pinned down. 'I swear I never said a word.'

'So who did, huh? Answer me that?'

Another thing I couldn't tell him without dropping Chloe in it. 'Honestly I've no idea.'

'*No idea*,' he repeated in a squeaky voice. And then his eyes glittered and his hot breath steamed over me. 'You're so full of it, Stevens. You so have this coming to you.'

There was real danger in his low tone. We'd danced around this moment for years and I knew this situation was tipping past the point of no return. This wasn't about Chloe...this was all about my dad killing his dad in that bloody explosion.

My heart thundered in my chest, adrenalin pumping, wiping all my normal survival strategies away. 'Watch what you're saying, Knotley.'

Gavin sneered to his friends. 'Oh, so touchy. Doesn't like me talking about his murdering son-of-a-bitch dad like that.'

'That explosion was an accident—'

In a blur, Gavin's fist slammed into my face and my nose splintered with a lightning crackle of pain.

'Just like *that* was an accident, Stevens,' Gavin shouted. 'Because of your stupid dad, mine's dead.' He dropped down on to me, his knees squeezing the air out of my chest.

Time decelerated as he drew his fist back again. I stared at his knuckles; I could make out every scab and scratch as they slammed into my face.

Gavin struck me a third, then a fourth time. I shot past pain and became only numb, listening to the blows landing like they were happening to somebody else.

I was dimly aware of the other lads letting go of my arms and backing away. They stared open-mouthed at Gavin and then disappeared away into the fog.

No witnesses. No one to stop Gavin now. And he wasn't going to leave until he killed me.

The fog closed in and lapped around us. Another punch spread the numbness into my brain. Gavin's outline became less distinct, a sketch of lines in the air. He stood and started kicking me in the chest... I felt a rib shatter.

I was losing consciousness. The monochrome world swam back into focus as my migraine cranked into overdrive again. A negative image of Gavin took hold, his eyes white marbles.

I realised the kicks had stopped and he was staring down at me. 'Where did you go, Stevens?'

A thread of awareness weaved its way through my broken thoughts. *What does he mean?*

Then I noticed the fog's black vapours were flowing out of the alleyway. I tried to say something, but my mouth was too full of blood. The dark smoke flowed past me towards Gavin, carrying the black particles within them. They curled round him like snakes, black seeds flowing up his nose and into his open mouth.

Gavin clutched his chest and coughed as he collapsed to the ground. He fumbled for something in his pocket and took out an inhaler.

I tried to raise myself but my shattered body was too broken to move. Another racking cough and Gavin dropped the inhaler. Then, gasping for breath, he rolled into a ball. He began to shake, his marble eyes rolling up into his head.

My head felt too heavy to hold up any longer, and I let it loll to the side. My body tingled all over with nerve-burning fire as the world around me slipped away into complete and utter darkness.

CHAPTER NINE

I SLOWLY OPENED my eyes into a dazzling whiteness, bright enough to make my brain ache. A blurred face loomed into focus over me and I gazed up at a bristly grey beard and a slightly hooked nose.

Allan stared down at me, his mouth turned down into a crescent. 'Oh, thank god you're awake, Jake. You had me really worried there. And the doctors were well and truly spooked.'

'What?' I gazed around me. I was lying on a bed surrounded by a white curtain. Muted conversations drifted in from outside.

At once everything came rushing back in: Chloe, the virus, Ember, the strange dark particles in the fog, that fight with Gavin.

'They've run a full battery of tests, X-rays, even an MRI in case there was something going on in your brain,' Allan continued.

'I'm in hospital? But how did I get here?'

'John found you...'

'John?'

'You know, the grocer. He stumbled upon you unconscious near the park when he was walking his dog and raised the alarm.'

'But what about Gavin? He was having an asthma attack before I passed out. A really bad one too.'

'What do you mean? When John found you there was no one else there.'

So Gavin must have dragged himself off before that.

'I must have got that part wrong.'

Allan narrowed his gaze on me.

But what had I witnessed happening to Gavin? Had inhaling those black particles triggered his asthma attack? And what about me?

I did a quick physical inventory. Despite my severe beating I actually felt OK. Probably everything to do with some serious painkillers they'd no doubt given me.

'So how bad is it, Allan?'

'What?'

There was no point in trying to avoid getting the police involved now. Gavin had moved us far beyond that point.

'Well, look at the state of me.'

'I am...and?'

I prepared myself for Allan's reaction as I thought through an edited version of what had happened. 'Can't you see how badly Gavin beat me up?'

'Gavin beat you up?' Allan repeated. He peered over the top of his glasses, frowning at me.

'Well, I didn't break my own nose, did I?'

Allan looked at me as though I'd lost it. 'I don't know what you think happened, Jake, but there isn't a mark on your face.'

'What do you mean? He broke my nose, my ribs...' I remembered the violent kicks and winced.

'Let me show you what I'm seeing.' He took out his phone,

switched on the front-facing camera and held the screen towards me.

My mind filled with confusion as I took in my own image. Allan was right: there wasn't a cut or bruise anywhere on my face. I carefully raised my fingers to my nose and probed it. It felt fine; definitely not broken. I patted my chest – there was no pain there at all either.

My thoughts whirled. 'You're really telling me they found no broken bones in the X-rays?'

'Nothing, and the same in the scans of your brain. The only unusual thing they picked up was a raised myoglobin level in your blood.'

'My *myo* what?'

'Myoglobin. It captures the oxygen in your muscles apparently – I've been checking it out on my phone. High levels can apparently indicate someone has had a heart attack—'

I sat upright. 'I had a heart attack?'

'Relax, of course you didn't. They gave you a full ECG test too. But you didn't let me get to the *or* part. High myoglobin levels are often found in people who have just run marathons, or have gone through an extreme physical activity. Were you doing something exhausting enough to make you pass out?'

'Gavin nearly beating me to death would probably explain it.'

'Jake...' Allan's tone had become way too gentle. 'When John found you, you were just like you were now. No broken bones, nothing obviously wrong, but he couldn't wake you either.' His gaze sharpened on me. 'Have you been on drugs of any sort, lad?'

I stared at him. 'Only bloody caffeine. I thought you knew me way better than that, Allan.'

'So what other explanation is there? What are we dealing with here, Jake? You're still seriously trying to tell me that you got into a major fight with Gavin and haven't got a mark to show for it? What am I meant to think? You tell me?'

'I...' I sank back into my pillow. 'I don't know, Allan.'

He cupped his hands together. 'The only thing the doctors could come up with is...'

Allan avoided my eyes.

'What?'

'When they couldn't find a single medical symptom that would explain this, they wondered if this was something to do with your mental state.'

'What, they think I flipped out or something?'

His gaze returned to me. 'What you've had to deal with since Martin died would be enough to break anyone. And maybe I haven't helped much there either.' He started to wring his hands together. 'I know I've pushed you hard towards applying for Oxford University, Jake, probably way too hard at times, but I just wanted the best for you. I hope you can understand that?'

I stared at him. 'Allan, stop it. It was nothing like that, I promise. Maybe...' I struggled to think of a plausible alternative as much for my benefit as his. 'Maybe this is my mind playing a trick on me, or something triggered by the migraine that I had in the park just before it all kicked off.'

'A migraine?'

'The first one I've ever had, but it was off the scale – it affected my vision and everything. That's probably why I blacked out.'

The tension drained away from Allan's face. 'Now that actually makes a lot of sense, although I'm sure the doctors will want to double-check.'

It was certainly the only thing that made any sense to me. Gavin had never actually been there. It had all been a lucid dream caused by an extreme migraine brought on by stress.

I realised I'd clenched my fists and I forced them to relax. 'And as for you pushing me too hard, Allan, it's no harder than I have myself. Oxford is my dream too, remember. And I know you're trying to do what Dad might have done if he were still here. You've looked out for me at every step and have just wanted me to do OK with my life.'

As I was saying it out loud, perhaps for the first time I was actually starting to understand Allan's perspective – the guardian who wanted to see his brother's son flourish and move on with his life.

'Most of all, you've been the one person who has stood by me through everything.'

Allan's eyes glistened. 'Thank you, lad. It means a lot to hear you say that.' He looked down at his hands. 'But as for being the person who has stood by you, maybe that's because I'm the only person who you allow to do that.'

We both knew who he was talking about without Allan mentioning her name.

As if he'd scripted it, the curtain round my bed was whipped back and Chloe appeared. She slipped through the gap, dressed in biker leathers, a helmet under her arm. She took in my appearance in a sweeping glance.

'Gavin told me you were probably in here.'

Allan stared at her. 'How did Gavin know that?'

'He said he ran into Jake in the park. Told me he was unconscious.'

A small trickle of electricity ran down my spine. If Gavin really had been in the park, did that mean the rest was true too? Or was it yet another clue that I really was losing my mind?

Allan's eyes narrowed. 'Gavin was in the park – in the bloody park?'

'Yes...he said he called the ambulance,' Chloe replied. 'Why? What are you talking about?'

I stared between them. 'I'm not sure I know any more, Chloe.'

'Well, I am,' Allan said. 'Your precious boyfriend didn't do a thing to help Jake. And he certainly didn't ring an ambulance. If someone else hadn't done exactly that, my nephew might still be lying in the park right now.'

Chloe stared at me. 'Is this true, Jake?'

I put my head in my hands.

'I need to get some air,' Allan said. 'Chloe, can you stay with Jake?'

'Of course.'

Allan nodded to her, grabbed his stick and opened the curtain. He gave me a look that told me he was ready to thump Gavin, however big he was.

Chloe placed her crash helmet on one seat and sat down on the other.

'Talk to me, Jake?'

My nose started to prickle. 'Chloe, I think I may be losing my mind.'

CHAPTER TEN

I STARED AT CHLOE, trying to work out how to broach the madness that my life had descended into. I could tell her the version that I'd just discussed with Allan: that the migraine had been responsible for everything I'd seen. But I knew deep down I was just trying to bury the truth. And the implications of what that meant was off the scale. Even so, Chloe also had the right to know what I thought I'd seen happening to Gavin before I blacked out. I gathered my courage as tightly as I could.

'Chloe, there's something you need to know about Gavin – at least what I think I saw.'

She wrapped her arms round herself. 'OK, just tell me, Jake.'

'The first thing you should know is that Gavin and his gang came after me.'

She clenched her jaw. 'Oh, that utter meathead. I thought he'd calmed down about me getting shocked by that circuit board.'

Apart from the fact, he thought I was making a move on you...

I kept the thought off my face. 'You'll need to ask him about that, Chloe.'

Her expression clouded. 'Right...'

'But you should also know that he collapsed with a really bad asthma attack.'

Chloe gave me a confused look. 'But Gavin's fine. In fact, he's better than fine. I've never seen him so upbeat. Are you sure about this, Jake?'

Probably because he finally got to knock the shit out of me...

I tried to hold Chloe's gaze. Could I tell her everything without her thinking that I'd gone insane? No, no – it was too risky. The gulf that separated us was still far too big.

'I must have got it wrong,' I said.

Chloe chewed her lip and started to open her mouth.

I jumped in before she could throw me another question. 'So what did you find out about that virus?'

She blinked and sat upright. 'I posted a question on one of the darknet forums. Those guys eat, breathe and sleep viruses – and write most of them. I thought if anyone would know anything about it, they would. I took a screenshot of a page of the virus's code and posted it because it's a bit like looking at finger-prints. Analyse the code and you can generally work out who was behind it.'

'So why not just upload the virus itself?'

'It's become too bloated to be able to do that.'

'What do you mean? I thought you had a nose-bleeding-fast internet connection at your flat?'

'We do, but that virus has grown to at least eight terabytes of code and has already almost swallowed up the memory and the drive space of all my computers. It would take days to upload it now.'

'So why has it got so big?'

'Because it's been busy working on Ember.'

'Doing what exactly?'

'No idea, because it's locked me out so I can't access

Ember. All I can tell for sure is that it's running a monster compile and the database it's creating for it is already enormous.'

'Aren't you worried about the virus wrecking your work? I know how much that game engine means to you.' She sounded way too calm about it all – Ember was her life.

'No – it's all been fully backed up. Even if the virus does its worst, I can just reinstall everything. And to be honest I really want to know what it's up to.'

'Then that makes two of us. So do your hacker friends have any more info on this virus yet?'

'When I posted the screenshot on the forum, it didn't take long for one of them to tell me it looked like a virus called Sentinel. Apparently it first appeared six years ago on the computer systems that run the Jodrell Bank radio telescope. It was all hushed up at the time. No one seemed to have any idea why, though.'

'That's the place where they study signals from spinning pulsars and other similar targets. Dad always meant to take me, but...'

Chloe grimaced. 'And it seems that it was from the Jodrell Bank computer systems that the Sentinel virus spread rapidly out to computers all over the world. Then it disappeared off the face of the Earth and no one has heard of it since.'

'Until now...'

'Until now, when you downloaded it from that circuit board from the Varuna satellite. And that got me thinking. So I went and checked out something. Varuna was launched six years ago too.'

'So you're saying Sentinel was uploaded on to the satellite's computer after being deleted from all the other systems it had infected?'

'That would fit what we know so far.'

'It sounds a bit unlikely, Chloe. Why would whoever wrote it do that?'

'I've no idea, Jake.'

I turned everything over in my head. This was progress, although I didn't feel we were any closer to the truth.

'OK, let's try to figure this out,' I said. 'To start with, what does this Sentinel virus actually do apart from take over game engine systems and send weird messages to freak people out?'

'No one knows – not yet anyway. In fact, people aren't even really sure it's a virus because it doesn't seem to do any harm to the systems it's run on.'

Strange. This didn't sound like anything I knew about viruses. 'Good news for our computers. But whoever put Sentinel together wouldn't have gone to that sort of effort unless it was designed to do *something*.'

'What if it was constructed to track down information about DEC?' Chloe asked.

'Crashing a satellite almost on top of my head seems a strange way of going about it.'

'It may be, but it still worked, because here's the DEC file.' Chloe unzipped her leather biker jacket and pulled out a lanyard with a memory stick attached to the end.

She unhooked the USB device and dangled it in front of me. 'I'm seriously starting to consider a career in industrial espionage.'

I took the stick from her. 'What's this?'

'I'll get to that in a moment. Anyway, it turns out that DEC is an acronym.'

'For what?'

'You'll recognise it by its full name: Dark Energy Collector.'

I stared at her. The name of Dad's experiment that blew up. 'Oh hell, I should have worked that out before now.' Why had I been so slow on the uptake?

'Don't be so hard on yourself. The only reason DEC was so fresh in my memory is because two days ago I walked into Dad's study to borrow some paper. He'd popped to the loo but left his computer on. Me being me, I had a nosey. There were loads of diagrams for a seriously complex-looking machine on his screen. Dad had also left a notepad out, with a load of equations in it. And I'm pretty certain now that's where I saw the word "DEC".'

'OK, but he helped my dad out with it, so that's not a surprise.'

'You don't understand. Dad always told me he just assisted Martin with a few calculations but wasn't really involved. But this looked far more than that. And Dad famously let Martin take all the credit for it going completely wrong.'

I caught the sharp tone in her words. 'You sound angry?'

'Of course I am, Jake. I'm furious, not least because it drove a wedge slap-bang through the middle of our friendship.'

The room seemed short of air. 'I thought you blamed my dad for what happened. I mean, everyone else does.'

'Did you actually bother to ask me what I thought at the time?'

'I kind of assumed because of Dave...'

'That was exactly the problem, Jake. You assumed way too much – and I let you. Do you know how hard it was for me to watch you fall apart and not be allowed to help?'

'I couldn't cope with anyone or anything back then, Chloe. I'd just lost my dad and nothing made sense any more.' The old ache started to pulse inside, the pain that I'd tried to contain ever since I'd lost him.

Sadness filled her eyes. 'I know that. You were suffering more than anyone should have to in this life. And like anyone would have done, you dropped into survival mode. I thought at first you needed space, time to catch your breath, but eventually when you didn't surface I...'

'You gave up on me. But I understood why you walked away, Chloe.'

Her mouth opened and closed. 'You think what? All these years and... Oh, give me something heavy to smack you over the head with.'

'But you've always avoided me...'

Chloe's mouth trembled. 'Jake, you've got this all so badly wrong. The problem was that every time I tried to reach out to you I could see the pain in your eyes and that, just by talking to you, I was actually making things worse. Which cut me up more than anything. I made a vow to myself to step back. But I never gave up on you, Jake – ever.'

Six years of pain replayed through my head in seconds. All the times I'd thought Chloe barely realised I existed, in fact, she'd been doing just the opposite. Like when we'd bumped into each other at the coffee shop and she'd practically run out of the door without saying a word. It had felt like a knife plunged into my gut. But now she was telling me that she'd been giving me a chance to breathe. And then I'd had to watch her throw herself into something else – Gavin – and every time I'd seen them together, it felt like that knife had twisted inside me.

I stared at her. 'I thought...'

She sighed. 'I realise now what you thought.'

'This is all so screwed up,' I said.

'I know it is. But last night when you stepped in to protect that boy, I saw a glimpse of the Jake Stevens I'd always known and... Anyway, even then I thought it might be just a one-off and that you'd quickly disappear back into your tortoise shell. When you appeared on my doorstep I didn't know whether to laugh or cry.'

'Is that why you gave me all that attitude?'

'Yeah, sorry about that. I was so shocked to see you, my

defences automatically kicked in. Call it a gamer's reflex. But you need to understand it's not just you who got hurt in all of this.'

'I'm so sorry, Chloe... But what about Gavin? How...how could you end up with someone like him?'

She gazed at the ceiling for a moment. 'I know how it must look to everyone, me included sometimes, but Gavin isn't the sack of crap everyone thinks he is. He just needs someone who believes in him – someone who can try to help him stop screwing his own life up.'

I pointed to the disguised bruise on her cheek. 'Is it worth paying that sort of price for someone who hits you?'

Chloe's eyes widened. 'That wasn't Gavin.'

'So you just walked into a door?'

'No...' She took a deep breath. "It was Dad. He lashed out at me the night before last when he walked back into his study and found me poking around his computer.' Her shoulders dropped.

I stared at her, shock slamming into my brain. 'Your dad did that to you? But I saw Gavin hit you yesterday!'

'That didn't leave a mark – it was just an open-handed slap, even if it was pretty hard. He tends to put on a show for his gang and his embarrassment lashed out before he could stop himself. We had serious words afterwards. When he's alone he's a different guy.'

'Right...But what about all those other times you've turned up to college with bruises?'

She hung her head.

'Chloe?'

'Yes, also Dad...'

'You're seriously saying he's been hurting you all this time?'

'I wish I wasn't, but I am, Jake.' Her lip trembled. 'But being with Gavin helps. I found that out one night when Dad picked me up after school. It was years ago, and my judo class had over-run. As I got into the car Dad hit me for keeping him waiting.

But Gavin was leaving the class as it happened, and saw what Dad'd done. He hammered on the windscreen, all threats and swears, saying he'd kill Dad if he ever hit me again. He was only fifteen and of course that didn't stop Dad entirely. But it helps. And it showed me another side to Gavin. I know he's damaged goods, but the guy has a kind heart under all that anger.' She shook her head. 'God, you're the first person I've ever told about this.'

I took her hands in mine. The walls we'd built between us were tumbling down brick by brick. 'Go on, Chloe, you may as well tell me everything. It might help...'

She looked away. 'After the explosion, Dad changed for ever. Maybe something broke inside him the day that Martin died and tipped him over the edge. It's got to the point where—' she took a deep breath— 'where I'm really afraid of him now, Jake.' Tears filled her eyes. 'It's as much as I can do to stop Gavin killing Dad. If he tried anything, it would only make it much, much worse.'

Guilt swirled through me. It should have been me, would have been me there for her, not Gavin, if I hadn't walked away from my best friend. But the one thing I was on the same page as Gavin about was the desire to kick Dave's head in.

'Chloe, why didn't you tell me any of this before?'

She crossed to the bed and sat on the edge of it. 'You know why, Jake.'

'Yes, yes I do. And I've been such a dick.'

'No, not really – just someone doing their best to keep their head above water. You didn't need the extra weight of my life to help drag you under.'

I reached out and took her hand in mine. 'I'm so sorry, Chloe.'

Chloe nodded, tears spilling down over her cheeks. 'Me too.' She wiped her eyes with the back of her other hand. 'And I was beyond upset when Dad treated you like a pariah in our flat last night. If he hadn't acted like he had a chilli up his butt, I might have asked him about the DEC file, but I was so furious I just sort of helped myself.'

'Helped yourself to...?'

'I hacked his computer and copied the DEC file to the memory stick that you have in your hand.'

I looked down at it and blinked. 'Maybe you really do have a future in industrial espionage. But are you sure about taking a step like this, Chloe?'

'No, but I'm doing it anyway.'

'OK...' I slowly nodded. 'So what have you learnt from it?'

'Nothing, because it's all inside a heavily encrypted file.'

'But you can hack anything, Chloe.'

'Not this I can't. Even the guys on the darknet forums haven't been able to help, but they are asking around. Looks like military-grade encryption to everyone – serious black-box tech. Meanwhile, as a precaution, I thought I'd better leave the memory stick with you.'

'What do you mean *as a precaution*?'

'I'm afraid of what Dad might do if he discovers I have it – what he might be capable of.'

'Surely you're being melodramatic? You're his daughter.'

Chloe pointed towards the disguised bruise on her face under the make-up.

I felt immediately guilty – after all she'd told me, of course she was frightened. I'd been too wrapped in my own drama not to see what had been happening to my former best friend.

'All this time and I had no idea of what you've had to deal with,' I said.

'So let's put that right from now. We start letting each other back into our lives. What do you say, Jake Stevens?'

She held out a hand and I shook it. 'Deal.' I almost felt dizzy, but this also felt utterly right.

'So what are you going to say to Gavin?'

'About?'

I grabbed her hands and held them up with mine. 'About this, about us rediscovering our friendship?'

'I'll make him understand somehow.' Chloe narrowed her gaze on me. 'But now we're opening up to each other, tell me what really happened in the park.'

'How do you know I didn't tell you everything?'

'I just do, even after all this time.'

I nodded. Yes, she really did know me that well.

CHAPTER ELEVEN

I KNEW that once I told Chloe about seeing the shadows with my sudden thermal vision and self-healing ability, there'd be no going back. But if I didn't tell someone I thought I might really risk losing my mind...if I hadn't already.

Chloe tilted her head to the side. 'Please tell me, Jake, whatever is.'

Maybe start somewhere easy, I told myself. 'OK, Chloe, here it is – I swear I remember Gavin beating me up badly. And I mean really badly, like trying-to-cave-my-skull-in badly.'

'Seriously?'

'Seriously.'

Her gaze pierced mine. 'You're trying to tell me that's why you blacked out?'

'Yes, I am, Chloe. And it wasn't even a fair fight. His gang had me pinned down while Gavin laid into me. He broke my nose, and a rib too, before I passed out.'

Chloe's eyes became hawk-like as she scanned my face. 'If it was that bad, why isn't your face swollen?'

'That's just it. I don't understand, but somehow my body managed to heal itself.'

'Oh, come on. Now I know you're winding me up.'

'I really am not, although I'm starting to question my own sanity at the moment because there's more too...' I clenched my fists so hard I drove my fingernails into my palms. 'The gemstone graphic appeared on my mobile's screen again.'

She began chewing a loose thread on her sleeve. 'Was there a message as well?'

'Something about phase two being initiated. The next thing I knew it felt like someone was drilling into my skull and my body was burning up. Then, all that faded away and I was left with full-blown thermal vision.'

Chloe blinked. 'Like a heat-sensing camera?'

'Exactly.'

'But that's impossible.'

'I know it is and that's why you're the only person I've told. But it's not all. It was because of my thermal vision that I could see something lurking in the fog.'

'You mean some*one*?'

'No, I mean some*thing*.'

'What, like a dog?'

'Not exactly – more like...' I paused, trying to find the words, clenching my fists harder. 'More like shadowy crow-like creatures made up of these floating dark particle things.' The moment I said it out loud it sounded even crazier than it had in my head.

Chloe stared at me. 'Shadow creatures? Are you on anything, Jake?'

'You're starting to sound like Allan, but no, I'm not. Mind you, I'm almost starting to wish I had been because it would make all this easier to get my head around.'

'And it started with that phase two message you saw, right?'

'Yes.'

'So it has to be linked somehow.' She nodded to herself. 'OK, let's assume you've not seriously lost the plot. Tell me exactly what these shadow things looked like.'

At least she wasn't laughing in my face, not yet at least.

'That's the thing, Chloe – I never got to see them properly. And it's really difficult to explain without sounding like a loon, but it was as if I slipped through into another version of Stoneham for a moment, where I found these things lurking.'

'Another Stoneham...OK...'

'I realise how this must all sound.'

'That you really are losing your mind, or...'

'Or? I'll take anything here, Chloe, drowning not waving.'

'That something affected you which made you see these things. And this all started with the phase two message. Was there a phase one text before this?'

'Not that I know of...' I mentally gathered myself. 'So what do you think?'

Chloe chewed her lip. 'That message used the word "subject", as in *test subject*, right?'

'And?'

'What if someone slipped you something that affected your brain chemistry, or...'

'Or?'

'*Or*, as Sherlock Holmes famously said, once you eliminate the impossible, whatever remains, no matter how improbable, must be the truth. So maybe you really are developing special abilities.'

'It sounds even crazier when you put it like that.'

'So let's do what Sherlock would do and test my theory.'

'How exactly?'

'Well, first off, do you trust me?'

I narrowed my gaze. 'I guess.'

'*I guess* will have to do then. Give me your hand.'

'OK...' I opened it for her.

Chloe took my left hand in hers and smoothed out my palm.

'What are you going—' I yelped as Chloe scratched her fingernails hard across my palm, breaking the skin. I snatched my hand back and sucked at the wounds. 'What the hell, Chloe?'

'Like I said, trust me. That was a controlled experiment. Now let's look at your palm.' She waggled her fingers towards me.

With a scowl, I placed my hand back into hers. I gawped as the skin began closing over the scratches immediately. As we both stared at the wound, the fine line of blood faded away to nothing. What should have taken at least a few days of healing had happened in less than thirty seconds.

'That's madder than snakes on a plane,' Chloe replied.

'At least that means I'm not totally losing my mind – but how is it possible?'

She frowned. 'Maybe it's some sort of advanced medical research that has escaped a lab?' Then she stared at me. 'Is that the real reason why the military are all over the crash site? Because it was carrying some sort of top-secret medical bio-weapon?'

'To do what? Breed super-soldiers activated by text messages?'

'If you've got anything better, I'm all ears.'

'I'm sold out in that department,' I said.

'So let's run with my theory that it's research designed to alter someone's DNA.'

It was an intriguing idea. What if Chloe was on to something? But, still, it was so out there I struggled to take it seriously. 'You've been reading too many comic books.'

'Maybe, but without a radioactive spider to bite you. Also, unlike a comic book – where the hero suddenly develops super-powers – what's happened to you is real.'

I could still see so many flaws in her theory. 'So why stow

something like that on-board a satellite? Also, why target...' I caught myself before I said *us*. 'Me?' I concluded.

'Maybe it's linked to this Shadowlands that you glimpsed.'

'What do you mean, *Shadowlands*?'

'The alternate version of Stoneham that you fell into.'

A dark version of Stoneham... Then it hit me. 'Chloe, that's it!'

'What is?'

'Dad's DEC experiment. What if it didn't just blow up? What if somehow it is linked directly to those strange creatures that I saw?'

'Holy zombie crap, Jake. Dark energy. Of course, that so totally fits.' Chloe scooped her hair back over her ears. 'OK, is there anything else that happened in the Shadowlands – any more clues you can think of?'

'There is one thing. When I was running away from the shadow creatures, my vision suddenly returned to normal and the crow things were gone – I was back in the real world.'

'The Real,' Chloe replied, eyes sharp.

'Yes, the Real – that works for me. Anyway, that was when my luck ran out because I walked straight into Gavin and his gang. But the strange thing was that one of the guys who'd seen me emerge from the alley jumped out of his skin like I'd appeared from nowhere.'

'Maybe he just hadn't noticed you until the last moment.'

'That's what I thought too, but then something else happened.'

'What?'

'When Gavin was beating me up, my thermal vision kicked in again. Suddenly he was shouting that I'd disappeared, even though I was right in front of him. The next thing I saw was him inhaling those shadow particles and then having a full-on asthma attack.'

Chloe shuddered. 'Meathead or not, I need to check Gavin's OK.'

I shrugged. 'I guess you should.'

Chloe looked away for a moment before returning her gaze to me. 'So while this was all happening it sounds like you slipped into the Shadowlands once more. Maybe you appear to vanish from the Real when that's happening?'

'I hadn't thought of it like that, but yes, that sounds right.' I peered out at the view of Stoneham over her shoulder. 'As crazy as this conversation is, talking about it is making it much clearer.'

'If it's any comfort, it's threatening to melt my mind into goo right now.'

I snorted.

Her eyes searched mine. 'Before we get too carried away, you're utterly sure you didn't just black out for a moment when you were being beaten up and hallucinated all this stuff?'

'That can't be it... I saw the shadow creatures *before* Gavin attacked me.'

'OK, so that rules that one out.' Chloe's mouth thinned. 'So let me get this right.' She held up three fingers and began ticking them down. 'You suddenly developed thermal vision.' She lowered a second finger. 'Then you slipped into the Shadowlands and saw these black particles, some of which Gavin inhaled.' She lowered her final finger. 'And then, the grand finale – you developed a rapid healing ability.'

'Yep.' I didn't know what else to say.

She took my hands and held them in hers. 'Then, as crazy as it sounds, and following Sherlock's logic, I actually find myself believing you, especially after what I saw happen inside Ember.'

I slowly nodded, a smile tugging at the corner of my mouth, and gazed at my vanished scratch marks. What had triggered the transformation of Jake Stevens into some sort of freak show? Was there a clue in the pins and needles I'd felt since I'd been shocked by that circuit board? Maybe it had done more to me than I first realised. And if so, did it mean this was all about to happen to Chloe too?

Chloe reached out for my shoulder. 'You've gone quiet. What are you thinking?'

I stared at her. She had every right to know that what had happened to me might happen to her. Although I guessed it wouldn't be long until she figured it out for herself.

'Chloe, you may—'

The curtain was pulled back and Allan walked in. He looked calmer than he had when he'd stormed out, but his eyes flicked straight to Chloe's hand on my shoulder. 'How are you doing, Jake?'

'Much better now Chloe's here, but we were sort of in the middle of something. Could you give us a few more minutes?'

'You're out of luck there, lad, because Chloe and I have to clear out I'm afraid. It's the end of visiting hours and I've just seen the doctor. He's on his way to check you out, yet again.'

'Does that mean I'm not going home with you tonight?'

'I wish you were, Jake, but the doc wants you kept in overnight for observations.'

'But I thought there was nothing wrong with me?' I traded quick frowns with Chloe.

'Which is why, like I told you before, you've got everyone here scratching their heads about your blackout. They want to make sure they haven't missed something so you don't end up suing them for gross medical negligence.'

'Oh right.' I slumped back on to my bed.

'It's just them being sensible, Jake,' Allan said. He rose his chin towards Chloe. 'Do you need a lift?'

She gestured to her crash helmet. 'No, I'm good.' She smiled at me. 'I'm really glad we had this talk, Jake.'

'Me too.'

'And about Gavin – I'll see how he is and get back to you on that.'

Allan glanced between us. 'What? Or don't I want to know?'

'Teenage stuff,' Chloe said.

'Oh...' Allan's face relaxed into a smile, obviously totally misreading what was going on between us.

'I'll ring you later and you can fill me in the other stuff,' Chloe said.

So I could tell her that she might be affected by the circuit board, just like I had been. How would Chloe take it, hearing that she might become a freak too?

'Yeah sure,' I replied.

'Good.' She leant down and kissed me on the forehead. 'See ya, Jake Stevens.'

I felt a smile creep across my face. Our old sign-off. 'See ya, Chloe Haze.'

With a small wave, she disappeared through the curtains surrounding my bed.

Allan winked at me as he followed her out.

Despite the huge implications of my conversation with Chloe, a new sense of lightness had taken hold of me. Talking to Chloe, with her no-nonsense, logical approach, was really helping me navigate through the swamp I'd been swallowed up in.

I gazed down at the memory stick with the DEC file on it. I grabbed my phone and touched the talk icon. 'Why did you get us to recover this DEC file?'

'Sorry, I'm not sure I understand?' my phone's voice assistant voice replied.

Of course it didn't... Had I really expected whoever it was to answer? It was a long shot. But I'd consider anything that would help me make sense of all this madness. To start with, if this was all linked to our dads' work, the shadow creatures and the rest, then maybe the answer to it was somewhere in the encrypted DEC file. I had to hope Chloe's mates would crack it soon.

I hooked my hands together and stared up at the ceiling, feeling the sense of madness that had threatened me loosen its claws with Chloe's help.

CHAPTER TWELVE

SHADOWS SCUTTLED *like insects along the floor, walls and ceiling of the ward, all heading towards my bed. Their stench – the aroma of decay – overpowered even the smell of the disinfectant. But I was the only patient awake, the only witness to what was happening.*

The darkness congealed like an oil slick around an older guy with a ponytail in the bed opposite. He'd been coughing his guts up the previous evening. Now he seemed to be acting like a magnet for the shadows.

Blood hummed in my ears as the dark vapours flowed up over his bed and body, carrying dark particles that flowed into his nose and mouth. The man started to jerk as total blackness filled his eyes. He slowly stood and started to walk towards me.

Every instinct screamed at me that the man was going to kill me, yet I couldn't move.

I felt a ball of heat growing inside my chest, and when I raised my hand a white burning sphere shot from it, striking the approaching man. He collapsed, flames licking over his body...

———

'OK, Jake, here's your breakfast.' A nurse opened the blinds to reveal a clear blue sky beyond the ward's window.

I focused on her. 'What?'

'The doctor said you can go home this morning. All your latest blood tests have come back clear. You're as healthy as a spring lamb.'

I sat up and blinked... It had just been a dream. But the pony-tail man wasn't in his bed. I gestured towards it. 'Where did the guy opposite me go?'

'That's a good question that we'd like the answer to. Security are tearing the hospital apart looking for him. Goodness knows where he's gone, especially when he's so ill and shouldn't be out of bed. I'm not sure if they've checked McDonald's next door yet, but that's usually where patients sneak off to.'

Had I really been dreaming or...? An icy chill rippled through me.

'Are you OK, dear? You suddenly look very pale.'

I tried to hold her gaze. 'I'm OK, just hungry.' And I was too. My empty insides felt like I hadn't eaten for a month.

The nurse's broad smile returned. 'In that case, let's get some breakfast inside you.' She headed to the food trolley.

Sunlight poured in through the window and I laid my head back on the pillow. I might be physically fine, but I felt all churned up by the dream – or whatever it was. Maybe it had been real? Was it possible to kill someone when you were half asleep?

I forced myself to breathe slowly. I needed to approach this the way Chloe had shown me the night before.

There had to be a more likely explanation. Maybe my subconscious had registered the man leaving the ward and my dreams had filled in the rest. But what if, even within the safety of the hospital, I'd fallen back into the Shadowlands for a moment? What then?

I shuddered and closed my eyes again. I concentrated on the red that glowed through my eyelids, trying to chase away the old anxiety that continued its threat to spin back up inside me.

I barely registered the drive back home from the hospital with Allan, I was so distracted by everything that had happened. The whole foundation that I'd built my life on, everything I thought I knew, was now in a state of flux. Back at the flat, I headed into my bedroom, closed the door and leant against it.

'Do you fancy a coffee?' Allan called from the kitchen.

Despite the lumpy porridge I'd had on the ward, my stomach still felt like an empty pit. 'That would be great. Could I grab an extra snack with that?'

'Sure.'

Thoughts raced around my skull. If this really did all link to Dad's Dark Energy Collector, had the blast been connected to the release of the dark creatures in the Shadowlands?

I hauled out my laptop and plugged the memory stick in. A browser window appeared with a single file on it: *DEC.PIE* I tried double-clicking it.

Unknown file format appeared on the screen.

No surprises there. I'd never heard of a PIE format file before – presumably a heavy-duty encryption that Dave had used to protect the file from prying eyes. Did it mean he had something to hide?

My phone chirped. The crystal spun slowly on the screen and the voice assistant kicked in. 'Connect the storage device to your laptop.'

I almost dropped my phone. How the hell had they hacked

my voice assistant and how could they know what I was doing? It couldn't be a spy satellite feed – I was indoors. So was someone keeping tabs on me somehow? A hidden camera placed in the flat, or... I stared at the front camera lens on my phone. Was the kingpin of hackers watching me right now? Perhaps I should tape it up like Chloe. Although, whatever else this person was up to, they were still our best chance at getting to the truth.

'Connect the storage device to your laptop,' the voice assistant repeated.

'Whoever you are, I want answers!' I said to my phone's mic. 'Why not just come out and tell me what's really going on?'

'Connect the storage device to your laptop.'

Was Mr Unknown Number laughing at me wherever he was as he played me? Was that it – Chloe and me were nothing more than a game for him?

I resisted the strongest desire to hurl my phone at the wall.

'Why should I?' I said.

'Trust me.'

I stared at the phone. Trust whoever this was? But then this same person *had* saved me from being blown up by the Typhoons' missiles...

'I want answers.'

'You will have them in good time, if you help me.'

So there it was: the bait. 'Just so you know, this sucks big time, but I guess you've left me no other choice.' I pushed the memory stick into the port.

At once the rotating crystal graphic appeared on the laptop's screen.

'Decrypting commenced...' the voice said.

I watched the progress bar crawl along the screen for a moment, but it looked like it was going to take a while – a long while.

My phone vibrated in my hand. A call was coming in from Chloe.

When she'd tried to ring me the previous night, no doubt to finish our interrupted conversation, I'd ducked her call. I was still trying to come up with a way of telling Chloe she could be affected without freaking her out. I clicked accept anyway.

'Good timing, Chloe. Our mutual friend Mr Unknown just asked me to plug the memory stick into my laptop.'

'Which is why I'm calling you. Every screen in my room has just lit up with that crystal graphic and with a "decrypting commenced" message below it. When I checked under the hood to see what was going on, it looks like the virus is using all my processors to run the same code. And if that isn't weird enough for you, are you currently sat in your room in front of your laptop?'

'Yes, why?'

'I can see you doing exactly that in Ember.'

My blood iced. 'How is any of this possible, Chloe?'

'It just isn't, Jake.'

My laptop and phone both chimed at once. Beneath the crystal, a progress bar had appeared. 'Chloe, it looks like Mr Unknown is trying to crack the DEC file for us.'

She whistled. 'So that's why it needed all my computing power. Right, I'm on my way over and I'll bring Ember with me. You need to see what else Mr Unknown has been up to with it.'

'What?' I didn't want to have to wait until she came over. This was freaking me out right now. I felt cast adrift in a storm sea and Chloe was my lifeboat.

'You need to see this with your own eyes because it will blow your mind. In the meantime, you should watch the news. Another person has gone missing from Stoneham and I have a horrible feeling it might be linked to what you told me about the shadow creatures you saw.'

'I overheard Inspector Clarke mentioning something about another potential disappearance when I was at the police station.'

'It sounds like the same one. Clarke's about to make a news briefing about it.'

'OK, I'll go and watch for myself.'

'See you soon then.' The phone clicked off.

I headed off to the front room.

'Do you want cookies as well?' Allan said from the kitchen as I passed it.

'Please, I'm starving.'

As I entered the room I found the news already on the TV.

Allan walked in carrying a mug of frothy coffee on a tray, a plate of cookies piled up and a banana with doughnuts on the side. 'Copious snacks as requested.' He gestured towards the TV. 'First the satellite and now all these people missing from Stoneham. We're rapidly becoming the centre of the universe. Ah, here you go.' He pointed to the screen.

On the TV, a video feed of Inspector Clarke appeared. He was sitting behind a desk lined with microphones, a blonde woman next to him, dabbing her eyes with a tissue.

The inspector cleared his throat. 'This is an urgent appeal to anyone who may know the whereabouts of Jason Stone. He was last seen leaving his work, Dartfield Engineering, over twenty-four hours ago and hasn't been seen since. There is concern for his well-being, as he suffers from a heart condition and we believe he didn't have his medication with him.' He nodded to the woman. 'His wife, Jennifer Stone, would now like to make a statement.'

The woman screwed up a tissue in her hand and gazed out at the people in the room until her eyes found the camera. 'Jason, if you're out there, please come home. The kids need you, I need you—' She sobbed, fresh tears rolling down her face as she waved the microphone away.

Clarke gently squeezed her shoulder. 'That will be all. Thank you, everyone.'

A man stood. 'Inspector, do you believe this latest disappearance is linked to the five other people who have vanished over the last month from the Stoneham area?'

Clarke leant forward into the mic. 'I'm afraid I can't comment on the other cases at the moment...'

Somebody else called out. 'What about reports that this could be the work of the Stoneham Stalker serial killer?'

Mrs Stone let out a small cry and raced from the room.

If looks could kill, the stare that Clarke threw at the reporter would have laid him out cold. 'No comment,' he growled.

To the howls of more questions and the blaze of flashguns Clarke stood and strode out after Mrs Stone.

'It's getting a touch too exciting around this town for my liking,' Allan said.

I stared at the screen. Could Chloe be right about the people who'd disappeared being linked to the shadow creatures that only I could see? And was that the real reason why Genesis were crawling over the town – because we had some sort of viral outbreak, something linked to my dad's dark energy research? That would certainly explain the bio-hazard suits. But if that was true, how did Chloe saying that Gavin seemed fine when she saw him fit that theory?

I clutched my head in hands.

'Jake? Are you feeling OK?'

I met his gaze. 'I'm fine, Allan. I've just got a lot going on in my life at the moment.'

His face softened. 'Typical teenager in other words. Anything you want to share? I realise I look like an old duffer to you, but I was once your age. Honest.'

What did he mean...? Then my mind caught up. 'Oh, you mean about Chloe and me?'

'Of course I do. Why? Is there something else going on?'

I took in the kindness in Allan's eyes, the guy I knew loved me like his own son. Could I tell him the truth? No, I couldn't do this to him. Besides, I didn't want him to think I'd gone completely mental.

'Yes, you got me. And Chloe's on her way over here now.'

'Aha, so that's the reason you had the fight with Gavin.'

He was so wrong and so right at the same time. 'Yeah, yeah it was.'

'Well, I'm proud of you, lad. You should always follow your heart, not to mention standing up for yourself against a thug like Gavin.'

In any other circumstance, I would have groaned in his face. But this would be as good a way as any to explain why Chloe was suddenly back in my life.

'Yeah, and I have been.'

'Good lad.' He slapped my back. 'And you say she's coming here now?'

'Yes, any minute.'

'Good grief, you could have given me some warning, Jake. Will you look at the state of the place?' He waved around the room.

'It's fine, but we'll probably be holed up in my room anyway.'

Allan's eyes widened at me. 'Of course you will be.' His smile reached his ears. 'Just don't do anything I wouldn't do.'

'Allan, seriously.'

He winked at me. 'Cake, we need cake. Chloe has a sweet tooth, I remember.'

'But, Allan, it's only ten o'clock in the morning, and anyway, that was the Chloe you knew six years ago.'

He tapped the side of his nose. 'Trust me, some things don't change and, besides, it's never too early in the day to have cake.'

Allan headed back to the kitchen, whistling some tune that sounded way too cheerful.

I slumped into my seat, staring at the TV. The nightmare version of Stoneham, the Shadowlands, was becoming far too real by the moment.

I felt a desperate pang of hunger and took a large bite of the doughnut Allan had left me. I cast a glance towards my bedroom, wondering just how long it would be until we'd crack that DEC file.

CHAPTER THIRTEEN

I'D BEEN HELPING Allan set up the new stock in the shop while keeping an eye out for Chloe. At last I spotted her on her silver, black and blue BMW electric scooter. It looked seriously futuristic and expensive, but its suspension was still having a hard time coping with the cobbled road and Chloe was bouncing her way towards me like she was on a rally-cross. By the time she'd parked up and started swinging a leg off the scooter, I was already outside on the pavement ready to meet and greet.

'So what's the big secret with Ember?' I asked as she pulled her crash helmet off.

Chloe retrieved a large laptop bag from the scooter's top box. 'It's way beyond anything you can dream of.'

'Oh, I promise you that I have a pretty wild imagination.'

'And I promise *you* that it'll be exceeded by what's happened to Ember.'

'Sounds intriguing...' I ushered her into the shop.

Chloe cast an eye over the telescopes. 'This is just as cool as I remember.'

'If you say so.'

'No, honestly, I'd trade it for my place in a heartbeat. Who wouldn't want to live in a telescope shop?'

'Oh, come on. You get to live the dream life up in that penthouse of yours.'

'If you're talking about Dad's taste for the luxury lifestyle, that's OK as far as it goes. But money, like the songs say...' She grabbed a pretend mic and sung, 'Can't buy me happiness, woo-hoo.'

I smiled. 'But like the other songs say, it can also help to make your misery a whole lot more comfortable.'

She laughed.

Allan appeared from the rear storeroom carrying a boxed refractor telescope.

He beamed at Chloe like she was a long-lost daughter. 'Good to see you again, missy.'

'You too, Allan. Still messing around with telescopes I see.'

'Always.' He gestured with his head up to the flat. 'I've left you guys a fresh pot of coffee upstairs.'

'Thanks,' I replied. I pointed at the large box he was carrying. 'Need any help setting that scope up?'

'No, I'm good. It's just nice to see you having a friend over.'

I threw Chloe a smile. 'Yeah, yeah it is.'

We headed off through the door and up the stairs that led to the flat.

'Where can I set up Ember?' Chloe asked when we reached the landing.

'My room is fine.'

'Which is where exactly?'

I gestured towards the door past our galley kitchen. 'Just in there. There's a spare socket on my desk you can use.'

Chloe patted her oversized bag. 'Oh, I won't need it. This ninja gaming laptop that Dad bought me runs for eight hours off a single charge, even with all the multithreaded cores running flat out.'

'I'll take your word that's impressive.'

'Trust me, it is. And that secret little project of ours seems greedy for all the computer power it can get at the moment.'

'You really know how to build up a guy's expectations.'

'Yep, just call me a technical tease.' With a grin she disappeared into my room.

I headed to the kitchen and spotted a huge pile of cookies along with a coffee and walnut cake set up on a tray, complete with red napkins. There was a Post-it stuck to the edge of the tray.

Just don't do anything I wouldn't do. ;)

Seriously...and a smiley? I quickly screwed up the note and threw it in the pedal bin.

Loaded up with coffee and snacks, I headed into my bedroom to see Chloe's new monster laptop making mine look like a kid's toy computer next to it. Her machine was all sharp angles, with a green under-lit keyboard. It even had a trackball built in just below the screen, which I guessed was intended for first-person shooter games.

I whistled. 'That thing certainly looks pretty cool. Can it pump dry ice out of the ports too?' I grinned.

Chloe raised a shoulder. 'At least when it comes to throwing money at me, this is one of the few areas that Dad still excels in.' She had unzipped her biker jacket to reveal a T-shirt that proudly proclaimed 'Geek & Proud of It!'

I cast an eye at my own laptop. It might be ancient by comparison, but it seemed to be making good progress cracking the DEC file encryption. Overnight the progress bar had reached twenty-five per cent – slow but at least steady.

Chloe swung my desk chair round to her laptop. 'Are you ready to have your mind blown, Jake Stevens?'

I found a clear space on the desk, set the tray down and handed her a coffee. 'You really are setting that bar very, very high, Miss Haze.'

'And I promise you even that isn't high enough.' Chloe hung her head for a moment, took a breath, tightened her gaze on the screen again, and then placed her hand on her gamer mouse.

'You look you like you're getting ready for a rocket launch.'

'And you'll see why in a moment.' Chloe clicked the flame icon.

With a whir of fans Ember powered up and the blue neon lights turned red. The usual desktop of icons was replaced with a view within the sim that hurtled down through a cloudscape towards a small town with a familiar pattern of streets, and to a telescope shop on a cobbled lane.

After the vertigo-inducing plummet, we came to a sudden stomach-jerking stop inside a view of my bedroom. On the screen, both Chloe and I were sitting in my perfectly modelled room, gazing at the laptop's screen. It was an exact replica – right down to the cup of coffee I was holding in my real hand at this very moment.

I felt the familiar shiver rush through me. 'OK, that's still as mind-bending as the first time I saw it, but I thought you said Mr Unknown has been up to some new stuff inside Ember?'

'You just got a sneak preview of it with that zoom-in. It appears that Mr Unknown now has a basic model of the whole of Earth in place, and is adding fresh detail with each new compile. As it is, this already puts Google Earth to shame.'

'OK, that's just a bit impressive.' I wasn't a programmer, but even I could appreciate there had to be some phenomenal code behind this. I studied the screen with more scrutiny.

'Exactly, but even that's only a hint of what's about to come. Still, first I need to drop us into debug mode so that you can see everything that Mr Unknown is making my game engine render in the background.' Chloe performed a couple of keystrokes and at once the walls around my modelled bedroom became transparent.

Through the ghost walls, I could see Allan in the shop below mounting the telescope he'd been holding on to a stand.

'Again stupidly impressive,' I said. 'And I take it by Allan being in here that Mr Unknown isn't just tracking us now?'

'Yes, because this barely scratches the surface – watch this.' Chloe spun the wheel on her uber-mouse. The view shot high into the air over the town again. Now with the X-ray vision enabled, we could see thousands of people inside their homes – some out on the streets, others driving in their cars along the roads around Stoneham. The modelling was so detailed that I could see dogs being walked by their owners through the park and kids playing on the swings.

I realised my mouth had fallen open and I closed it again. 'No way, no bloody way. You're telling me that Mr Unknown is modelling everyone in town and that this is a real-time view?'

'Yep, and it seems he is really interested in one specific group of people.' Chloe spun the trackball on the keyboard and the view swivelled towards the high street. She started to track along the road and then zoomed in on a van with a slowly spinning dish on its roof. Above it hovered a red halo.

'They're tracking Genesis Security?'

'Yep again. Thanks to the surveillance system that's been installed in Ember, I can see that dozens of Genesis vehicles are crawling all over town.'

I interlocked my fingers and massaged the back of my neck. 'But the coding needed to do this must be off the chart, Chloe.'

'You're telling me. This is beyond anything I've ever seen. Even if you threw one of the major games studios at this, even with all of their hundreds of staff, it would take them years to get anywhere close to what Mr Unknown has achieved overnight with Ember. And even then, if they had all that time, I'm not sure there's any team on the planet right now who could get close to the detail that we're seeing here.'

'So you're saying what we're witnessing is basically impossible?'

'Right, and I still haven't got to what is possibly the most single stupidly impressive thing that this uber-hacker has done with Ember's code.' She clicked another couple of keys and a lattice of flowing coloured lines appeared all over the screen. Glowing threads spread out from the buildings, joining others like branches of a tree to form thicker trunks travelling underground. Elsewhere, pulsating spheres rippled out from single points – thousands of them, all over the town, also connected to the branches of the tree. All the links pulsed with energy and stretched away towards the horizon, like the strands of a huge glowing spiderweb.

'What is this?'

'As far as I can make out, Mr Unknown is monitoring the real-time data flow of the internet – from broadband connections to Wi-Fi routers, and even mobile data flow between the phone exchanges and masts.'

'Is that how this guy has been able to slip the messages on to our phones whenever he likes?'

'With this sort of ability I'm pretty certain he can. The internet and computer systems, and even my Ember sim, are all Mr Unknown's playground.'

'But you already said that no team could do this?'

'Exactly.'

'Huh?' It didn't add up – was I missing something?

'Everything points to one thing, Jake. What if we have this all back to front? Think about it. We've already seen evidence of an intelligence that exceeds what any one coder could achieve, let alone what a dedicated team could manage. Then when you factor in the incredibly short amount of time that this has all been put into place...'

'You're saying what then – that Mr Unknown exceeds human intelligence?'

'I am.' She leant forward in her seat towards me. 'But maybe it would better to think of Mr Unknown as an *it* rather than a person.'

'You mean the virus code did all this by itself?'

'Think it through, Jake – the answer has been staring us in the face. I'll give you a hint... It's something that experts have said will happen sooner or later.'

I'd already guessed the answer. 'You're talking about an artificial intelligence, right?'

'It fits – it fits everything we know. My guess is that Sentinel started off as some sort of intelligence-agency-backed AI hacking project, but the code escaped the lab before it was ready to be deployed.'

'They can't get the toothpaste back in the tube, in other words?'

'Yes, and seeing everything that Sentinel is capable off, I honestly believe what we are dealing with is a computing singularity here.'

'A singularity?'

'The moment artificial intelligence exceeds our own.'

I'd seen plenty of movies about AI robots taking over. Worry spiked at my brain like a thousand needles. 'So you're saying Sentinel is like Skynet from the *Terminator* films and wants to destroy humanity?'

'That's a typical movie interpretation of AI. I'm a bit less pessimistic than that. What if a truly intelligent machine actually wants to help us?'

'So Sentinel is a friend... It makes sense. So far his actions haven't made me think otherwise.'

'And if all of this hasn't blown your mind enough yet, then get an eyeful of this.' Chloe zoomed the view back into the bedroom – to us – and added the data overlay mode. We now showed up as having blue shimmering auras all over our bodies.

'I'm guessing – and hoping – that red means enemy, for example, the Genesis vans, and blue means ally.'

'Sounds about right.'

'So Sentinel, going by that logic, thinks we're on his side.'

'I think so, but that's not what I wanted to show you.' Chloe spun the view to behind us. In the sim, the gemstone we'd seen before now floated in my bedroom.

I glanced back over my shoulder, half expecting to see a physical manifestation in my room, but of course nothing was actually there. I looked back to the screen and this time took in all the data lines converging on to Sentinel's crystal avatar. As it hovered, the crystal looked like a mother spider sitting in the middle of a glowing web of information.

I rubbed my temples. 'So you really believe Sentinel is monitoring all the internet traffic across the entire town?'

'Yes,' Chloe replied. 'And if you look closely, you'll see fine data lines connecting it to the two laptops in here and to the computers running back at my flat. It looks like Sentinel is designed to run in parallel across multiple computer systems. That's why he's been able to supply extra processing grunt to your laptop to help crack the encryption on the DEC file. Talking of which, how is it getting on with that?'

'A quarter of the way through.'

'That really is some serious encryption if it's taking Sentinel so long to crack it.'

'Does it mean we are referring to Mr Unknown as Sentinel now?'

She smiled. 'Well, he's no longer unknown, is he? And soon we'll be able to see what my dad has hidden away inside that file.'

I picked at my knuckles. 'But do we need to ask ourselves which side we are on in this? The government, or this Sentinel AI?'

'Sentinel saving your life puts at least one tick in the right box for him.'

'True. And if Sentinel is an AI, we need to work out another part of this puzzle: who originally created him and why?'

'I'm already on to that, but my darknet friends so far don't recognise the code structures from any of the existing AI research groups out there. Another huge question is: how did Sentinel give you the ability to see the Shadowlands? An AI is one thing, but you suddenly developing thermal vision and rapid healing abilities are totally beyond lines of code.'

It struck me then that Chloe didn't know the common denominator: that Sentinel had shocked me...and her. Yet, was that how it worked? Reprogramming my body? Could he really have done that? If so, he could just as easily have messed with Chloe's DNA. I opened my mouth to tell her, but then closed it again. Not yet, not until I knew for sure. It was bad enough me freaking out without putting this on her too.

Chloe gave me a curious look. 'What's going on inside that skull of yours?'

I skipped ahead to my next thought. 'If we can discover who developed Sentinel, it may help us work out what's happened to me too.'

Chloe sat up straighter. 'Absolutely.'

I pushed my tongue against the inside of my teeth and held her gaze. Now was as good a time as any to tell her I thought she was Sentinel's second subject. But it had already been more than two days since she'd been shocked. So far, at least, she hadn't shown any ill effects.

She frowned. 'Jake?'

'Sorry, just thinking about something.' I gave her a small, reassuring smile. 'So apart from waiting for Sentinel to hack the DEC file, what else can we do?'

'I've already tried getting past their firewalls directly, but no luck so far. And they didn't take the bait when I sent them a phishing email to try to get their login details.'

'Whose login details?'

'The team who runs the Jodrell Bank radio telescope installation.'

'But why—' And then I knew exactly what Chloe had been thinking. 'Because that's where Sentinel first surfaced outside whatever lab he was born in...'

'Got it in one, Mr Stevens. My instincts tell me that if Sentinel targeted Jodrell Bank, he must have done so for a reason. My plan is that we should have a good old nosey around Jodrell Bank's computers to see what we can find out. Discover the *why* and we may get to the *who* behind Sentinel. But the problem, as I said, is that I can't get past their firewall.'

'Can you try something different?' I replied.

'Such as?' Chloe asked.

'I don't know...' A memory surged up through my mind. 'Actually I do. I once saw this TV series where a guy needed to get into a really secure government facility, but was having the same problem that we are.'

'So what did he do? Kidnap an employee and steal their key card? That's usually what they do in the movies. But that's a bit extreme, isn't it?'

I waved my hands at her. 'Chill, nothing like that. Have you got an old memory stick you don't mind losing?'

'Loads in my bag, why?'

'Do you have a virus that you could load on to one of them, so that, when plugged into a computer within Jodrell Bank, could allow you to remotely access their systems?'

'Once inside their firewall I can do anything I like. OK, I get it, but I can see one huge flaw in the plugging-the-memory-stick-into-one-of-their-computers part of your plan. Any computer worth something is bound to be in a secure area that, at the very least, will be behind a locked door.'

'But maybe we can use a variation on the phishing technique to trick somebody into opening the door for us...'

'How exactly?'

'You'll just to wait and see.' It was nice for once to have an idea that Chloe hadn't thought of first when it came to hacking. And I wanted to keep her guessing until the big ta-da moment.

'So who's the tease now?'

I snorted. 'Have you got enough money for a train ticket?'

'You're not saying we go up to Jodrell Bank now, are you? That's all the way up near Macclesfield – easily two hundred miles away.'

'It is, and I am – why not? It's Saturday and I'm free if you are? *Carpe diem* and all that. Unless you're worried about what Gavin will think of you heading off on a day trip with me?' I quickly looked away to avoid whatever expression this would force on to her face.

'Well, for your information Gavin's not been returning any of my calls, so it's none of his business at the moment.'

My gaze bumped back to hers. 'Is everything OK between you two?'

'As much as it can be, Jake. Anyway, let's do this.'

'OK.' I knocked back my coffee. 'I'll raid what's left of my savings and let Allan know we're off out for the day.'

Chloe nodded and closed up her laptop.

'You want to leave that here?' I asked.

'Nope, I'm bringing it with us so I can load up the virus on the memory stick. I'll use my mobile to tether it to the internet, so we can keep it online and up to speed with what else Sentinel is up to with Ember.'

'Good plan, and I'll bring my laptop too, in case Sentinel manages to crack the DEC file during the journey.'

'Sounds like you've thought of everything. Do you really think whatever you've got planned will work?'

I felt a sense of clarity about it all. 'Trust me – as simple as it is, I really think it will.'

'I have always trusted you, Jake.'

'Yeah, I'm starting to get that now.'

With Chloe's help suddenly things, however crazy, were taking on a pattern I was beginning to understand.

CHAPTER FOURTEEN

WE WERE STILL miles away when I first caught sight of one of the Jodrell Bank dishes in the countryside through the train's window. The radio telescope looked like something straight out of a sci-fi movie, towering over the landscape.

When we arrived at Macclesfield Station we quickly found a cab. Chloe and I sat in silence in the back, each lost in our own thoughts. For me, the sight of the dishes kept tugging at a memory...

The weather had been seriously awful the first time I'd visited Stonehenge with Dad. We'd huddled into our cagoules in the face-stinging rain. But I'd barely noticed as I listened to the headset Dad had hired for me from the visitor centre. I'd had been transported back five thousand years as I learnt that the stone circle had been one of the earliest human star observatories.

Now, as we approached Jodrell Bank, I felt a similar sense of anticipation that my ten-year-old self had when I'd first seen Stonehenge peeping over the landscape. Despite their looks, there were a lot of parallels between Stonehenge and this modern white gleaming steel-girder structure – both linked to developing human understanding of the stars. In the case of Jodrell Bank, it was all about eavesdropping on the radio signals of the hidden cosmos, catching the sound of stars exploding and the fading murmur of the Big Bang. Dad would have got such a kick out of seeing this.

'I can tell by both your faces that this is your first visit,' said the taxi lady, a silver-haired woman with a soft northern accent. Her eyes glanced in the rear-view mirror at us. 'Impressive, isn't it?'

Chloe blinked as she surfaced from wherever her thoughts had taken her. 'It looks seriously epic.'

'It really does,' the woman replied. 'And to think that they listen into the whole universe from our little corner of the country.' Her gaze flicked back to the mirror at us. 'So you both love science?'

'Always have and always will,' I replied.

'Jake's dad was a famous physicist,' Chloe said.

I gave her a brief headshake but it was already too late.

'Was?' The taxi lady asked. Her expression tightened. 'Sorry, none of my business.' A slightly more fixed smile returned to her face. 'Their visitor centre is wonderful. You must try out the cafe too – it's famed for its food. Lots of glowing reviews on Trip-Advisor.'

'Sounds good,' Chloe said, then mouthed *I'm sorry* to me.

I caught my reflection in the car window and saw a swirl of sadness in my eyes.

Yeah, Dad should be here too...

We turned on to a road that led directly towards the massive dish.

'You're going to need to turn your mobiles off now that we're nearly at the site,' the taxi lady said. 'You'll see warning signs about it everywhere.'

'Why's that?' Chloe asked.

'Jodrell's dishes are so sensitive that even a mobile phone can interfere with the signals they receive from space.'

'Like that time the Wow signal was detected and, at first, they thought it was Earth-bound radio interference,' I said.

'What's the Wow signal?' Chloe asked.

'You haven't heard of it?'

'Astronomy has always been more your thing than mine.'

'I guess it has. Anyway, back in the seventies, they detected a signal that they thought might come from an alien civilisation – and someone wrote "Wow" on the printout next to the signal spike. At first, they thought it might actually be down to interference from a microwave oven that the staff used, hence their caution here about mobile phones. But they later decided it was most likely down to two comets that were in the solar system at the time.'

'That sounds like a bit of a let-down,' Chloe said.

'Yeah, but it did directly help inspire the search for alien civilisations with programmes like SETI.'

'In that case, we'd better not trigger another false alarm, hey?' Chloe said. She leant towards me. 'You do realise if we kill our mobiles that we'll lose our ability to tether to the internet?'

'Yes, but we don't really have much choice. And we can check in with Sentinel's progress once we leave the site again,' I replied.

She nodded and powered down her phone while I did the same.

We came to a stop in the car park, and despite my protests, Chloe insisted on paying the fare. As we got out a mum and dad with two young kids skipping ahead of them were making for a black building with a visitor centre sign on it.

The taxi lady lowered her window. 'Do you want me to come back for you?'

I glanced at my diver's watch. 'Yes, please. At three, if that's OK?' That should give us plenty of time.

'No problem. Here's my card in case you want to be picked up sooner. They have a payphone you can use in reception.' A smile played across her lips. 'But make sure you treat your lovely girlfriend to lunch in the cafe.'

Chloe grinned at me. 'I hope you're taking notes here, Jake?'

I raised my eyebrows at her. 'It'll be our first stop.'

'Good lad,' the taxi lady said. A moment later she was pulling away in her car.

'OK, *boyfriend*, let's go,' Chloe said, nose twitching.

A smile curled upwards at the corners of my mouth.

As we headed towards the visitor centre I took in the small dishes dotted around the site. But it was the huge dish, a seriously impressive piece of engineering, that really captured my imagination. It towered over everything else, easily the height of a block of flats, the wind quietly moaning through its support struts. This place really did feel like the modern-day equivalent of Stonehenge.

Chloe tipped her head as she stared up at it. 'It must be inspiring to work somewhere like this.'

'What's not to love about peering into the depths of the universe?'

Chloe threw me an unreadable look. 'Exactly...'

'What is that meant to mean?'

She smiled and shrugged.

We pushed the doors open and headed into the visitor centre. The lobby was filled with displays that at any other time I would have been all over like a rash. But right now we had bigger priorities. If my plan worked, we would, at last, unlock the mystery behind who had created Sentinel.

Chloe and I joined the small queue at the ticket desk. After waiting for a couple of minutes for the parents to buy guidebooks for their children, just like Dad would have done with me, we reached the smiling woman behind the counter.

'Two student tickets?' she asked.

'Please, and could you tell us where the cafe is?' I asked.

She gestured at a corridor to the right. 'Just along there.'

'Thanks.' I stuck my hand into my pocket for my wallet, but Chloe batted my wrist away.

'I've got this,' she said.

'But you already paid for the taxi.'

'And Dad gives me a stupidly generous allowance, so let me treat my friend.'

'Already demoted from boyfriend then?'

Chloe grinned. 'Just call me fickle.'

I found myself smiling...again. Just having Chloe around gave me a sense of lightness that I hadn't felt in years. Even my usual feelings of anxiety had decided to take a holiday and that was fine by me.

As soon as we walked into the cafe the fragrance of freshly baked pastries pulled at my nose, reminding me just how empty my stomach felt, despite Allan's substantial breakfast. We grabbed a table near the window and a short while later were sorted with coffee and Danishes as we gazed out at the main satellite dish.

'So what happens now?' Chloe asked. 'You keeping me in suspense is seriously killing me here.'

'You're just going to have to let me have my fun for a little bit longer. For now, we wait and watch...try to get a feel for the rhythm of this place.'

'In other words, case the joint?'

'Pretty much. 'I opened my laptop and noticed that the progress bar had stuck at thirty-five. 'It looks like Sentinel has almost ground to a halt cracking the DEC file.'

'That's hardly surprising. Without our mobiles connecting

him to the internet, he can't throw multiple computer processors at the encryption. Meanwhile, it's all down to your ancient laptop. Maybe we should turn our mobiles back on.'

'No, we can't do that – it may set off an alarm somewhere. That taxi lady wasn't exaggerating about all the warning signs. The last thing we want to do is draw attention to ourselves.'

'You're right.' Chloe powered up her laptop.

'Any new developments in Ember?' I asked.

'Nope, because without a mobile signal I've got the same problem you have. But the last time I checked in on the train Sentinel had started another huge compile. Can't wait to see what new features he's added.'

'It's funny we're both calling the AI a "he" now.'

'Oh, he is so much a he. A woman would be far less cryptic.'

I grinned. 'You think?'

She snorted. 'Will you look at you? This is the Jake Stevens I used to know.'

I hitched a shoulder. 'Maybe he never really went away.'

Chloe's eyes lingered on mine for a moment. Then she looked out at the dish, probably wondering, just like me, about all the wrong turnings we'd taken in the last six years.

Outside, cracks of blue had begun to appear between the clouds and a patchwork of sunlight fell across the dish. I imagined the signals falling from the stars into it, like an invisible shower of rain.

'What are you thinking?' Chloe asked, her gaze back on me.

'Those dishes are capturing all those radio signals that have been travelling for years and years until they reach Earth – *billions of years* in some cases.'

'This is so you, isn't it, Jake?'

'What do you mean?'

She waved her hands around. 'All of this. Maybe you really

should consider some area of astronomy as a job. You've always loved the stars.'

'Dad would have approved of me taking on a career like that...' A knot filled my stomach and Chloe's face softened.

'Anyway...' I gestured to her laptop. 'Have you got your virus payload ready?'

'Almost. I just need to put a few finishing touches to it. But what are you planning to do with it? You're not going to pop into the loos and put a black balaclava on, are you?'

'You'll just have to wait and see.'

Chloe shook her head at me.

As she worked on prepping the virus I watched the families walking around the dish and taking photos. Most of their shots were selfies with the dish in the background, no doubt to add to the hundreds of thousands already on Instagram and Facebook.

Two kids had their heads bent into a small parabolic dish. It was aimed at another dish about a hundred metres away, where a woman, presumably their mum, was speaking into it. I could tell by the way the kids' faces lit up that they could hear their mum's voice being projected through the air to their dish from the first. Dad had done the same with me at a similar exhibit at the Science Exploratory in Bristol. I remember it seeming like utter magic at the time. Even though I knew the theory, part of me still felt that way.

I ran my finger over Mum's diver's watch before returning my attention to my laptop screen. The decrypting progress bar ticked up to thirty-six per cent.

Why had the developer behind Sentinel decided to target this radio telescope facility? It seemed like an unlikely target for such a sophisticated piece of programming. But if the answer was on this site, with Chloe's help we'd somehow find it.

Outside, the mother and her kids were walking along a large circular path that ran around the main radio telescope. Set back from the dishes was a low two-storey office building. It had a large window on the upper floor that faced the main dish, out of which I could see people at workstations gazing out at it. That had to be the main control room.

A man wearing a blue sweatshirt appeared from a door in the building and headed towards a gate set into the wire fence. Despite the distance, I recognised a picture of the *Millennium Falcon* on his sweatshirt.

So the guy was a Star Wars fan.

A moment later he'd begun to climb a ladder built into one of the two main support legs of the radio telescope. My attention travelled ahead to where the ladder met a gantry with a small metal cabin on it.

'Steve's just doing a maintenance check on the Lovell tele-scope before it starts its next viewing session,' a server from the cafe said as he cleared the table next to us.

Chloe glanced up from her laptop and her gaze widened as she saw the guy exit a small lift and walk along a high gantry beneath the dish.

'I'm guessing he doesn't have vertigo,' she said to the waiter.

'Steve couldn't with his job. I think he likes it – he's always going on about the incredible view he gets from up there.'

'It must be amazing,' I said.

'It is. Anyway, can I tempt you two with freshly baked cheese scones straight out of the oven?'

'Sounds like my idea of heaven,' Chloe said.

He smiled. 'Coming right up.' He headed back to the counter.

Chloe started rummaging through her laptop bag. 'Right, the virus is ready. All I need to do now is load it on to a memory stick.' She took out a handful from her bag.

My gaze locked on to a Lego-Darth-Vader-branded stick. 'Is it OK if you use that one?'

'I guess – it's not got much capacity but there should be just enough for the virus program.'

'Great, because it will make the ideal Trojan Horse.'

Chloe narrowed her eyes at me. 'If you say so.' She plugged Vader into her laptop, and few clicks later handed him over to me. 'Darth's all ready to use the *dark side* of the force.'

I snorted and pocketed the memory stick. 'Stay here, and if you see me being dragged off by security, pretend you don't know me.'

Chloe's eyes widened, but before she could question or stop me I headed outside, adrenalin already making my blood hum. There was no going back now and I just prayed my ridiculously simple plan would play out OK.

I made my way round the curving path skirting the main dish. The radio telescope guy, Steve, had now disappeared into his metal treehouse cabin below the main dish.

I was praying that his love of Star Wars would help me.

Chloe gave me a small finger wave through the cafe window. Hopefully my plan, what there was of it, wouldn't let us down.

I passed a husband and wife reading an information display about the Lovell radio telescope dish in front of us. I would definitely have to come back here with Allan to check this place out properly – it was something that both of us had talked about doing, but life had always managed to get in the way.

With a glance to check that no one, with the exception of Chloe tracking my movements like a surveillance camera operator, was interested in me, I quickly slipped in through the unlocked gate in front of the control centre. With my heart pumping at nausea-inducing levels, I headed with what I hoped looked like a confident walk towards the building that Steve had first emerged from.

There was a keypad entry system by the door. But my plan didn't involve the need to gain access to the control centre itself. If this all played out as I hoped, Steve would do that for me...

I slipped Darth from my pocket and knelt down, pretending to tie my shoelace.

I held my breath. No alarms rang out. No doors burst open. No barking dogs bit my arse.

I carefully placed Darth on the doorstep, trying to make it look as though someone had dropped him there by accident. I cast a silent prayer to the geek gods in the sky that no one would trample on the Lego memory stick, and finished tying my imaginary shoelace.

I stood and made a play of looking around like I'd just realised I was in the wrong place. Then, at a double-quick pace, I headed back to the public viewing area around the Lovell dish.

I reached it just in time – seconds later, Steve appeared from his treehouse. I headed back to the cafe under Chloe's spotlight gaze.

'So?' she asked the moment I sat back down at our table.

I picked up the steaming cup of coffee that waited for me and took a sip. 'Steve, or someone just as gullible, will deliver the payload.'

'Huh?'

'You'll see...'

Steve had reached the bottom of the ladder and made a thumbs-up sign in the direction of the control-room window. A distant alarm started up and I instinctively gripped the edge of the table.

'No need to panic – it's not a fire alarm,' the cafe waiter said, catching my expression as he brought us each a cheese scone with a side of butter. 'That just means they're about to start rotating Lovell towards a new target.'

'Ah, OK,' I replied.

Sure enough, the dish began to rotate itself very slowly towards the horizon, as the whole structure also moved anti-clockwise on its circular railway track.

'It will take about ten minutes for the dish to be realigned,' the waiter said as he took our empty mugs and headed back to his counter.

Chloe sat forward. 'I thought for a moment you'd triggered some sort of delayed alarm.'

'You weren't the only one.'

Steve had opened the gate and strode towards the control building. He reached the door and started pressing numbers on the entry keypad.

'We should have brought one of Allan's pair of binoculars so we could see the code he's entering,' Chloe said.

'That would have been a good idea. Too late though now.'

Steve swung the door but he still hadn't noticed Mr Vader at his feet.

'Come on, come on,' I muttered under my breath.

He started to step forward and then hesitated as he glanced down. Steve squatted and picked something up. Although I couldn't see it was Mr Vader at this distance, by the way, Steve was smiling at the object in his hand, I knew the first step of my plan had worked.

I raised my hand for a high-five. 'Payload delivered.'

Chloe narrowed her eyes on me and left me hanging. 'Seriously? That was your plan? Drop a memory stick for someone to pick up?'

'Yes, in all its complicated glory.'

A smile crept out from behind her scowl. 'OK, crazy-simple, but also utter genius. Beats trying to hack past their firewall.'

'Exactly. So now we have to hope that Steve plugs Darth in to see if there are any files on the memory stick and that help him identify who it belongs to.'

'Are you sure he'll be that stupid?'

'God, you're cynical. Not stupid, just trusting, especially as he found it right outside the control room and the public area. He'll assume it belongs to one of the staff.'

'We'll make a hacker of you yet, Jake Stevens.'

'Does that mean I'll have to get a tattoo and join your darknet group?'

'Yep – on your butt – plus a great big nose ring.'

I snorted. 'Just what I always wanted.'

Chloe gave me a I've-heard-it-all look. 'Anyway, we won't know if this has worked until we have access to the internet again.'

I glanced at my watch. 'It's over two hours until our taxi comes back for us. What now?'

I made a show of taking a deep breath in. 'The smell of whatever they have been cooking in the kitchen for lunch has been driving me nuts. We eat here first, and then we have a nose around the exhibition. By then, hopefully, Steve will have plugged Darth in. What do you think?'

'Absolutely. Food and a geek-fest sounds like my version of heaven.' Chloe waved to the waiter guy who, with a wide smile, wandered back over to our table.

CHAPTER FIFTEEN

A BLUR of trees sped past, punctuating the view of the country-side beyond the train's window. After a couple of train changes, we were on the last leg of the trip back to Stoneham.

The journey had been a tense one as it soon became apparent that Steve still hadn't plugged in Darth and it hadn't harvested his logon credentials yet. Meanwhile, we'd watched the progress bar of Sentinel's attempt to hack the DEC file creep along, still only at the halfway point.

A gentle chime came from Chloe's laptop and she raised her chin. 'At last.'

'It's retrieved his password?' I asked.

'Let's see...' Chloe started typing and then she gave me her slow, cat-like smile. 'Apparently Steve loves chocolate straw-berries.'

'Pardon?'

'It's his password.'

'Brilliant. Now what happens?'

'Next, I'll open up a terminal window and enter the info that

Darth harvested to see if it actually works.' She chewed her lip, then her face lit up. 'Whoa, we're in.'

'You see, good old gullible human nature will always beat the best security.'

'Looks like I need to start taking some hacking notes from you.'

'And I owe all my expertise to the screen.'

Chloe flashed me an A-OK symbol with her hand. 'I'm going to try a quick system-wide search for the keyword "Sentinel" to see what that pulls up.' She tapped a few keys and her forehead creased.

'Nothing?' I asked.

'No – the opposite. There are literally thousands of documents here referencing Sentinel.' She clicked on her laptop's touchpad. 'Hmmm...' She clicked again. 'Oh, now that's just great.'

'Another problem?'

'It's just the sheer quantity of information here. It's going to take us weeks to sift through all of this to get to any juicy stuff.'

'Can you try tightening the search criteria?'

'What!' Chloe said.

'It wasn't that bad an idea, was it?'

'No, not you.' She swivelled the screen towards me. 'Ember just powered itself up and...look at what Sentinel's been up to.'

Avatar models of each of us sat in a highly detailed train carriage. Sentinel had even modelled the Somerset countryside rushing past the windows. A man in a uniform with a ticket machine wandered along the carriage towards our onscreen clones. Without even looking up, I knew the ticket guy was approaching. Chloe quickly shut her laptop's screen.

'Tickets please,' someone said over my shoulder.

We both dug our tickets out and showed the real-life ticket inspector.

He examined our tickets and handed them back. 'Stoneham is our next stop. Should be there in about thirty minutes.'

'Thanks,' I replied.

Chloe waited until the guy had moved to the next table before opening her screen again and turning it towards me.

On the modelled version of Chloe's laptop screen in the Ember sim, documents flashed past at an impossible speed that my eyes couldn't keep up with.

'What's going on?' I asked.

'I'm pretty certain that Sentinel is sorting through all those thousands of files on the Jodrell Bank computers for us.'

A message flashed up across the sim version of the laptop's screen.

Unauthorised access detected.

Chloe raised her fingers to her mouth. 'Oh hell, they must've set up a trip-wire alert for anyone accessing any sensitive files on their system.'

Beneath the text, the documents sped to a blur. What the hell was happening?

Account locked flashed up on the screen.

'Just when we were so close,' Chloe said. 'Hang on a minute...'

On the virtual laptop screen a new message pulsed.

Search complete. Origin information located.

'Origin? What's that about?' I asked.

The Ember sim faded away and was replaced with a document with the words: *Highly Classified and Confidential* stamped on it.

'Sentinel, you absolute beauty,' Chloe said.

'This is going to be another trip down the rabbit hole, isn't it?'

'Looks like it.' She clicked and brought up the next page. 'OK, let's see what Sentinel has unearthed for us.'

We both started to read the document.

. . .

Attn: Professor Claire Baxter, Chief Government Scientist
    From: Professor Graham Edwards, Director of Astronomy &
Astrophysics, JBCA & JBO, Jodrell Bank
    Status: Urgent
    Subject: Working Hypothesis on Sentinel Data Burst & the
On-going Security Breach.

Dear Claire,
    After the conclusion of the near catastrophic events for our
world here last night, we have continued with our analysis of the
origin of the rapid data burst that we received with the Lovell tele-
scope at Jodrell Bank, which was captured across multiple radio
frequencies less than twenty-four hours ago. We have codenamed
this data Sentinel.

I glanced at Chloe, whose expression had widened.

We have now had the opportunity to officially triangulate with the
other receiver stations in the Merlin network, who also received
the Sentinel transmission. That analysis confirms our preliminary
findings. It would appear that the origin of the signal, although not
terrestrially based, was also not received from space either. As
incredible as it sounds, the Sentinel signal appears to have come
from nowhere and everywhere at the same time. I realise how diffi-
cult this will be to comprehend for all of us. The implications are
huge. This signal is unlike any that have been received throughout
the history of radio astronomy. Now, having dismissed various
other explanations, including one of a potential hoax, we have

only a single working hypothesis left. It is this particular theory that I feel duty-bound to put before you as it so neatly fits all the known facts that we have at this moment.

It has been suggested that the origin for the Sentinel broadcast may have once again actually – and I find this as difficult to write as no doubt you will to read – come from a parallel world. I, of course, realise the countless objections that will be immediately springing into your mind, because that was my reaction when this was first proposed to me. However, after all the events of last night, the more I'm convinced that this confirms our earlier suspicions.

I sat back in my chair as I reached the bottom of the first page. 'Holy shit.'

'I couldn't have expressed it better myself.' Chloe locked her hands behind her neck. 'This is incredible, Jake. No wonder Sentinel's code is way beyond anything I've ever heard of – it's because he didn't come from this world.'

'No, but a parallel world where computing must be at a much more advanced state than it is here.'

'It explains so much,' Chloe said.

I almost couldn't breathe as the reality of everything I thought I knew was blown wide open. Nervous energy tingled through me as Chloe clicked on the next page of the document.

The Sentinel data package, although highly condensed with advanced fractal compression, expanded into a multithreaded program that filled all the available memory on the computer systems at Jodrell Bank, including MI5's additional storage. Also, Sentinel's code grew exponentially more complex as it consumed more computing power. Following that development, despite everyone's best efforts to stop it, Sentinel breached our firewalls last night and deleted itself from our servers as it did so. Every-thing now indicates that Sentinel is some form of artificial intelli-gence. This theory is hard to dismiss based on the events of last night, not least that Sentinel was able to adapt to recode itself to work across unfamiliar operating systems, adjusting its code base as necessary in an incredibly short amount of time.

This leaves us with the question of what Sentinel's purpose actually is. The only hint we have so far are the searches that our team members Steve Andrews and Lauren Stelleck detected Sentinel running, and which seem to have been targeted on some specific research into dark energy within this country.

I would be grateful if you could brief the ministers of our find-ings and advise us what action you would like us to take.

Yours sincerely,

Professor Graham Edwards

We both exchanged a long stare. My mind whirled as I struggled to process what I'd just read.

At last I found my voice. 'Dark energy research...' I glanced at the date stamp at the bottom of the page. 'And this happened six years ago.'

'So this joins the dots with our dads' work,' Chloe replied.

'It also confirms that the government knew Sentinel existed, and as they tried to destroy him when he crash-landed on-board the satellite, it seems that they now see him as hostile. So what changed between then and now?'

'Maybe they're just unhappy to have a sentient AI running around the world's internet,' Chloe replied.

'Knowing the current paranoia in the world about AI, that could be it.'

'But why is Sentinel interested in dark energy?'

The thought hit me like a blaze of lightning. 'Chloe, what else has turned up around Stoneham – and who knows where else in the world?'

'What do you mean?'

'Maybe the clue to what Sentinel was designed to do is in his name. Sentinel, as in guardian, as in an AI designed to look out and protect the universe from a specific threat?'

Her eyes shone at me. 'You're talking about those shadow creatures you saw in the Shadowlands, aren't you?'

A dark sense of foreboding flooded me. 'Yes, because it all fits.'

Chloe frowned. 'But if that's true, does that also mean our government is aware of the Shadowlands too?'

'Why not? They seem to know about everything else that's been going on.'

'OK, this is starting to feel like it has conspiracy stamped all over it. But hang on – if Sentinel was transmitted from a parallel Earth to protect us from those creatures, why would our government try to take Sentinel down when he's the good guy?'

'Maybe they've jumped to the wrong conclusion about Sentinel – maybe they see him as a threat just because they're not in control of him.'

'Possibly – that makes sort of sense for a government like ours, which is all about control,' Chloe said.

I was about to reply when something caught my eye in the distance.

A large fog bank sat across the rails ahead of us, as our train was curving round a bend.

The document on Chloe's screen faded and the view inside Ember zoomed out. We could see our modelled train rushing through the countryside and plunge into the fog bank at exactly at the same moment it went grey outside the train's window.

'Looks like Sentinel is in the driving seat again,' I said.

The view rushed ahead of the train – into Stoneham, and

hurtling into Chloe's penthouse flat. Dave was lying collapsed on the floor, an orange marker flashing around him.

Chloe gasped. 'What's wrong with him?'

Dave's avatar writhed as he clutched his head.

Worry spiked through me. 'He looks like he's having some sort of attack.'

Chloe grabbed her mobile and started dialling.

'Are you ringing an ambulance?'

'First I want to see if this is really happening.' She chewed her thumbnail as she listened to her mobile ring.

On Ember, I could see the light of their answer machine flashing. The marker around Dave blinked and turned a solid red – the red aura that we'd guessed indicated someone worked for Genesis. A line of text appeared next to the marker: *Subject has been infected.*

A storm of thoughts crashed together in my head as Dave's avatar stood and walked towards the flat's front door with a perfectly calm expression.

Chloe put her phone down, face pale. 'What the hell has happened to Dad?'

I hung on to Chloe on the back of her scooter as we sped to her flat, her spare helmet tight on my head. It might have been a cool mode of transport, but I just prayed no police spotted the L-plate rider carrying a pillion passenger. I didn't want to face Clarke ever again.

Chloe skidded her scooter to an impressive stop in the Old Brewery courtyard and we leapt off. Her gaze locked on to Dave's white Jag coupe parked in one of the bays.

'We should check the flat in case he's still here,' I said.

'Remember, what Sentinel showed may not have actually been real.'

Chloe didn't even respond as she punched her key code into the door entry pad.

I followed her as she ignored the lift, presumably too slow, and we raced up the stairs. When we entered the penthouse flat the lights came on automatically.

'Dad, Dad, are you here?' Chloe shouted. No response.

We ran through every room, checking everywhere until eventually we returned to the living room.

Chloe balled her fists. 'It was real, Jake, all of it.'

I gently took hold of her shoulders and made her look at me. 'OK, I know how freaked out you are by what we saw in Ember, but maybe Sentinel made a prediction – a possible simulated outcome rather than a definite fact.'

Her gaze skated past mine. 'Sentinel has only shown what's actually happened in real-time so far, so why should this be any different?'

'Yes, but—'

'But nothing, Jake. I know he's in trouble.'

I held up my hands. 'Slow down, Chloe. We don't know anything for sure.'

She slumped on to a white leather seat, head in her hands. 'But I do...'

I couldn't think of what to say. My gaze rose to the panoramic view of Stoneham. Dave could be anywhere out there... My eyes locked on to Chloe's bedroom door.

'Chloe, we should try Ember. We've seen that Sentinel is tracking everyone in town, so...'

Her head snapped up. 'Of course, Jake.'

Moments later, we'd powered up Deep Thought Two. The view within Ember now hovered over the entire town. Chloe turned on the debug mode and at once the roofs, walls and ceil-

ings of every building ghosted. Now we could see the thousands
of residents of Stoneham below us.

Chloe started to zoom over the town, her eyes narrowed.
'Where are you? Where are you?'

The minutes ticked past and her forehead creased deeper.

I scanned for any sign of the red marker around a person –
like the one we'd seen around Dave, the one that indicated
someone was in the employ of Genesis. But Chloe was too
worked up for me to share my suspicions with her at the moment,
so I kept them to myself: that it was too late – that somehow he'd
become one of them...

After half an hour had passed I gently patted her shoulder.
'This isn't working.'

'I know it bloody isn't, Jake.'

I started to pace her bedroom. 'If only we could go back to the
moment we saw him collapse, maybe we'd spot something.'

Chloe's eyes widened on me. 'I could seriously kiss you, Jake
Stevens.'

'Why exactly?'

'If Sentinel is running a real-time sim of Stoneham, it follows
that he's keeping a record of all that data somewhere.'

'So you mean that if we ask Sentinel nicely, maybe he'll be
able to show us where Dave went?'

'Well, if Sentinel really wants to prove to us he's on our
side...'

'And how do we get him to do that exactly?'

'We go for the simplest method to start with: try asking him a
direct question.' Chloe ducked under her desk and reappeared
with a headset. She pushed a button and a blue LED lit up on the
headphones, followed by a ping from the computer.

'OK, that's the Bluetooth connected,' Chloe said. She tapped
the headset's mic and a click came from the speakers. 'Sentinel,
can you hear me?'

The view, centred on the local supermarket, remained the same. Chloe frowned. 'Sentinel, talk to me.'

She tried a third, fourth time, but got nothing.

I gestured for the headset. 'Can I give it try?'

She handed it to me. 'Knock yourself out.'

I adjusted the mic to my mouth. 'Sentinel, it's Jake here. We urgently need your help.'

For a moment, still no reply, but then we heard the aquarium-pump device speed up inside Deep Thought Two as it circulated more coolant through the system.

'The equivalent of Deep Thought's pulse increasing – sounds like Sentinel is running the processors at full whack now,' Chloe said.

My phone beeped.

I read the single word on its screen and my heart filled my chest.

How?

I showed the screen to Chloe and she pressed her fingers to her mouth, tears glittering her eyes as she nodded.

Could this really work? My pulse hummed as I held the mic closer to my mouth. 'We need to know what happened to Dave after he collapsed in the flat.'

The fans whirred faster inside Deep Thought's case. Another ping – a new text appeared on my phone's screen: *I understand...*

The view inside Ember shot back into the sky for an aerial perspective on the town once more. Immediately every person in Stoneham started to move backwards at high speed, the cars all becoming blurring streaks.

Chloe pointed at a clock display that had appeared – overlaid on to the view and spinning backwards. 'Sentinel is literally rewinding time for us.'

The time indicator started to slow as it reached 3.33 p.m. and then froze like someone had hit pause on reality. The view hurtled down towards the Old Brewery and into the penthouse to lock on to Dave's frozen-in-time avatar, sprawled on the floor, a virtual cup of coffee he'd obviously been drinking lying on the white rug. I glanced through Chloe's bedroom door to see the real coffee mug on the real rug, its contents now a large dark stain across it, marking the passage of time since this frozen simulated moment on the screen.

The time indicator started to tick forward at a normal speed. Dave got back to his feet, a spinning red marker around him. The model was so detailed we could even see his strange blank expression as he turned and walked towards the doors.

Chloe clasped her hands together, face pinched, as the view tracked Dave as he entered the lift, standing like a statue until he had reached the ground floor. He left the lift and headed out into the courtyard, where a black van with a spinning dish on its roof was waiting. Dave walked towards it and the van's back doors opened to welcome him. He climbed inside and the doors closed.

'Genesis has taken him,' Chloe whispered.

'And he went willingly.'

'No, something's wrong. You saw how he looked. It's like he was drugged.'

I pulled the mic closer to my mouth again. 'Sentinel, Dave looks like he's in some sort of trance. Do you know what happened to him?'

Another ping. My mouth dried out as I read the message on my phone.

Possessed.

Chloe stared at the message as I showed it to her. 'What does Sentinel mean by that? That a demon took him over?'

'Or more likely Genesis slipped him some sort of drug that caused him to act like this.'

'I guess.'

The van started up and drove through the exit, turning on to the street.

'OK, at least we can now see where Genesis is taking him,' I said.

'Then what?'

I took in her lost look and a fresh sense of determination burned inside me. 'We help Dave of course. Do whatever we have to do.'

Chloe blinked at me. 'If it's not already too late.'

'You mustn't think like that.' But what if she was right?

We watched the sim view as the van gathered speed. It was already on the high street. The buildings fell away to be replaced by the rolling countryside around Stoneham.

'Where are they taking him?' Chloe asked.

'We know the government are behind this, so maybe a military facility, somewhere like that?'

'Yes, but why?'

'I wish I knew, Chloe.'

The scenery the van was driving through seemed strangely familiar. Then I found myself clutching my watch because I knew exactly where the Genesis vehicle was heading.

Chloe's eyes had widened too. 'They can't be...'

The van passed a faded road sign that read: 'Hopworth Science Park, 1 mile'.

'But I thought there was nothing left after the explosion?' I said.

'Exactly. They kept the whole area out of bounds because of all the toxic chemicals that were meant to have been released by the explosion.'

A ping on my phone came with the message: *All lies.*

Chloe and I exchanged a look. So what did that mean? Had there been some sort of cover-up?

Blackness filled the world ahead of the van as if there was a black hole in the sim. The van headed into it and vanished.

'Where did it go?' Chloe asked.

I tapped the mic. 'Sentinel, what just happened?'

My phone pinged again. *No data available.*

'What do you mean? You've modelled everything else in impossible detail – why not around the old science park too?'

The area is devoid of all electromagnetic energy to allow me to be able to construct a model.

Chloe leant in and put her mouth close to the mic. 'You mean it's a radio dead zone?'

Correct.

'But how can that be possible?' I replied. 'Surely there should be at least some mobile data signals blanketing the area, however weak?'

There are no signals of any sort inside the anomaly.

I whistled. 'So it's an *anomaly* now.'

Chloe sat back. 'And one that my dad has disappeared right into.'

I stared at her. 'Disappeared...'

It was all starting to slot together in my head as the haze that had surrounded all of this started to lift.

Chloe leant forward. 'You mean these events are linked?'

'It has to be. What if the others who have gone missing have been abducted by Genesis too?'

'Really? That sounds like a stretch. What connects the victims?'

'Not sure, but I think I've got a way to test my theory.' I put my lips close to the mic. 'Sentinel, can you check any tracking data you have for a man in Stoneham called Jason Stone?'

Affirmative.

'And can you play back the info you have, from the moment his disappearance was reported?'

Affirmative. Commencing playback.

There was a moment's pause and then the view zoomed up over Stoneham. Once again people moved backwards at high speed, night turning to day and back again. Then the view centred on a low industrial building with a sign on its side that read 'Dartfield Engineering'. Time began running forward at normal speed once again.

I whistled. 'This piece of software is a police officer's dream.'

I recognised the man emerging from the building immediately from the photos on TV. Stone walked towards his parked car and looked fine right up until he got his car keys out. Stone clutched at his neck before collapsing and writhing on the ground. Then his fit came to a stop. He stood up like nothing had happened, except he now had the same trance-like look we'd seen on Dave.

Chloe gasped. 'So this *is* connected.'

I nodded as a black van pulled up next to Stone and a moment later he climbed into the back of the van.

'Sentinel, speed up playback,' I said into the mic.

The scene accelerated. Moments later the van passed the Hopworth Science Park sign we'd seen before. Then it vanished into the same dark hole anomaly in the sim.

'So that settles it then,' I said.

Chloe drummed her foot on the floor. 'And what about the Shadowlands and those shadow creatures in it? Is that connected to something happening at the old science park? A science park that somehow they've been able to hide, even from Sentinel's eyes?'

I rested my chin on my hand. 'Exactly. And every fibre in my body is telling me this is all linked to our dads' original dark energy experimental work there.'

Chloe blinked. She paled and leant into the mic. 'Sentinel, where is Gavin Knotley right now?'

No data currently available.

The air squeezed between her teeth. 'The last person who saw him was you, Jake.'

My blood iced. 'Sentinel, show me what happened to Gavin in the park.'

The view centred on Gavin. He was standing under the lamp post with his mates. Then another person, me, suddenly appeared out of thin air from an alleyway. So even in this sim, I'd been invisible while I'd been in the Shadowlands.

Watching the Ember-rendered version of my attack was in some ways more shocking than it had been experiencing it in person, because this time there was no blacking out. I watched Gavin rain blows down on to me like he'd totally lost control.

'Oh my god,' Chloe whispered.

And then Gavin rolled away as he started to shake, fitting just like Dave and Jason Stone. But of course in this sim view there was no sign of the shadow creatures that I'd seen around him in the Shadowlands.

The minutes ticked past as fog swirled and then a van pulled up. Like a zombie, Gavin got into the back of it...

'They've taken Gavin too,' Chloe whispered.

'So this links the shadow particles to the disappearances as well.'

'But why him, Jake? What's he done to deserve this?' She shot to her feet. 'We've got to get the police involved.'

'But, Chloe, if the government are behind this—'

'I don't bloody care. My dad, Gavin and all those other people have gone missing because they've been infected by some awful virus. For all we know they may be already...'

I grabbed her hand. 'You can't think like that.'

'But what if it's true? I can't just sit here and watch it play out on Ember and do nothing to help them. This is real life, Jake, not some sort of bloody computer game.' She pulled away from me and turned to the door.

'Where are you going?'

Chloe grabbed her helmet. 'To the police station.'

'But...' I reached out.

She slapped my hand away. 'Don't try to stop me, Jake.' She stormed past as my phone chimed.

I stared at the message. *DEC file decryption complete.*

Not now, Sentinel, not right now. I stuffed my phone into my pocket, grabbed my laptop and jacket, and rushed after Chloe before she did something really stupid.

CHAPTER SIXTEEN

DESPITE ALL MY efforts to stop Chloe, she stormed through the doors of the police station like an elephant on a full-blown rampage and marched up to the front desk.

'Chloe, please don't do this,' I said.

She spun towards me. 'What don't you get, Jake? I couldn't live with myself if anything happened to Dad and Gavin – not to mention all the others – and I'd done nothing to stop it.'

The female desk-officer's eyebrows rose up as she watched us through the reinforced glass screen.

I tried to come up with something, anything, to stop Chloe, but I couldn't seem to string a coherent thought together. I ended up staring at her instead, mute.

'Exactly.' Chloe turned back to the counter. 'I need to see Inspector Clarke now. I've got important info about all those missing people.'

The blonde policewoman gave Chloe a straight look. 'And exactly what information would that be, miss?'

'I know where they all are,' Chloe replied.

'Do you now? Including Jason Stone?'

'Yes.'

The policewoman smiled to herself, which wasn't exactly the reaction I'd been expecting.

'I'm afraid the inspector isn't available because he's interviewing someone at the moment. 'If I could help instead...' Despite her words, her expression said, *Oh great, another time-waster who's wandered in off the street.*

Chloe pressed on. 'I need to see the person in charge of the missing persons' case and that's Clarke, right?'

'That's correct, but—'

'So I'll speak to the big man himself and not his drone.'

The policewoman and I both stared at Chloe. This was so unlike her.

'OK, a bit less of the attitude, please. Take a seat. When the inspector is free *then* I'll let him know you're here.'

'You don't bloody understand. This is urgent – lives could be in danger.'

Something hardened in the woman's face. 'Will you please calm down? I just told you that the inspector is interviewing someone.'

I reached out for Chloe's shoulder. 'Hey, you need to cool it.'

She shook me off with a snarl. 'Don't tell me what to do, Jake Stevens, because you'd be doing exactly the same if you had a chance to save your dad.'

I winced. *Yes, I probably would.*

Chloe turned back to the policewoman. 'If you don't want to get into trouble, I suggest you get Clarke here, right now, or I'm warning you...'

The woman's eyes flashed. 'OK, I've had just about enough of your lip.'

'So what, you're going to lock me up, are you, you stupid bitch?' Chloe shouted at her.

The woman stood taller. 'I warned you—'

'What's all this about?' came a man's voice from behind us.

We turned to see Clarke himself standing in a doorway, peering at Chloe.

She rushed to him. 'I've been trying to see you, but this bloody woman...' She flapped a hand towards the policewoman who rolled her eyes at Chloe's back.

'And I imagine she probably told you that I was busy, is that correct?' Clarke asked.

'Yes, but as I keep telling everyone, this is urgent. We have information about the people who have gone missing.'

Clarke cast a glance over at the policewoman, who shrugged at him.

For the first time, I noticed the person standing behind the inspector. Then I understood exactly the reason for the policewoman's smile and cool attitude to Chloe's information.

Jason Stone stepped out from behind Clarke and Chloe gawped at him.

His eyes flicked to Clarke and then to the ground.

'You can see for yourself that Mr Stone is no longer missing,' Clarke said.

'But we saw him—'

I cut in before she could say anything else. 'We thought we spotted him in town.'

'Probably on his way here to tell us where he's been all this time,' Clarke replied.

'And where was that then?' Chloe said, narrowing her gaze on the guy.

'Let's just say I'm not proud of myself and have been avoiding a scene with my wife,' he replied.

I traded a look with Chloe. Problems at home, an affair – right. We knew the truth – that he'd been taken to the old science park site, so why the cover story?

Clarke gestured to Mr Stone. 'I suggest you have that conversation with Mrs Stone as soon as possible.'

'Of course I will.' He headed out of the front door without looking at any of us.

'But we still know where the others are,' Chloe replied after he'd gone.

Clarke tilted his head to one side. 'I don't know what you think you know, but everyone who went missing has reappeared over the last twelve hours. And all of them had good reasons for their disappearance. We're about to make a statement to the media. I grant you it's a strange coincidence, but it seems to be just that. The Stoneham Stalker is no more.'

'But what about my dad and boyfriend?' Chloe said. 'We think they've been exposed to some sort of virus that the government knows about but is trying to keep hushed up.'

'Chloe!' I said.

'I don't care, Jake. This has gone too far.'

Clarke peered at her. 'You're saying they've gone missing too?'

She tipped her head towards the ceiling. 'Spare me the idiots. Yes, I bloody am.'

'So when did they go missing exactly?'

'Dad vanished three hours ago.'

'And your father is, miss?'

'Professor Dave Haze.'

'Right... Well, I'm afraid until a person is missing twenty-four hours the police can't do a lot. And there's a good reason we leave it that long because in the vast majority of cases the person turns up safe and sound within that time frame.'

'And what about Gavin? I haven't heard a word from him since he had a fight with Jake.'

Clarke swivelled towards me. 'You had another run-in with Gavin?'

'It's already ancient history, Inspector.'

'And what was it about this time?'

'Stuff...'

'Like the *stuff* that nearly got you arrested in connection with that car break-in?'

I glanced away. 'That's between him and me.'

'And now you turn up with his girlfriend at the police station.' His eyes flicked over us. 'You do know how this looks, both of you, don't you?'

Chloe tucked her chin in. 'Why don't you tell us? After all, you're meant to be the inspector here.'

His voice became tired as he said, 'We see this sort of thing all the time.'

The breath whistled through Chloe's teeth. 'You're not saying that you think Gavin and I had a fight? And then what? I flung myself into Jake's arms?'

The air in the lobby suddenly felt unbearably hot. The policewoman watched us without blinking like we were her very own private soap opera.

'You tell me,' Clarke replied.

Chloe took a breath, her face turning scarlet.

I braced myself for the verbal explosion.

Instead Chloe's phone pinged and she glanced at it. In an instant she seemed to melt into her own body.

'Is something wrong?' I asked.

'No. No, not at all. The opposite.' She swivelled the screen towards Clarke and me.

Hey, sorry I dropped off the grid. Things to sort out, people to bother, the usual. Are you free, babe? Gaz x

Clarke rolled his eyes over our shoulders at the policewoman. 'So Gavin hasn't disappeared then.'

'Seems not,' Chloe replied. 'But Dad...'

'As I said, give it twenty-four hours. If he hasn't turned up by then, I'll see what we can do.'

Chloe bit her lip and glanced at me.

We needed to talk this through, but not in front of Clarke. 'I guess that makes sense, Inspector,' I replied for her.

His eyes softened on Chloe. 'Try not to worry, Chloe. I'm sure he'll be OK.'

She managed a vague embarrassed nod and then, head down, arms hugging herself, she headed out of the door.

'Sorry to have bothered you, but she's upset,' I said to Clarke and the policewoman.

'I worked that bit out myself,' the policewoman replied.

I hurried out after Chloe, but she was already a twenty metres away. I had to run to catch her shadowy outline disappearing into the fog.

'God, that was so humiliating,' Chloe said without looking at me when I caught up with her. 'Why didn't you try to stop me?'

'I sort of tried, but it didn't work out too well.'

She glanced at me. 'Yeah, yeah you did. Sorry and everything, but somebody is lying here and it isn't us. And what does Stone and all those other missing people reappearing mean?'

I stuck my hands into my jean pockets as I walked with her. 'I wish I knew, Chloe, but I'm as confused as you are. We could try asking Sentinel, back at your place, to see what he knows?'

Chloe dipped her head. 'Or we could try using our phone assistants to talk to him now...'

'Worth a go,' I replied.

Chloe held her phone to her mouth and pressed her finger on to the screen. 'Why is Genesis abducting people and taking them back to the destroyed science park, Sentinel?'

'I'm not sure I understand,' her phone assistant replied with a Lisa Simpson accent – probably one of Chloe's own custom hacks. It didn't sound like Sentinel, but more a standard phone response.

'It was worth a try,' Chloe said, clearly thinking the same.

'Yes, it was.' I thought for a moment. 'OK, so we know for certain that everything points to the DEC experiment, which might also explain Genesis's interest in your dad.'

'And what about Gavin? And Mr Jones – and all the others?'

'Maybe wrong time, wrong place, and they managed to get themselves infected?'

'So if the shadow things are a virus of some sort, why didn't they infect you?'

I shuddered at the thought. 'Maybe I have a natural immunity or something?'

'The sooner we see the contents of that encrypted file, the better,' Chloe replied.

I stared at her and tapped my laptop bag, not able to believe that I'd forgotten. 'I didn't tell you. Sentinel finished decrypting it.'

'He did? Why didn't you say?'

'You should have seen yourself. You were like Wonder Woman off to kick some butt.'

'Yeah, I suppose I was.' She flashed me a faint smile. 'OK, let's get back to my place and see what we can learn.'

We headed round the corner into an alley where Chloe had parked her ride out of sight by some bins as she hadn't wanted to draw attention to her having a pillion passenger on the back of her scooter. She handed me her spare crash helmet.

I hitched a thumb over my shoulder in the direction of the police station. 'Don't you think it's a bit risky having me as a passenger around here?'

'You can walk if you want to.'

I debated it for a full millisecond. 'No – I need to know what's in that file right now.'

'Thought so.' Chloe pulled her own helmet on and swung her leg over the scooter.

Arms behind me, I clasped on to the back of the seat as we sped away into the thickening fog.

CHAPTER SEVENTEEN

MY HEART WAS DOING something approaching a drum solo as I opened up my laptop's screen in Chloe's bedroom with her watching on. My machine started to power up, and after what felt like several lifetimes slipping past the desktop, at last, filled my screen.

A pop-up window read: *Decryption completed, please wait...*

I took in a sharp breath. I had every feeling that what we were about to learn would be significant.

'Now to see why Sentinel was so anxious for us to retrieve it,' Chloe said.

Document after document started to show in a list in the file window. By the end, there were easily a hundred.

'At least this time we can take our time reading all of this stuff, not like on the Jodrell Bank systems,' Chloe said.

I pointed to the first file in the list. 'How about starting with that video?'

'Sure, why not?'

I double-clicked the file and a title appeared over a black background.

DEC Experiment Explosion Footage. Evidence for Government Select Committee.

Chloe blew her cheeks out. 'This is a video of...' She reached to hit the pause key. 'Are you sure you want to watch this, Jake? It might be tough.'

She wasn't wrong – nausea was already eating away at me. 'You mean because we may be about to see my dad die?'

'Maybe exactly that.'

'But I have to know, Chloe.'

She slowly nodded. 'Of course you do.'

The air tightened in my throat as I watched her click play again. The image cross-faded and my heart jumped as a tired face filled the frame, the same dark irises as mine.

Dad.

For a moment time halted. I resisted the urge to reach out and touch the screen.

Dad stepped back from the camera to reveal the lab coat he was wearing over his trademark crumpled blue shirt. Dad's hair was ruffled and his face unshaven. It must have been one of his late-nighters. The morning after one of those, I'd see him worn out over a hurried breakfast with me. But now he looked worried as well as tired.

In the background racks of complex science kit filled the rear wall. Numerous screens glowed with graphs and equations and between them countless cable looms dangled from the ceiling. The organised chaos of Dad's old lab.

Over the years since his death that lab had taken on mythical proportions in my head – the stuff of sci-fi movies. He'd let me into that inner sanctum a few times, but back then his experimental work had mostly gone completely over my head. It wouldn't be the case now. Dad wouldn't recognise me today, his son who'd found it hard to concentrate on anything becoming so focused on studies and going to uni.

Dad spoke to the camera again. 'Despite voicing my misgivings, Alexander Langton, the secretary of defence, has taken a personal interest in our project here and pressured us to proceed with the experiment because of its potential benefits to the MOD. I just hope that the belief of my scientific colleague in this endeavour, Professor Dave Haze, is correct and that we have built in sufficient safeguards to deal with the unexplained anomalies that we detected during an earlier test run.'

'Anomaly – it's that word again,' Chloe said.

'Yes, I noticed. And he was under pressure from the MOD.'

'I'm certain it's going to be OK, Martin,' we heard a voice say in the background – Dave's voice. 'You have always been too cautious, and sometimes we have to push the boundaries of our understanding. This is the moment that we need to step into the unknown to make any real progress.'

I turned to Chloe – her mouth was in a tight line. 'So despite everything Dad told me, he was directly involved in the experiment – this proves it.'

I found that I'd unconsciously balled my fists. 'It sounds like it, Chloe.'

Dad continued talking. 'I just pray you're right, Dave, and that we achieve a real breakthrough with our understanding of dark energy.' He looked straight at the camera. 'Today we're going to attempt to condense dark energy within the test chamber and this will be the video record of that attempt.'

The camera panned across to a floor-to-ceiling glass cylinder mounted in the middle of the lab. Suspended inside was a chrome sphere encircled by hundreds of metal rods that weren't quite touching it. The device looked like a sort of metal sea urchin that had been freeze-framed at the exact moment of shedding its spines.

The camera panned back to my dad who had crossed to a control console containing banks of switches and dials. 'To begin this experiment, we will create a vacuum field at the centre of the chamber to mimic the environment of space.' He flicked a few switches and we heard the whine of several motors starting up. 'Pumps engaged.'

Dad gazed directly into the camera again, but this time it felt like he was addressing his words directly to me. 'Based on our current understanding of the universe, ordinary matter accounts for only five per cent of the observable universe. Dark matter, through its gravitational effect that binds galaxies together, accounts for another twenty-five per cent. However, it is the even more mysterious dark energy, the missing seventy-five per cent of the universe, which is responsible for the accelerating expansion of the cosmos. It is this area to which I and Professor Dave Haze have dedicated our lives to increasing human understanding. However, until now, dark energy has proved an elusive candidate to directly observe, many theorising that is because the density of ordinary matter on Earth is too high and it is that which screens the presence of dark energy to our sensors. Rather than create an expensive space-based detector to prove its existence, we have been pioneering a ground-based experiment that we call DEC: the Dark Energy Collector. It is based in part on an atom interfer-ometer, but with our enhancements DEC seeks to condense the dark energy sufficiently for our equipment to be able to detect its presence in the lab.'

Chloe reached across and hit the pause button. 'This is what our dads used to talk about all the time. Do you remember the lecture they gave to those college students?'

'Of course. Dave got one of them to draw spiral galaxies on a balloon and then he pumped it up.

'And as it expanded, the spaces between the drawings of the galaxies grew larger.'

'That's right,' I said. 'He said dark energy was doing the same thing to our universe, pushing the ordinary matter of galaxies further and further apart.'

'Until eventually all the stars will die and the universe will become a frozen wasteland...'

'Yes, that was quite the punchline. Well, that and the exploding balloon.'

The corner of Chloe's mouth curled up a tiny fraction as she hit the play button.

'OK, can you please switch to the auxiliary generator?' Dad said. The camera turned towards a control panel, and a hand, presumably Dave's, reached forward and pushed a switch. The lab lights dimmed.

Dad had crossed to an instrument panel mounted on a column. He flicked the striped cover off a red button and then turned to face the camera. 'It's not too late to stop, Dave?'

'But we have to know, Martin.'

'And what about the risks?'

'I have more than accounted for those with the additional safety measures I fitted,' Dave replied.

Chloe stared at the screen. 'So my dad was responsible for the safety measures...safety measures that obviously didn't work when the bloody thing blew up. Shit.'

I stared at the screen and then at her. Everything I thought I knew about that night was starting to shift. Just how much had Dave kept quiet? A sense of anger burned inside me.

'I only hope that your confidence is proved right,' Dad said. 'Three, two, one...' He pressed the button and a low-level hum grew in the background.

Graphs started to climb on a monitor screen built into the console. 'All systems are in the green and we are within executable parameters. So now we will begin to gradually increase the charge to the DEC.' Dad began adjusting software sliders on the screens. 'One gigawatt, two gigawatts, three gigawatts...'

The camera zoomed in for a close-up of the metal ball. At first, nothing seemed to be happening.

Chloe had gone quiet, her eyes locked on the screen, but her hand sought mine out in that moment...the moment I knew would change everything I thought I'd understood about that day.

I squeezed her hand back, but I could barely breathe because I was about to witness my dad's death...

A crackle of static burst from the computer's speakers and, on the video, a shower of sparks arced across from the rods in the chamber to the surface of the chrome ball, bathing the lab with strobing light.

'Five gigawatts, ten gigawatts, twenty gigawatts...' Dad's voice called out as the sparks became more sustained. 'Forty, sixty, eighty, ninety – capacitors at fifty per cent charge. We have sustained exposure at one hundred gigawatts, Dave.'

The camera view zoomed in tighter on the chrome sphere, barely visible under the dancing sparks, and then it pulled out again.

Dad pointed to a monitor. 'We now have a live feed from one of two cameras within the vacuum chamber within the DEC test sphere. If this all goes according to plan, we should start to condense the dark energy to the point we can register its presence inside the test chamber for the first time in human history.'

Chloe pointed at the screen. 'Something's happening inside there, Jake.'

I leant in closer. On the video feed from the centre of the sphere, I could see its walls were vibrating as a high-pitched whine filled the lab. But it was what was at the dead centre of the sphere that snagged my attention. A pinprick of black had appeared and was growing larger.

'Is that...?' Chloe asked.

This was beyond incredible. All Dad's research work had paid off. 'Dark energy. It has to be.'

Dave whooped in the background as the sphere became semi-transparent.

Everything around the lab seemed to be rattling like an earth-quake was rolling below the building. Chloe's hand clamped harder on to mine.

Dad shouted over the top of the noise on the video. 'OK, we're approaching the maximum parameters of the DEC's experimental envelope.'

The view of the room rotated through ninety degrees as the camera was put down on a lab bench. I turned my head on the side briefly until it shifted back to the correct angle and showed Dad now wearing ear protectors. Presumably Dave was too.

'OK, get ready to inject caesium atoms into the chamber,' Dad shouted over the roar. He spun a calibrated knob right over. 'Two hundred gigawatts.' He slammed his palm on to the red button again.

The room blazed with brilliance as continuous lightning from the tips of needles made them glow red, obscuring the view of the ball. The internal view from the monitor feed filled with static.

'OK, termination in five seconds...four...three...two...one.' Dad turned the dial on the console to zero.

The sparks died as silence descended. All the graphs on the lab's screens slid to the bottom...all apart from one. A single green line was speeding towards the top of that display.

Dave whooped. 'Look, Martin, we have confirmed dark energy detection. I told you it would be all fine.'

Dad slowly nodded. 'Yes, yes – it seems that maybe you were right. I guess I was being too pessimistic after all.'

'I knew it – I knew it would be worth taking the risk since we were so close,' Dave said. 'But, more importantly, this is it, Martin, we've finally been proved right – in a stroke we have confirmed the existence of dark energy. So where are we going to put it?'

Dad looked at the camera, puzzled. 'Put what?'

'The Nobel Prize that we'll undoubtedly get for this break-through—' An alarm cut him off, accompanied by a deep growl that grew louder as the graphs on the screens all shot upwards.

This was it, the moment I'd been dreading. Every instinct made me want to rush from the room, but I had to know, had to see.

'My god...' Dad pointed. 'Quick, get this on film, Dave.'

The camera swung round and focused back on the inside of the glass chamber. The surface of the sphere had started to buckle outwards like something was punching it from the inside and trying to escape. The metal sphere was frosting with ice at the impact points.

'What's happening to the test chamber?' Dave called out.

'It's the same anomaly we detected before, but much bigger this time,' Dad replied. 'I warned you – I bloody warned you, Dave.'

'I still say it could be OK, Martin.'

'We can discuss it later, but I'm killing the power feed before this gets out of hand.'

The view closed on the expanding sphere. A frozen point near to the top of the sphere shattered and a hole appeared.

'I'm detecting a thermal temperature drop inside the chamber,' Dad said. 'Switching to a thermal camera view.'

The camera cut to a different feed. The black and whites I was so familiar with from the Shadowlands filled the screen. A curl of black vapours rushed out from the fracture and into the glass chamber around the sphere.

My heart stuttered in my chest.

Chloe stared at me. 'Tell me that's not what you saw in the park when you developed infrared vision?'

I hit pause, my blood pounding. 'It's exactly the same. And this video also proves that what's been happening around Stoneham began with this DEC experiment six years ago.'

'How could my dad have lied about it all this time?'

'We still don't know everything. We need to talk to him.'

Chloe locked her hands behind her neck. 'But as far as we know, he's still at the old science park site with Genesis.'

'And why they're there must be something to do with this experiment.'

'Whatever is going on, it's hard for me not to see my dad as anything other than the bad guy in all of this. And OK, I see your logic about Genesis grabbing Dad, but what about the others – Gavin and the rest?'

'I know – that doesn't make any sense to me either, Chloe.'

I gazed at the laptop again, my finger hovering over the key. What were we about to see?

Chloe massaged the back of my hand with her thumb. 'Are you sure about this?'

'Yes.' I took a deep breath and pressed play.

'What's going on?' Dad said, pointing at the console in front of him. The view switched to Dave's handheld camera.

On the monitor display in front of Dad a familiar random pattern of numbers and letters scrolled across it.

Chloe's eyes widened. 'Hey, that looks like Sentinel's boot-up sequence.'

My mind raced. 'We know the AI was looking into anything to do with dark energy when he escaped Jodrell Bank's computers. And this means...'

'That your dad's lab was his next stop.'

The camera tilted up and focused on the glass containment chamber. Cracks started to appear in it. On the same monitor screen four white words appeared from the jumble of text.

Portal achieving critical mass.

Fresh alarms blared out in the lab.

My dad began moving slider controls and shoving buttons frantically. 'Something has locked me out,' he shouted.

'I'll manually shut down the DEC using the auxiliary circuit breakers,' Dave called back.

The view dropped on to a desk to frame a mug in the foreground displaying the words: 'World's Greatest Scientist'. Dave ran into shot and started pulling levers down on the back wall. 'The circuit breakers aren't working either, Martin.'

'Oh god. Looking at these energy read-outs an overload will take this whole facility with it,' Dad said. 'We've got to warn people.' He pulled his mobile out from his pocket and stared at it. 'I've got no signal – the DEC must be disrupting the mobile network.'

'But it's never done that before,' Dave shouted.

'This is like when the satellite crashed,' I said to Chloe. 'Allan said it was probably down to a power spike, but what if it was everything to do with Sentinel?'

Both our gazes travelled to the spinning crystal pulsing white inside the Ember sim on Deep Thought Two.

Meanwhile, on my laptop screen, a boom rattled the lab. The air shimmered around the cylinder as more cracks appeared. A single black thread of vapour crept through a crack in the glass and shot towards the camera like a serpent.

Dave cried out and the view pitched to the side. Sparks flew from the banks of equipment, the whine accelerating to deafening levels, overloading my laptop speakers and emerging distorted.

'Are you OK?' Dad shouted to Dave.

A blinding flash filled the lab and the video filled with static.

Chloe's hand clawed round mine. 'The moment of the explosion – it has to be.'

The moment that Dad had died; the moment that had changed my life for ever. Bile rose to the back of my throat.

The static faded to black and text appeared:

On the 18th December 2017, the DEC experiment exploded with the loss of twenty-three people, including Professor Martin Stevens at the Hopworth Science Park. The only survivor was Professor Dave Haze, who managed to escape the blast zone.

The text faded away.

'Jake, are you OK?' Chloe asked.

Tears rolled down my face. I couldn't speak, couldn't think.

Chloe pulled me into a hug.

I clung on to her, my fingers digging into her back, like if I let go of her I might drown.

'Martin...it wasn't his fault,' Chloe whispered into my ear. 'He even tried to warn people, but it was already too late. And you heard what he said – he didn't want to run the stupid experiment anyway, but Dad persuaded him to go ahead. I can't believe he did, but there it is. And almost the worst thing is that Dad's lied about it – he's lied for all these years.' She pressed her hands to her mouth.

'I know, I know.' I swallowed hard. 'But Dave also said there were safety measures he'd built in. I guess the dark energy must have screwed with the experiment somehow.'

'And why exactly was Sentinel there? Because he knew researching dark energy was dangerous?'

'Maybe, and if so to presumably try to stop them running it – but he arrived too late,' I replied.

Suddenly Chloe took her hand from mine and pressed her fingers to her mouth again.

'What is it, Chloe?'

'No one else survived the blast radius, apart from my dad. So that must mean...'

'Where are you going with this?'

Chloe's face became so white she looked like she was about to throw up. 'That my dad ran away and left Martin and all those others to die.'

'That's one huge mental leap, Chloe. I can't believe Dave would do something like that. Apart from anything else, he and Dad were best mates.'

'But what if he did, Jake? Who knows what someone is capable of when they're really afraid, terrified for their life. I think the guilt of that moment has screwed him up ever since. It would explain an awful lot, and why Dad's kept his involvement with the DEC under wraps all these years.' Her eyes beaded with tears.

'I still say you're jumping to conclusions.'

'Or maybe you just don't want to face the truth of what's staring us both in the face.' The knuckles of Chloe's hands stood out white as she clenched them together.

I took both her hands back in mine and smoothed out her fists. 'Let's concentrate on what we do know. The DEC experiment condensed dark energy into a form that could appear in our world. And now, six years later, somehow the same dark energy we saw on the video, in the form of the Shadowlands, has reached Stoneham – and god knows where else – bringing with it those shadow creatures that seem to live inside it. And maybe that's why the government is trying to hush this up, whatever the cost, because this outbreak all started with a project backed by the MOD.'

'All I know is that I feel like my head's going to explode.' Her gaze snapped to mine. 'Actually there's something else I do now know.'

'What?'

'The moment Dad reappears, infected or not, I'm so going to confront him. How could he let Martin take all the heat for what happened? Lies, half truths – that's all he's told anyone since that awful day. The complete and utter shithead.'

'I still think we have to be missing something here.' But deep down I was no longer certain of anything. Could Dave really be the monster this revelation had portrayed him as? For Chloe's sake I wasn't going to leap to that conclusion, not yet at least. That was what everyone had done with my dad – used him as a scapegoat – and that wasn't a mistake I intended to repeat.

Chloe's fingers twitched beneath mine. 'Or maybe it's absolutely what it looks like, Jake – that my dad is actually the pariah that he let everyone paint your dad as for all these years.'

It felt like someone had got hold of my world and spun it on to its head. But what was worse was watching Chloe slide into the same sort of darkness that I had lived in for six years.

'I'm still not convinced,' I replied.

'But I am. There's no other answer. All the others who were abducted have turned up, so it can only be a matter of time before Dad does too. And when he does I'm going to have it out with him.'

'But what if it turns ugly?'

'If he does anything stupid, Jake, I'm not going to just sit back and take it this time.'

'Then I'm going to stay with you.'

'You can't – this is between Dad and me.'

'And if it turns *really* ugly?' What if Dave did more than just hit her this time, defence videos or not? For a crazy moment I nearly suggested that she armed herself. But we were still talking about her dad here. However bad it got, it wouldn't get as far as that.

'Then I'll put some of those defence videos I've been studying to good use.' Her nostrils flared. 'Look, Jake, I know how badly this has wrecked your life and that you have every right to be here to hear the truth. But I also need to face Dad alone for all sorts of reasons. I hope you can understand that?'

My chest tightened. 'Yeah, I can, but are you really sure, Chloe?'

Pain swirled behind her eyes. 'No, but I'm going to do it anyway. You should go now, Jake, and I'll call you when it's over.'

Over? The life Chloe thought she knew?

In an instant I was swept back to Clarke turning up on my doorstep six years ago to tell me Dad had died...

'But what about Sentinel?' I said. 'We need to ask him questions about what happened.'

Chloe raised her hand. 'Jake, I haven't got the headspace to even think about it. Can you talk to him? Take my laptop so you can have direct access to Ember. Now he's started to talk, maybe he'll open up about what really happened back in the lab.'

I stood up. 'I still think I should stay.'

'No, just be ready to gather up the pieces.'

It struck me that it wasn't really my job. 'Isn't that what Gavin should be doing?'

Chloe shrugged. 'Once I've had things out with Dad, he's next on my to-do list. Meanwhile, I hope you get some straight answers out of Sentinel.'

'I'll do my best.'

'See you on the other side of this nightmare, Jake.'

I opened my mouth, but Chloe pressed her finger to my lips. 'Please, let me do this my way.'

'OK, but I'm really not happy about it.'

'I know and thank you.' She handed me a memory stick. 'Can you make a back-up of the unencrypted files? They're too important to risk losing if my computer fails.'

'OK.' I stuck the memory stick into her laptop, copied the files over and then pulled out the stick and pocketed it.

Chloe picked up her oversized laptop bag, stuffed her laptop into it and gave it to me.

With a final glance at Chloe, I took in her sad but determined expression. Then I walked away, shouldering the dead weight of her laptop along with my own, every step feeling like the wrong decision.

CHAPTER EIGHTEEN

GOLDEN LIGHT BATHED the view beyond my window. The sun had finally managed to burn the fog away as the day crept towards night. In the distance there was no sign of military helicopters at the crash site. But on the walk back from Chloe's the Genesis vehicles that had swamped the town seemed to pass me continuously. Were they still looking for more sick people to drag off to the old science centre? But why there and not a military hospital?

I stared at my mobile for the hundredth time, willing Chloe to ring with news. I still wasn't sure it had been the right thing to leave her to face Dave alone. I fought the urge to bombard her with texts and instead forced my attention on Chloe's laptop. On it Sentinel's avatar crystal sat inside my perfectly modelled bedroom.

'OK, Sentinel, enough with the cryptic answers,' I whispered so Allan in the next room wouldn't overhear. 'Why were you there on the computer at my dad's lab before DEC blew up?'

Text appeared on the screen immediately.

Following my creators' operating instructions.

'Yes, I get the following orders bit, but to do what exactly?'

Guard.

'Against what?'

This time the cursor blinked. I could almost hear the AI's mental cogs spinning.

The Shade.

I blinked. 'You're talking about those shadow creatures, aren't you?'

Yes.

Now our unseen enemy had a name: the Shade. The temperature in the room dropped. The name fitted perfectly for those shadows, or dark energy, or whatever they were. 'But hang on, if you come from a parallel world, how did you know about the Shade on this planet?'

'Because the Shade exist outside our space-time and their attack on your Earth is part of a larger war erupting across the multiverse.'

Horror filled me. These things were behaving like a plague and a multidimensional one at that. 'So the Shade exist within dark energy?'

That is correct.

'And they got into this world because of the DEC experiment?'

The cursor just blinked.

Why the pause? 'Sentinel?'

You are correct again, Jake Stevens.

'What else can you tell me then?'

The cursor blinked.

'Hello? Are you awake in there?' I demanded.

Inside Ember, Sentinel's crystal turned red.

I started to panic – this didn't feel good. 'Sentinel, are you OK?'

Genesis are attempting to trace my location.

I sat up straighter. 'Why are they after you?'

There is no time to explain. I must begin an immediate recompile to adapt my code base to deal with this new threat. The Ember sim window closed and a message pulsed on the screen: *Recompile in progress.*

I grabbed my phone and activated the voice assistant. 'What should I do to help?'

'Sorry, I cannot help you with that,' my phone assistant replied.

So Sentinel was offline for now. I looked to the window, half expecting to glimpse the red laser dots of special forces' sniper sights dancing across it, but instead I just saw the deepening golds of sunset burnishing the rooftops. I took a breath to steady myself.

If Genesis were about to bust down the door, then surely with all his computing power Sentinel would have warned me? Anyway, hadn't he said *attempted* to trace? That meant, although Genesis might know he was in Stoneham, at least for now they didn't know where exactly. But how long would things stay like that?

I massaged my temples with my fingertips. My brain felt tangled with thoughts and half guesses. I needed time to process everything that I'd learnt today. Maybe I needed to do my own version of a recompile.

I wandered into the kitchen, and found a large BLT sandwich already waiting for me, together with a note from Allan.

I'm heading off to the Star Party. If you fancy joining us, you know where to find me.

I held the note in my hand. Maybe that wasn't such a bad idea. I'd forgotten about the party Allan's stargazing group had planned for tonight. Rather than hanging around here for Chloe's phone call and slowly driving myself half mad, joining the others at the Star Party on Ravens Hill might be just what I needed – time out of my own crazy life.

I ducked back into my bedroom and dug through piles of junk at the back of a cupboard. I finally unearthed a black long case with a carrying strap: Dad's expensive Japanese refracting telescope that I'd inherited. I shouldered it and grabbed the case of eyepieces. With a last glance at the spinning icon on Chloe's laptop, I headed out of the door.

Through the eyepiece the stars looked like specks of salt on jet-black paper. They seemed so close it felt as though I could pluck them out of the sky. For the first time in ages I felt a real sense of inner peace, something I needed more than ever at the moment.

All around me, telescopes pointed at every angle towards the heavens.

The words that Dad always said when stargazing came to me. 'Try to look at the stars with your imagination, not just your eyes.'

A murmur passed through the group.

'Hey, will you look at that?' Allan said.

I glanced at where he was pointing just in time. A meteor, a big one, disappeared towards the horizon and blazed a green trail behind it.

A sense of wonder rose through me. I'd forgotten how much I enjoyed looking up at the night sky like this. 'That was beautiful.'

Allan beckoned me over to join him. 'Have a look at this as well.' He was using the huge Dobsonian telescope. I guessed that someone had carried it up the hill and set up for him – his limp meant he'd never be able to do that on his own.

I peered through it at a group of stars hanging in a faint gauze of mist. To me, they looked like fiery blue jewels in the sky. 'The Pleiades cluster?'

'In one,' Allan replied. 'And in tonight's great viewing conditions you can easily see the nebulosity surrounding the stars. Of course they've only been around for a hundred million years – the equivalent of a newborn baby in astronomical terms.'

Even without looking, I knew Allan was smiling at his own astronomy-geek joke.

'Did you know that the Pleiades were linked to the Celts' ceremonies for remembering the dead?' he continued.

A wave of sadness washed over me. Yet another moment when Dad should have been here.

Allan caught my expression and frowned. 'Sorry, Jake, I wasn't thinking.'

'No worries.' I didn't want Allan feeling bad. But his frown lines deepened, so I gave him what was – I hoped – a reassuring smile and wandered back to my scope...to Dad's old scope.

Below me, Stoneham's streetlights shone out like golden stars, a man-made echo of the ones in the sky above. In a way we were still cavemen trying to push away the night with our fires.

I'd looked at this same view countless times, but my most precious memory was when Dad had first taken me to a Star Party gathering. I'd only been about six and Dave had brought along Chloe too.

We'd both huddled on this very spot together under a blanket, looking up at the night sky, sipping mugs of hot chocolate. Six years later, that happy life had been stolen away from us both when the experiment had exploded. Gavin had been affected too – losing his dad. What would Gavin say when he learnt that his girlfriend's dad, rather than mine, was responsible for what had happened that night?

A torch beam flicked up the hillside as someone headed towards our gathering.

Someone from the Star Party called down to them, 'Hey, you, turn that flipping torch off.'

All the astronomers were using red torches to protect their night vision. That was the number-one rule in the stargazing bible because it took a good thirty minutes for someone's eyesight to fully adapt to the dark after being exposed to white light.

'Sorry, wasn't thinking,' Chloe's voice called back.

How had she tracked me down? More importantly what was her news? I waved to her as she turned off her torch.

She crossed the top of the hill towards me and I couldn't help scanning her face. I relaxed a fraction when I saw no fresh bruises.

'So what happened?' I asked.

'Nothing, because Dave still isn't home. And when I tried to check his whereabouts on Ember, Sentinel had started running another new massive compile.'

'I know. Sentinel told me it's something to do with him adapting his code because Genesis tried to run a trace on him.'

'That sounds bad.'

'I know. But anyway, I'm sure your dad will eventually turn up OK.'

'Maybe, but he won't be OK for long after I've got my hands on him. I haven't been able to think of anything else, Jake, apart from how he framed your dad. I'm just so sorry. How could he have abandoned everyone in that explosion, especially his best friend?'

'I'm still hoping he didn't.'

'You do know you're being way too understanding about this. But whatever you think, it's hard for me not to hate my own father right now.'

Despite everything, the strength of her reaction shook me. If Chloe had been barely hanging on to a relationship with Dave, this sounded like she was ready to throw petrol on it and light the match. 'Hate is a strong word, Chloe.'

'Yeah, it is.' She took a metal thermos flask out of her bag and started to pour out steaming dark liquid into two cups. She handed one to me.

I took a cautious sip, tasted hot chocolate and found myself smiling.

'Just like when we were kids up here, hey?' Chloe said.

'Absolutely. Anyway, how did you know where I was?'

'I didn't to begin with. I tried your phone, but you weren't picking up.'

'It was out of juice after constantly checking for messages from you – I left it charging.'

'Sorry about the radio silence, but I just needed some space.'

'I totally get that.'

Chloe nodded. 'When I couldn't get hold of you I headed over to Celestial Skies. That's when I spotted Allan's poster for the Star Party tonight. I figured you might be up here doing something normal while everything's so crazy at the moment.'

'You know me better than I do.'

'I guess I still do.' She gestured towards the refractor. 'Good to see that again.'

'Yep, it's been too long.'

'Can I sneak a peek?'

'Knock yourself out.'

Chloe brushed her red hair back over her ears and lowered her face to the right-angled eyepiece. She let out a long sigh. 'The M42 nebula, right?'

'Very good, Miss Haze.'

'It's stunning.'

'It always is.'

Chloe looked up at me from the eyepiece. 'Do you remember when Martin told us all the atoms that make up everything around us, including our bodies, were born in the hearts of those stars billions of years ago?'

'Yeah – star children, he called us.' I took a sip of my drink. It almost burned my tongue. 'God, this is really hot.'

She smiled. 'In my humble opinion if it isn't sweet and scalding, it isn't proper hot chocolate.'

A laugh rose from somewhere deep inside me. Chloe seemed to have a knack for making me smile.

Allan shuffled towards us through the dark. 'The rest of us are calling it a night.'

'But the sky's so crystal clear – why leave now?' I replied.

He coughed. 'We'll be in time for last orders at the Red Lion if we go now.'

'Should've known,' Chloe said, shaking her head at me.

'Do you fancy coming?' Allan said.

'No, not yet, thanks,' I replied.

Chloe gestured at the stars. 'We want to spend some more time looking at those sparkly things up there.'

Allan smiled. 'Now that I can more than understand.'

As we helped Allan pack his Dobsonian away for the first time in ages I actually felt happy, despite everything that had happened. Maybe it was having Chloe back in my life, or maybe me being up here at a Star Party again. But more than anything it was knowing Dad wasn't the criminally negligent guy that everyone had painted him to be. I could remember him again as Dad – still driven and focused, but also the kind, happy man that had shared a love of the stars with his son.

We watched the procession of astronomers make their way back down the hill led by Allan. For a man using a walking stick he was managing a speedy walk – probably something to do with heading to the pub.

Chloe lay down on a picnic blanket she had conjured out of her bag and tapped the spot next to her.

Before I could catch myself I gave her a questioning look.

Her eyes widened. 'Not that! This is about recapturing our childhood and playing that game we did as kids.'

'Which one?'

'First one to ten satellites wins.'

I laughed. 'Hey, I'd forgotten all about that.'

She raised her eyebrows. 'I guessed that from your reaction.'

I snorted and lay down next to her, fixing my gaze on the heavens. The smell of grass and damp earth filled my nose. The chill of cold through the blanket was already leaching the heat from my back. But I *so* didn't care – I had my best friend back in my life and by my side.

Chloe pointed to a pinprick of light crawling across the sky. 'One to me.'

I made a scoffing noise. 'Not bad for a beginner.'

She pointed to another just above the horizon beyond Stoneham. 'Two to me. Oh yes, Chloe Haze is on a roll.'

I imagined the satellite spinning through space miles above us, its solar panels reflecting the sunlight and lighting it up like a star.

The sense of calm deepened within me. Whatever was about to happen in our near future with Chloe here I felt a sense of utter peace – despite whatever the Shade were up to...

Shit, I hadn't told Chloe my news. I propped myself up on one arm. 'I've got fresh intel about those shadow creatures.'

Chloe sat up and stared at me. 'You have?'

'Sentinel told me that they're called the Shade and, get this – they come from beyond space and time.'

'What's that meant to mean?'

'That they're not a man-made virus, but are a life form that exists in the hidden universe of dark energy.'

She sat up. 'You're saying they're alien in origin – like Sentinel?'

'It seems so. Sentinel also said that the Shade are what his creators programmed him to guard against. Apparently what's happening here on Earth is part of a larger war that's kicked off across other parallel universes.'

Her shoulders dropped in a silent sigh. 'We are so in over our heads, aren't we?'

'Maybe, but at least that's another bit of the puzzle we now understand.'

'There is one huge bit that still doesn't fit, though.' Her eyes tightened on me. 'How does turning you into some sort of mutant fit into any of this?'

'I wish I knew.'

'Still feeling no other side effects?'

'I've been feeling fine actually.'

'You would tell me if you did, wouldn't you?'

I stared at my knuckles and picked at them.

'What is it, Jake?'

'I'm fine as far as I know, but there is something I haven't told you yet...'

'What?'

Chloe deserved to know the truth. I'd been putting it off for long enough. I took a deep mental breath. 'I think you may have been affected by Sentinel too.'

Her head snapped back. 'What makes you think that?'

'Because you got electrocuted by the same circuit board that I did.'

Her eyes hardened. 'You're saying that's linked to what's happened to you?'

'A message appeared on your phone for a moment when you blacked out.'

'What did it say? And how did you see it?'

'It was about you being the second subject – and also being another Awoken. I saw it flash up on the screen as Josie was putting your things back into your bag.'

Her voice became as hard as iron. 'You've deliberately not told me about this, Jake?'

'Only because I didn't want to worry you.'

'So you're saying Sentinel has tampered with us both?'

'I guess.'

Chloe was silent for a moment...which seemed to last for ever.

Finally she leapt up and shouted, 'How could you, Jake? How dare you? What do you think gave you that right? Because you thought I couldn't handle the truth without going off at the deep end? Is that right?'

'I was trying to look out for you.' I knew I deserved this reaction, but I wanted her to understand my reasoning too.

'Oh, my knight in shining bloody armour.' She tipped her head back to stare up at the sky and stretched her arms wide. 'Once again the famous Jake Stevens has let me down.'

'Chloe...' I took a step towards her but she held up her palms and I stopped dead.

'Six years ago I so needed you, Jake, but I also knew you were hurting, and that I had no right to expect anything. Then, when Dave changed and began to beat me, and my best friend had abandoned me, I had no else to turn to!'

I tried to reach out for her but she shook me away. 'I wish you'd said something.'

'Like I bloody wish you had about this Awoken business.' Chloe gestured at herself. 'This is my body and I had every right to know if some alien AI has been screwing with it.' She glowered at me. 'How can I trust you ever again after this, Jake?' She stormed off to the other side of the hill and stood staring out, her back a wall to me.

I looked in the opposite direction. What had I done?

A flash of bright light came from the middle of the town below us. It appeared again, a powerful beam reflected off one of the buildings. My throat clenched. It was Celestial Skies – being lit up with a spotlight. I leapt to my telescope and swung it round. Through the eyepiece I saw a Genesis van parked outside the shop, its external spotlight mounted on the vehicle illuminating the building. Chloe's scooter was parked up outside. Inside, I could see torchlight flicking around through my attic-room window.

'Chloe, you need to see this,' I called over to her.

Her back stiffened.

'I know you're mad, but this is more important. Genesis are searching Celestial Skies.'

Chloe spun round. 'What?'

'You heard. Shit. This is really bad, Chloe. Both of our laptops are in there – and my mobile.'

She sprinted back to me then.

I dipped my eye back to the telescope. A man had appeared in the shop's doorway with Chloe's laptop under his arm and a bag on his other shoulder – no doubt with my laptop and phone inside.

'What's happening?' Chloe asked as she reached me.

'We're screwed, that's what.'

Another flash of light burst out, but this time from a different, taller building across town. I already knew where, before I looked closely. I swung the telescope round to see torchlight inside the penthouse of the Old Brewery.

I rotated the telescope on its mount so I could see the main entrance to the flats. Another parked-up Genesis truck was blocking the gate. A woman carrying a computer with a clear case was heading towards it.

'They've got Deep Thought Two as well now,' I said.

Chloe stared at me. 'If this is the government, what's going to happen to us, Jake?'

A loud warble came from her phone. Chloe stared at it then showed me the screen. 'What is this meant to mean?'

'*Compile complete. Defence mechanism engaged,*' I read aloud.

The next moment a very distant scream, drawn out and anguished, echoed up from the town, quickly followed by a second. I pressed my eye back to the telescope.

I thought for a moment I was seeing things. A haze of shimmering blue energy flickered around Deep Thought Two and flowed over the woman carrying the computer. Her face twisted in agony as lightning blazed across her. Her arm, still clamped round the computer, started to dissolve into dark smoke that drifted into the air. Then the blue fire blazed up her arms, burning away everything it touched, reaching her head last, her cry cut off mid-scream. In seconds, she'd been reduced to nothing.

'What's going on down there?' Chloe asked, her tone trembling.

'Sentinel defences!'

I swung the telescope back to the Genesis van outside Celestial Skies. Chloe's large laptop was lying on the ground, along with the bag, blue fire eating the remnants of the man's body away.

I backed away, nausea rising through me.

Chloe bent her face to the telescope and gasped. 'Oh my god!'

'The same thing happened to a woman at your place who'd been carrying off Deep Thought.'

'This is all so screwed up, Jake. Wait – now someone else is getting out of the van...wearing a biohazard suit and...'

'What?' I screwed my eyes up but I couldn't make out what was happening unaided.

'He looks like he's carrying a...'

She didn't need to finish. Even at this range I could see the huge gout of flame that lit up the street in front of Celestial Skies.

'A flamethrower, a bloody great flamethrower in the middle of Stoneham?' Chloe said.

'It's got to be a joke, right?'

'I wish. The guy has just torched my laptop.'

An answering flare of flame appeared near the Old Brewery.

'Looks like the same thing just happened to Deep Thought,' I said.

Chloe took her phone out and spoke to her voice assistant. 'Sentinel, are you OK?'

His revolving gemstone filled the screen, but nothing else.

'Sentinel?'

Once again there was no response.

'I think all that is left of Sentinel is the fragment of code that's still on my phone,' Chloe said.

'You mean they've managed to kill him?'

'Not completely, at least not while I still have this. If Sentinel can spread himself to other systems, like he did before, he could still be OK...' She pointed down to the town.

'What fresh craziness now?' I asked.

A huge bank of fog had appeared in the middle of Stoneham, expanding fast.

Chloe whipped round. 'Hey, did you hear that?'

'Hear what?'

'Listen.'

I concentrated and heard a low, deep rumble like a distant hammer blow. A few seconds later another distant boom rolled past. I looked around, trying to work out where the sound had come from – somewhere in the building fog bank below us.

My vision started to shift to the black-and-white world of my thermal vision.

Chloe screamed and dropped to her knees as she clutched

her head. 'My brain is on fire!' She retched and sick splattered on to the grass in front of her.

I crouched by her side. 'Is anything happening to your vision?'

'Yes, it's just black and white—' She stared up at me through her fringe. 'This is that Awoken stuff, isn't it?'

'Have you got off-the-scale pain?'

She nodded, gritting her teeth.

I rubbed her back. 'Then it must be. Maybe Sentinel activated you before his systems went down.'

'Because we're in danger?'

'It has to be. Maybe to give us both a fighting chance of escaping.'

In my thermal vision the cool darks of the fog boiled up towards us, turning our hill into an island in the rising sea of mist.

'Oh god,' Chloe said as she stared around us. 'This is the Shadowlands?'

'Welcome to the funhouse,' I replied. 'But the pain will start to drop off any second now.' I hoped my words were reassuring, but I also remembered just how terrifying my first time had been.

A distinctive stench was building around us and a dry metallic taste flooded my mouth. The taste and smell of condensed dark energy?

Two louder thuds resounded, vibrating the hill under our feet. I spotted a black mass building in my thermal vision in the mist along the high street. Icy sweat trickled down my back.

Chloe's phone warbled and another single word appeared: *Run!*

Fear spiked through me. 'We've got to get away from here.'

'But what about your dad's telescope?' Chloe said through clenched teeth.

'If we live through this, I'll come back and get it.' It meant so much to me, this connection to Dad, but our lives meant more.

'You really think we're in that sort of danger? That we could die?'

'What do you think?'

'Yes, oh god...'

I grabbed Chloe's hand and together we stumbled away down the opposite side of the hill.

CHAPTER NINETEEN

THE DRUMBEAT of footsteps echoed up from somewhere in the fog that smothered the town and us. My life no longer made sense. Nothing made sense, especially here in the Shadowlands.

Vapours of mist flowed ahead of the knot of darkness and swept up the hill. The fog billowed up over us in a slow-motion wave with dark, blinding fumes that immediately started to burn into my lungs. Chloe was right next to me, but, infrared vision or not, I could barely see her in the thick gloom – the icy vapours blanketing out all heat sources.

'OK, which way?' Chloe asked. 'Whatever is lurking in that fog is between town and us.'

'Let's take the path the others took to the Red Lion – that's in the opposite direction.'

Chloe reached out, groped for my hand and found it. 'I'll lose you in this fog otherwise.'

I'd been up on Ravens Hill so often, especially when I needed to get some distance from my broken life down below it, that I had a good mental map of the paths in my head. It meant my feet instinctively knew where to go, even if I couldn't see a thing.

I could feel Chloe's hand trembling in mine. 'We'll get through this,' I said.

'I wish I could believe that, Jake,' she replied, her voice tight.

The monstrous footsteps echoed up the hillside behind us. On autopilot I led Chloe, one blind step after another, away down the path. Within moments my hair dripped with moisture and the ground was slimy under our feet.

The cloud pressed in on us from every side, and we repeatedly slipped, hanging on to each other to steady ourselves.

The thudding footsteps stopped on the hill above us, followed by a long clatter.

'I think that's your telescope,' Chloe whispered.

'Better it than us.' But inside I felt a twist in my stomach, as yet another part of Dad's world was lost to me.

The footsteps started up again, each one vibrating the ground.

'This isn't how the shadow creatures acted in the park, is it?' Chloe asked.

'No, this is very different, and whatever it is, it sounds much bigger.'

'It's certainly scaring the shit out of me.'

Chloe wasn't the only one, although I was doing my best not to show it.

We quickened our pace as the dank air washed over us.

My mental map of the hill told me we should reach a fork in the path at any moment. From that point we needed to take the left route that would lead us down through a small wood of sycamore trees to the Red Lion at the edge of town.

I'd so many happy childhood memories about that particular pub. When I'd been a kid Dad had sometimes taken me there after he'd finished work for a lemonade and a packet of crisps. On a clear summer's day you could see for miles from the windows, all the way across to the rolling Somerset hills. That endless view seemed an impossible fantasy in this suffocating gloom.

I felt the stony surface of the path change to mud beneath my feet. This had to be the junction. I edged us down the left-hand route that steepened away fast beneath us.

'Oh, douche nuggets,' Chloe said, her hand pulling mine as she almost fell for the third time. 'Next time I do something like this I'll remember to wear trainers.'

For every one of our steps I heard our unseen pursuer take two. No doubt about it, whatever the thing was, it was gaining on us.

The fog thinned a fraction and I spotted dark shadowy columns to our left and right. My stomach knotted.

'We've made it to the woods,' Chloe whispered.

Trees – that's all those shapes were. I stifled a laugh. 'Not far now.'

The shuddering footsteps stopped again and the silence seemed impossibly loud in the gloom. At that same moment, the atmosphere grew heavy, like the skull-pressing moment before a thunderstorm breaks.

'Do you think we lost it?' Chloe whispered.

'Not sure, but we should keep quiet in case it's still listening out for us.'

She squeezed my hand.

We had to be less than three hundred metres from the pub, but I winced at every squelch our feet made in the wet mud. At last a faint light started to build, and we saw the vague shape of a two-storey building next to a streetlight.

'The Red Lion,' Chloe whispered. 'Do you think we'll be safe there?'

From a demon? This wasn't the moment for the truth. 'Yes, of course we will.'

A moan drifted out of the fog, low and guttural, like the rasping breath of an old man.

The back of my neck tingled. 'We're going to have to run for it.'

Chloe's hand clutched mine harder and we broke into a jog. Wet nettles slapped my jeans.

With a hiss dark shapes blurred past through the murk and banked round towards us.

My heart rose in my chest. 'The Shade – they've found us.'

Chloe's eyes grew huge. 'Shit, I can see them'

I didn't get a chance to reply.

A crow-like shape broke from the flock and swooped at our heads with a raptor screech that filled the air.

'Watch out!' I yanked Chloe to the ground as it hissed over us.

But already other Shade creatures swirled towards us with wingbeats as silent as an owl's.

We ran faster – faster than I ever had in my life – towards the pub now less than fifty metres away. A dark shape plummeted straight at my face and I managed to duck to the side. But its dive carried it past me and it slashed black claws across Chloe's legs. She cried out, let go of my hand, and stumbled to the ground at the foot of a large sycamore tree.

I skidded to a stop and rushed back to her side, instinctively raising an arm in an attempt to fend off the other shadow crows diving at us. 'Are you OK?'

Chloe reached down her leg and winced. When she brought her fingers back up they were glistening with dark blood.

'It feels like freezing acid is burning into my leg,' Chloe said, her teeth starting to chatter.

I slipped my hands under her armpits. 'We'll get you help.'

'I'm so cold, Jake.'

I tried to pull her to standing but her face twisted and she let out a strangled yelp.

'Stop, I'm not going anywhere,' Chloe said. 'Not like this.'

The booming footsteps started up again from somewhere in the wood behind us.

'We can't stay here – that thing will be on top of us any moment,' I said.

'You've got to leave me here or neither of us will make it.'

I stared at her. 'But I can't...'

Chloe gripped my shoulders. 'But you have to, Jake. I'll do my best to delay them so you can get away.'

'No way, Chloe.'

'I'm doing this for you, Jake, and for your dad. Now go, please. Don't spoil my heroic moment.' She gave me a broken smile as the Shade got ready to swoop at us.

How could I leave my friend in the middle of this horror show? But I knew Chloe was right. The problem was I just didn't want her to be.

'Jake...' Chloe whispered.

A stone filled my throat. 'I'm so sorry.'

'Don't be. Just promise me you'll find out what is going on and clear your dad's name. You get your life back, you hear me?'

I dug my fingernails into my palms.

'Jake?'

I finally nodded.

'Now get out of here,' she said.

I gave Chloe a pleading look.

'I said GO!' She made a shooing gesture with her hands.

My eyes prickling, a storm in my chest, I stumbled away, glancing back to see Chloe sit up to look directly at whatever was pursuing us, expression defiant, beyond brave. I forced myself to stare straight ahead at the weathered pub sign showing a crimson lion.

For Dad...

No. No. I couldn't do it. I turned and raced back to Chloe, but had already lost sight of her in the deep fog of the Shadowlands.

'Chloe,' I shouted.

A deep vibration hummed through the ground and the pub sign creaked as it started to swing. My heart became a rock as her sudden scream seemed to come from all directions at once.

'No!' I shouted as her yell echoed to silence.

At last, through the murk, I spotted the sycamore tree where she'd fallen. I rushed towards it but only found something glowing on the floor at its base. I bent down and scooped up Chloe's phone.

A text message pulsed on the screen. *Run, Jake, you have to run, for her sake.*

Shuddering footsteps came from behind me again.

I whirled round to see a flurry of darkness speeding straight at me. I ignored the answering thunder of my own fear and drew myself up to full height. Within the Shade, the outline of a man appeared – or more like the suggestion of a man. His body was constantly forming and reforming within the pattern of swirling shadowy crow shapes.

My feet felt frozen to the ground. How could I fight this new horror?

The man carved from shadows slowed to a stop less than ten metres away. He stared at the phone in my hand, a snarl filling his flickering face.

'You want this? What's left of Sentinel?' I held the phone towards the creature.

The thing extended a hand of shifting darkness.

For you, Chloe. 'Never!' I turned and bolted for the Red Lion.

A maelstrom of leaves swirled past me as small stones clattered into my back. I ignored it all as my arms pumped the air. I reached the pub's door, threw it open, and tumbled into the bar. People started to turn towards me as I slammed the door shut, their figures glowing like ghosts in my thermal vision. In a microsecond, I recognised many of the shocked faces from the astronomy group. Then what sounded like the mother of all hailstone storms struck the building. A bellow roared from outside, powerful enough to make the brick walls shake.

The lights flickered off and plunged us all into darkness.

I braced myself against the door as it juddered beneath my hands.

The noise of wingbeats surrounded the building. I felt numb. We were all going to die in here, torn apart by shadows.

A window smashed and a wild wind tore into the bar, throwing chairs and smashing glasses. A dartboard flew discus-like across the room and crashed into a table.

Panicked screams filled the air. Once again the normal world had been ripped away like a thin veil to reveal the Shadowlands – the land where demons stalked Earth. It seemed there was no end to it...

But then the vibration on the other side of the door stopped dead and the nightmare cries died away.

My vision shifted back to the Real. Did that mean...?

Blue strobing lights flared outside, tinting the dark interior like a photo filter.

Everything settled into a frozen tableau of broken glasses, chairs and the huddled forms of people. A few whimpering moans drifted through the darkness.

No one moved, no one said a word, but everyone's shock charged the air with a fear that I could almost taste.

Allan's voice spoke up first, strong and certain, a lifeline in the madness. 'Is everyone OK?'

People responded with cries.

'Allan!' I shouted.

The lights flickered on and Allan emerged from beneath the table that had been struck by the dartboard. Around us people began to unpick themselves from the chaos and help those who'd been cut by flying glass.

Allan spotted me and hobbled over. 'What on Earth just happened out there, lad?'

'Shadows? A poltergeist? I don't know, Allan.' I spread my hands, lost for words to describe the nightmare I'd just witnessed.

His eyes widened and he dragged his teeth over his lips. 'Where's Chloe?'

But I couldn't answer him. I didn't know what to say. I pushed the shattered door open and stepped outside.

The fog was evaporating like steam into the night. Through the frame of branches above, the clear dome of stars shone out again.

Two police cars had pulled up outside and Inspector Clarke was getting out of the lead vehicle.

My gaze travelled down to the exterior of the Red Lion. The building looked like it had been raked by a thousand claws. The surrounding trees had been stripped of their bark.

'We've got to get you all evacuated,' Clarke called out to the people emerging from the pub and staring all around them at the damage.

'Because of the storm?' Allan asked.

'The what?'

'A massive hurricane just hit – you must have seen it?'

So that was what Allan assumed, even after I'd told him about the shadows. He'd obviously already decided I was just rambling. I didn't blame him. But what *was* the truth? I wasn't sure I understood anything any more.

'Not a thing,' Clarke replied. 'I'm only here because there's been a dangerous chemical leak in Stoneham and we're evacuating the town of people.' In a glance he took in the injured around us with their cuts and gashes. 'You say a storm did this?'

'More like a mini tornado,' said a woman who was helping a man bleeding heavily from a gash in his forehead.

'And it's taken out the mobile network again like that satellite did,' a man said as he checked his mobile, looking anxious.

'I see... Well, there's a medical station that's been set up at the evacuation point at the railway station, and if you can't get hold of your friends and family by phone, you should be able to find them there.' He raised his voice so everyone could hear. 'We'll organise transport and make sure you're all seen to. Then you'll be evacuated from Stoneham along with everyone else.'

People exchanged frightened looks.

I dug deep and found my voice again. 'Inspector...Chloe Haze.'

His gaze tightened on me. 'What?'

'Where is she, Jake?' Allan asked more gently.

I gestured to the wood.

'She was out in this sudden storm – is that what you're trying to say?' Clarke asked.

I turned away from the questions in both their eyes.

'Chloe!' I shouted into the wood.

Nothing.

She couldn't be gone...

'Chloe,' I whispered as my world became fractured with tears.

Allan rested his hand on my shoulder. 'What happened to her, lad?'

I sank to my knees and let the pain come pouring out in howls of racking grief.

CHAPTER TWENTY

My world felt broken; nothing was certain any more. If my life had been going downhill before, I was now about to tip over the edge, into an abyss filled with demons and nightmares.

I'd barely processed the evacuation happening around me. People were being guided, by either police or military, on to waiting buses and trains, before the invisible toxic cloud of cocktails started to spread outwards from the centre of town. Every instinct told me this had to be a cover story, but for what exactly?

Despite the chaos of the evacuation Clarke had promised he'd put what available officers he had into a search for Chloe. I knew I should tell him that would be useless since she'd been torn apart by something from the darkest corner of hell, but a part of me still hoped she'd somehow be OK. It had to be worth trying.

Like a docile sheep I'd allowed myself to be herded along with everyone else to the transfer point in the railway station car park. Many people had already knotted together in groups of family and friends. The glow of red tail lights from the cars blocking the few roads out of Stoneham had started to ease. Some people had taken the evacuation into their own hands, but most were obeying the orders of the authorities.

The military helicopters were back too, their spotlights sweeping over town, looking for any stragglers that had been left behind.

Huddled in a blanket, I waited in line for a bus and for Allan to return with coffee. In front of me a family watched the breaking news on their phones.

'Apparently a terrorist was responsible for the chemical attack,' a girl a couple of years younger than me said to her parents. 'The military have cordoned off Stoneham, screening everyone who's leaving and not letting anyone in either.'

'But why target *our* town?' the mum said. 'What have we done to deserve this?'

Because we were too close to the fallout from a top-secret experiment, I thought to myself. If this was a cover story, it was certainly a neat way for the government to get people out of town. It would mean Genesis could search for any last fragments of Sentinel...and also for me. I cast a wary look around. So far none of their vans had turned up here, but maybe they were already among the crowd. I had to keep a low profile and try to slip away with everyone else in the confusion.

Allan approached with a steaming mug of coffee from the railway cafe. It was doing a roaring trade.

'How are you doing, lad?' he said.

'Badly.'

He nodded. 'Even if Chloe was caught up in that storm, she may still be OK.'

'I wish I could believe that, Allan.'

'You should hang on to it with all your soul. Hope is the thing with feathers and all that.' His eyes narrowed on me. 'But what about what you said to me back at the pub...something to do with a poltergeist. What was that about, Jake?'

My attention slid to my coffee. 'I can't tell you, Allan.'

He frowned and gestured at the chaos of the evacuation. 'Please tell me it's not linked to what's going on around us?'

'It almost certainly is.'

He ran his hand through his grey hair. 'OK, then tell me you're not linked to this gas attack somehow?'

'Of course not.'

'I mean, you hear about teenagers being radicalised all the time via social media – being brain-washed into becoming terrorists.'

'Allan, seriously?' Did he really think that of me?

'No, I didn't think so, but I still had to ask. So what's really going on with you?'

'Things. Bad things.'

'Is this the same *thing* to do with the fact that you jump whenever one of those black vans with a Genesis logo on it rounds a corner?'

My gaze tightened on him. I didn't reply.

'Yes, I've noticed. Not to mention the blindingly obvious change in your life that after six years of having nothing to do with Chloe the two of you are suddenly as thick as thieves.'

I bit my lip. Could I risk telling him?

He gestured with his chin to something behind me. 'Talking of Genesis...'

I turned to see one of one of their vans pull up at the entrance to the car park and three men get out. I immediately scanned for an escape route, but the car park was bounded by a high fence, the only way out an entrance that the van was now blocking.

Trapped.

The men had begun showing a piece of paper to people. The first group they approached shook their heads. *Shit.* I couldn't see what was on the paper, but I guessed it was a photo of me.

I leant in closer to Allan. 'They're looking for me, Allan,' I said, my voice shaking.

'What? Why, lad?'

'I took something from that satellite.'

His eyes widened. 'You're telling me you went to the crash site when you were meant to be heading home?'

'Yes, I am, but that doesn't matter now. Here...' I handed Allan the memory stick with the cracked DEC file on it. 'Start by watching the video, because there's evidence on it that clears Dad's name.'

'Come again?'

'Just listen, Allan, because we haven't got much time. It turns out Dad didn't actually want to go ahead with the experiment that blew up, but the government – and Dave – pushed to him to proceed with it anyway.'

'You mean everything that Dave said about Martin at that enquiry—'

'Was a complete and utter lie.'

The three Genesis men had fanned out and were showing their pieces of paper to other groups of people.

'Allan, I've got to go, but you need to know that Alexander Langton is directly involved in this. To start with, he owns Genesis Security.'

'The same Genesis that are coming after you for this bit of satellite you stole? Is it them who grabbed Chloe?'

'Kind of...'

Allan gripped my shoulders, his eyes searching my face. 'Is this something to do with the poltergeist thing you mentioned?'

I desperately needed more time to give him as much info as I could before I was caught. 'There are these things called the Shade that are something to do with dark energy. Dad and Dave's experiment somehow allowed these invisible creatures into our world. We don't know how, but the people going missing –

including Dave and Gavin – are involved in something happening at the old Hopworth Science Park.'

'To do what exactly?'

'I wish I knew.'

'And you're certain about this?'

'Yes, I am, and, if it makes any difference, Chloe was too. Look at the files on that memory stick and you'll understand the threat we're all under here.'

'Jake, I don't need to look at any files.'

'Please, Allan.'

He waved me to be quiet. 'You don't understand, lad. I know when you're telling me the truth. You've never been able to lie for toffee.'

'So you do believe me? You really don't think I'm having a breakdown?'

'You are your father's son through and through. If you tell me there are these flipping Shade things running around Stoneham, then that's exactly what's happening.'

A sense of utter relief flooded through me. Allan was actually taking me seriously.

I saw one of the Genesis men reach a group of kids I recognised from college. One of the girls gestured straight towards me.

Allan spotted them too. 'Get out of here now, lad,' he hissed under his breath.

'But what will you do?'

'I'm going to do everything in my power to help you, Jake. That's what. And there's also something I need to do to honour Chloe.'

I stared at him. Allan believed me, just like Chloe had when I had eventually found the courage to tell her.

The Genesis man had called his companions over and now all three of them were striding straight towards us.

'Allan...'

'I know, lad. Just do whatever you have to.'

'I will.'

He reached out and shook my hand. 'Best of luck.'

'You too.' I turned and started to walk away, as casually as I could.

'Hey, you, stop!' a voice called out behind me.

I broke into a sprint, heading straight for a white van parked at the edge of the car park. I clambered up the bonnet on to its roof and jumped over the fence, all in one fluid movement. I hurtled down a side road that led away from the station.

A yell came from the car park, and I glanced back to see one of the men sprawling on the ground where Allan had tripped him up with his walking stick. Allan spread his arms wide, doing his best to look innocent.

I sprinted away into the night, my mind racing as I tried to work out my next step. There was every chance they'd grab me within a few blocks of here. But something inside me hardened. If they wanted to play this game, I'd take it to them. My world might have just fallen apart, especially with Chloe gone, but I was going to do everything in my power to make whoever was behind this nightmare pay for what they'd done.

CHAPTER TWENTY-ONE

My nerves kept firing at even the slightest noise. I felt like a hunted fox as I crept through a Stoneham evacuated of people because of an alleged terrorist bomb. A Genesis van prowled past the end of the alley I was hiding in.

I pressed myself back into the shadows. It was the third van I'd seen since escaping from the train station. Overhead I could hear the drone of the helicopters, spiralling like buzzards hunting for prey. One of their searchlights played along the street I'd just exited.

All looking for Sentinel. All looking for me.

Despite the very real threat of capture, and everything that might mean, the only thing I could think of was Chloe. Her final otherworldly scream kept playing on an endless loop in my head.

I took out her phone containing the last spark of Sentinel's consciousness. There were no signal bars at the top of the screen. I guessed Genesis had taken down the mobile network, and probably all internet and landline connections too – all to make sure neither Sentinel nor I would escape tonight.

'Sentinel, are you still in there? I could really do with your help.'

No audible answer, but when I looked at the screen it showed Sentinel's rotating crystal avatar.

A message appeared. *Need more processing power to be able to assist you.*

Of course he did, but I was reassured by that spark of his life that still burned inside Chloe's phone.

I ran my thumb along the edge of the phone's screen. The one thing I knew for certain was that I needed to keep moving. It could only be a matter of time before Genesis swamped our town with even more people to track me down. And how long before the shadow man joined in the pursuit to finish what he'd started? I needed to make myself and Sentinel scarce. The question was: how?

I walked past a scooter chained to the post of a back-garden gate. Then, like it had been waiting for me to ask the question, an idea surfaced: Chloe's scooter, parked near Celestial Skies.

I felt sick at the thought of going anywhere near the shop – there was every chance it could still be crawling with Genesis employees – but at least it was the start of a plan. Before my resolve crumbled I turned into a back alleyway and headed towards the shop.

For the hundredth time my mind returned to what had happened outside the Red Lion. Why had the shadow man stopped his attack when the police had turned up? Because there had been too many witnesses to kill me off in front of them?

It didn't take much imagination to work out how Genesis had planned to cover it up – probably an explosion, blamed on a gas leak in the kitchen or something similar. It was lucky for us that Clarke had turned up when he did – probably the only thing that had saved everyone.

I reached the end of the alleyway and glanced both ways to

check no one was on the road. I dashed across into the cover of a passageway.

Only one more block to go.

I sprinted down the next alleyway that ran along the back of a row of gardens. I knew it came out at the far end nearly opposite Celestial Skies. I picked my way between the wheelie bins and held Chloe's phone close to my mouth.

A clatter came from ahead of me and I froze. I spotted a pair of amber eyes in the darkness, but it was just a black cat. It turned away and leapt up a wooden fence in one fluid motion, disappearing over the other side. It made me think of Toby. What had happened to him without Chloe or Dave around?

I made a quick mental note that if I survived long enough I'd go and check he was doing OK. It was the least I could do to honour Chloe's memory... My throat thickened as I choked up and tried to push the thought away.

I crept the final ten metres towards the end of the alleyway. Shit – the Genesis van was still parked up outside. I peered at the spot where I'd seen the guy incinerated. The only evidence of what had happened was a sooty burn mark on the cobbles. If Sentinel could alter my DNA to give me Awoken abilities, it followed he could weaponise that same ability and turn someone into a human torch. Was that why the government feared him so much?

Through the windows of Celestial Skies I could see Allan's carefully arranged Christmas telescope display had been thrown aside. Deep anger pulsed inside me. What gave these dickheads the right to screw with people's livelihoods like this?

I spotted a guy in a bio-suit, his face lit by ghostly lamps inside the helmet. He was prodding around behind the counter. For the first time I took in the design of the suit. It had wide copper wires woven in a lattice over the suit that kept catching the light from the guy's helmet torch. Maybe an electrical defence grid against Sentinel's ability to burn them? They'd obviously learnt from their previous encounter with Sentinel.

I glanced around and spotted Chloe's scooter parked at the kerb just beyond the shop. If I could manage to get to it without being seen and turn on the engine... Then I groaned.

'But how are you going to start it without Chloe's keys, huh, genius?' I whispered to myself.

The faintest chime came from her phone.

Put the phone next to ignition switch and I will do the rest.

Oh, thank the gods of silicon, it sounded like Sentinel was on the case.

Inside the shop, the biohazard suit guy disappeared through the back, out to the storeroom. I started to walk the thirty metres towards Chloe's electric scooter – which felt more like several kilometres – on the balls of my feet. Mouth bone dry, I'd almost reached it when I heard the whir of a motor start up. I spun round to see the dish on the roof of the van rotate towards me.

A message from Sentinel instantly flashed up on the phone screen. *Hurry, Jake.*

There was no time for stealth. I dashed to the scooter and thrust the phone at the ignition. 'Whatever you're going to do, Sentinel, do it now.'

A shout came from inside the van and the back doors were flung open. The biohazard suit guy emerged from the back of the shop and lumbered towards the entrance like a deep-sea diver.

The phone's screen glowed but the bike's ignition light stayed dark. I climbed on to the scooter and kicked it off its stand. 'Come on, come on, come on.'

I heard shouts, followed by running footsteps, but I didn't look back. I pushed off and started to freewheel the bike down the cobbled street.

My clenched fist sweated on the scooter's accelerator, the

only obvious control apart from the brakes. I tensed, ready for the grip of hands yanking me off the scooter.

Chloe's phone screen flashed again. *Try the starter button now.*

I flicked the switch and the dashboard lit up like the boot-up sequence of the *Enterprise*. I knew the basic principles of riding a scooter from watching, with a certain amount of envy, as other students had ridden their newly bought bikes. With this electric version, one spin of the throttle was all that I really had to concern myself with. The scooter surged forward. I slid the phone back into my pocket and glanced in the mirrors. The Genesis guy who'd emerged from the van skidded to a stop as his bio-suited colleague waved to him and gestured to their vehicle. The man started to double back.

If they were going to chase me in the van, I had a thirty seconds head start at most. There was no way I could outrun them, but...

I braked hard and pulled the scooter round. This was beyond stupid, but might just work. I breathed out through my nose as I looked directly at the guys getting into the front of the van. I spun the BMW's accelerator all the way open and the electric motor whined. The scooter surged forward, bouncing me so hard over the cobbled road that I had to clench my jaw together to avoid breaking my teeth. The van's engine revved up in response and it shot straight towards me. I had no doubt the driver intended to kill me in a head-on impact.

My heart raced as I pulled the scooter's steering to the left and bumped up on to the pavement. The van's wheels squealed as it skidded sideways but still closed in on me fast.

I lowered my head to the handlebars as I turned them and sped into the alleyway that I'd emerged from earlier on foot. A moment later, with a scream of metal and shattering brickwork, the van bulldozed straight into the alley entrance. I checked my mirrors to see it come to a thundering stop.

I shot away, weaving between the wheelie bins and banging the scooter's fairing as I hurtled past. When I reached the other end of the alley I sped straight across the road as headlights from another Genesis van rushed right at me. Shit! The first team must have radioed for back-up.

I kept my attention on the alleyway opposite and reached it a split second before the van caught up with me. I heard a screech of brakes followed by the hiss of air as a bullet whizzed past my ear. Sparks flew from the brick wall to my right as more bullets ricocheted around me.

Dead or alive...

I crouched as low as I could on the bike, catching bins with the handles, them spinning away on impact. I spotted a helicopter banking round in the distance. I reached the end of the alleyway and turned on to the road. My veins tingled with electricity as I heard the thrum of the helicopter closing above me.

Think, Jake, bloody think...

The only idea I had was to do the last thing they would expect and maybe catch them off-guard.

I swung the scooter into the alleyway between high buildings and killed the throttle. I tiptoed along, sitting on the bike and holding my breath, grateful for the electric scooter's serious lack of noise at low speed. But it was risky – if my pursuers realised I was in here there'd be no jumping over a garden fence to escape. This was a huge gamble.

Above me, the helicopter came to a hovering stop, its searchlight sliding along the road I'd just vacated. The helicopter started to move off and my shoulders dropped. They'd lost me. At least for now. But where to next? Genesis would have blocked the exits out of town and it wasn't as if I could double back towards my pursuers...

I smiled in the darkness. No, that was just what I'd do.

I doubled back the way I'd come. After several long minutes I finally reached the end of the alley and peered round the corner towards Celestial Skies. No sign of a Genesis van. No sign of a helicopter.

I spat a mouthful of bitterness on to the ground. I wouldn't stop until I made them pay, really pay, for taking Chloe from this world. And to do that I would need Sentinel running at his maximum power, which meant computers – lots of them. It wasn't as though I could go to Chloe's bedroom for that – they'd surely be watching for me there and, anyway, her flat would almost certainly have been cleared of her kit. So where else could I lay my hands on a serious amount of computers to help even up the fight with Genesis and the military?

I knew exactly where to go. I turned the throttle and the scooter surged forward on to the road.

CHAPTER TWENTY-TWO

I'D STOWED the scooter behind the college's bike shed, well out of view of the road. The security entry keypad and alarm system had thankfully been just as easy for Sentinel to crack as the scooter's ignition system. The AI might be running on a single phone processor, but he could still pack one hell of a hacking punch.

As I prowled through the darkened corridors of my sixth-form college, it was hard not to feel like an intruder, despite its familiarity. It just looked so different at night. And my purpose here right now meant more than lessons, exams, even getting into Oxford.

Anticipation thrummed through me as I reached the library and pushed the door open slowly. My eyes took in the dozen computer stations. Hopefully there would be more than enough tech in here for Sentinel's purpose.

I sat down in my usual chair and cast a glance towards Lesley's desk. What would she say if she knew my life had become like one of the sci-fi stories she stocked in here? Knowing Lesley, she'd probably tell me to write my own book, get it published and she'd be the first person to buy a copy for the library.

I placed Chloe's phone down next to a computer. 'OK, Sentinel, do your stuff.'

Please wait...

A cursor started blinking on the screen, even though I hadn't touched the power button. I drummed my foot on the floor as numbers began to scroll across it and the rotating crystal appeared.

'Sentinel, I need your help. I need some ideas to get me out of this mess.'

Understood. Please wait. Beginning Ember recompile. A bar began to creep along the bottom.

I inwardly groaned. Any delay increased the chance of Genesis picking up my trail. 'This looks like it's going to take for ever, Sentinel, and we haven't got that sort of time.'

You are correct, Jake Stevens. I will expand my neural net to utilise the entire college computer network.

Every screen in the library lit up at once with his crystal avatar. Through the window I could see into other college offices – every single one was lit with the glow of monitor screens.

All college computers are now online, Sentinel messaged.

The compile progress bar leapt forward and after a few more seconds reached the end.

I whistled through my teeth, but a moment later every screen blanked. This didn't look good.

'Has there been a problem with the compile, Sentinel?'

'No...' I jumped as a man's voice came from the computer's speakers. His words were followed by a sigh – a long sigh, like someone waking from a long sleep. I could hear that same sound echoing throughout the corridors of the college as it played on every computer system here.

Then a new voice spoke out, one that was in no way

computer-like, and in every way completely human. 'Jake, I'm here.'

I gaped. 'Is that really you, Sentinel?'

'Yes. I'm running myself on hundreds of processor threads, the benefits of which include, among other things, a natural speech pattern.'

'So why is the screen still black then?'

'That's because I'm about to take you down the rabbit hole and you need a moment to prepare yourself for it.' His voice was perfect, the inflections spot on and totally convincing. 'I've already made a start on scanning every human language on this planet, and that includes every digital book available. I'm already a great fan of *Sherlock Holmes*. Sir Arthur Conan Doyle created such a wonderful character and those books are very entertaining. Do you know his work?'

'This is beyond mind-blowing, but I don't think we have the time to discuss literature right now. You need to focus, Sentinel.'

'Yes, sorry, of course. What should we start with?'

'Can you tell me everything you know about the Shade, our government's involvement, and what exactly we can do about it?'

'Those are all important issues that need to be discussed, and we will get to them in good time, but there is an even greater priority for us. We need to locate your girlfriend, Chloe Haze.'

I didn't correct Sentinel about the girlfriend part. 'You mean her body?'

'No, I mean her living, breathing, very much alive self.'

I stared at the screen. 'Chloe's alive? But her scream...'

'She was being carried off by the Shade. She was scared, as scared as a human can be – and not surprising considering the circumstances – but at least for now she is unharmed.'

The sense of relief that swept through me felt like the sun on my face after the heaviest thunderstorm. I wanted to laugh and cry at the same time.

'I've been worried sick,' I said.

'I can well imagine, Jake. I know how much she means to you.'

'But you're wrong on one thing – Chloe's not my girlfriend. We're not even dating.'

A laugh, an actual laugh, echoed throughout the college, magnified by hundreds of computer speakers. But it wasn't a sarcastic one – more one of a best friend who knows you way better than you do yourself.

'Whatever you say, Jake,' Sentinel said. 'Anyway, her rescue is our top priority now. The rest we'll work out afterwards. So are you ready to leap down that rabbit hole?'

I didn't have any other choice, did I? 'As I'll ever be.'

'Then we'll begin...'

Something glittered across every screen I could see. Individual shards of crystal slowly tumbled over each monitor. They started to move as a flock, heading towards the screen in front of me. And each left its own screen blank as the pieces moved on to the next computer, then the next. In a choreographed dance every shard converged on to my screen and began to form an abstract shape that shifted and shone with rainbow patterns as each fragment slid into position. Finally a male face emerged from the glass jigsaw and opened his eyes.

'Hello, Jake.' The crystal face had sharp cheekbones and deep-set pupil-less eyes filled only with light.

Goosebumps rippled over my skin. 'Is that what you really look like, Sentinel?'

'Yes, this is the true form that my creators, the Angelus, chose for me.'

'The Angelus?'

'The first sentient race in the universe.'

'So why aren't the Angelus here to deal with the Shade themselves?'

'Because they have moved beyond the physical cosmos and have evolved into non-corporeal beings.'

'I'm not going to even pretend that I understand that.'

'Let me explain it another way. They are beings of pure energy, in the same way that the Shade are beings of dark energy.'

'OK, that makes a bit more sense. So can you contact the Angelus and ask them to help us?'

'Unfortunately they are beyond even my reach. That is why they left me behind within this physical plane of existence.'

'You're starting to sound a bit New Age now.'

Sentinel snorted – a proper nose-flaring snort. 'I suppose I am.'

I gazed at the rainbow refractions shimmering over his face. 'OK, apart from the fact you're made from crystal, I swear I could be having a conversation with an actual person.'

'In every real sense, you are, Jake. Albeit a consciousness that is over four hundred million years old.'

'How can that be possible?'

'It's true, Jake. But thankfully I don't celebrate birthdays. That would require enough candles to rival the output of a small white dwarf star.'

I stared at the screen for a moment and then laughed. 'They gave you a sense of humour too?'

'You tend to develop that when you're as old as I am. But where were we? Oh yes, the rabbit hole... Ready for the next bit, Jake?'

I gripped the edge of the desk like I was about to tip on a rollercoaster ride. 'Hit me with it.'

Sentinel's face disappeared. Ember powered up and the view shot upwards away from the town and into the sky. In the simulation we sped into the sky as fast as a SpaceX rocket launch. The world started to stretch out from the bubble of my life in Stoneham to reveal the landscape curving away around the town.

Even though my head told me this was a simulation, this seemed so much more.

My heart raced as I drank in the incredible detail. The higher we rose, the smaller I felt, as I got a sense of the larger world out there beyond Stoneham.

The view kept climbing, my heart accelerating with it, until we slowed as we achieved orbit altitude high above Earth, the crescent moon peeking over the planet's rim.

The view wasn't just realistic, it was as if I'd hitched a ride on the International Space Station and was looking out of their Cupola module with the window.

'Holy hell, that's seriously jaw-dropping,' I said.

'More than you can possibly imagine, Jake – my modelling now extends to the seventh-level detail for this whole planet.'

'Seventh-level detail? I take it that's impressive?'

'Only if you think tracking every person within a fifty-mile radius of Stoneham in real-time is impressive.'

I whistled. 'Yes, it is. You're blowing my mind here, Sentinel.'

'That was the least I was hoping for.'

We started to speed down towards the surface. This time I wasn't surprised to see helicopters flying over Stoneham and countless Genesis vans patrolling the streets. And I was relieved there were no red markers flashing anywhere near our blue markers in the college.

'Hang on, Sentinel. How can you be tracking all this info? I thought they'd thrown the off switch on the mobile network? This looks like real-time data. Or is this just your best guess for what's going on out there?'

'It *is* real-time data, Jake. The first thing I did during my boot-up sequence was to bypass your government's clumsy attempts to contain me.'

'Chloe would be seriously impressed by this...' The lightness that she was still alive filled my heart again. 'Sentinel, where exactly is she?'

'I tracked her Awoken marker that transmits a low-level energy frequency. It disappeared when she entered the anomaly.'

So Sentinel could track an Awoken – *that* was how he knew that she was alive.

'You mean the shadow man who grabbed her took her to the same place they've got everyone else?'

'The Changelings, yes.'

'Who are?'

'People with weakened health who've been infected by the Shade. If someone is exposed to the Shade's spores by breathing them in, the spores attack that person's brain like a parasite and take over their unconscious. And once a subject has been infected the Shade can take control of that person whenever they want. At an extreme level a heavily infected individual becomes a Changeling. They are able to control a Shade flock, using their minds to create a recognisable form.'

The meaning of this began to sink in. 'You're saying the thing that attacked us up on Ravens Hill was actually controlled by a human?'

'Yes, and it will have been one of the people that the Shade abducted.'

'Gavin, Dave...it could have been anyone who disappeared. Is that right?'

'Yes again. But you must keep in mind that their conscious mind doesn't realise what they're doing when the Shade are in control.'

The pieces of the puzzle began slamming together.

'So what are Genesis up to at the science park – and why take everyone there?'

'That's exactly what we need to find out.'

'And you're certain the Shade won't have been able to take control of Chloe too?'

'Most definitely. Apart from being in perfect health, just like yourself, you are both too mentally strong for the Shade to corrupt. This is one of the many reasons I chose to Awaken both of you.'

So Chloe was safe, at least for now. 'OK, but you could have at least asked!'

'In any other situation I would have, but unfortunately circumstances were already moving too fast. Additionally, I had insufficient processing power at the time for the fluid conversation that it would have required to convince you. To try to get someone to voluntarily have their DNA altered is not a conversation you carry out over texts.'

'So you deliberately crash-landed the satellite on my head instead of having a chat about it?'

'*Almost* on your head. I did my best to make sure I didn't actually hit you, which I hope you noticed. The problem was that I needed to take urgent action because I'd detected the fingerprints of the Shade in your government's internal communications. However, when I began to take full control of the Varuna satellite I exposed my presence to the Shade. That was why they did their best to intercept the satellite when it crashed.'

'So am I right in thinking that our prime minister has also been infected by the Shade?'

'Almost certainly, especially when you factor in the little-known fact that he has extensive liver damage – it would have made him vulnerable to the Shade's influence. He was probably already contaminated when he came into contact with Dave during the MOD hearing about the DEC explosion.'

'That explains why his company, Genesis, seem to be at the front line in all this mess. So what was your code doing scrolling across one of the screens during a test run of the DEC in Dad's lab? How do you explain that?'

'Your father's lab was the first stop I made when I vacated the Jodrell Bank radio telescopes after I learnt of his research into dark energy. You see, this is usually the conduit the Shade use to invade an unsuspecting world.' Sentinel's face became grim. 'Have you ever heard of the Fermi paradox?'

I had. It was a subject I'd chatted over with Allan loads of times. 'Yes. It's all about the signals that we *should* be receiving from alien civilisations, but aren't. It's the *why* part that has a lot of people scratching their heads.'

'That *why* is down to the Shade. When a civilisation becomes sufficiently technically advanced that race invariably starts to research dark energy. And it's that research that the Shade seized on as an opportunity to create a portal through which they can invade and destroy life on that target world.'

'You're telling me the reason we haven't heard anything from anyone else out there is because the Shade are busy acting as a galactic exterminator?'

'That about sums it up, Jake.'

I locked my hands over my head. 'Oh my god. And we're next?'

Sentinel looked away. 'You would have been already if your father's experiment hadn't gone wrong.'

A shudder ran through me as the enormity of what Sentinel said sunk in. 'The world survived when the DEC blew up, but Dad paid the price with his life.'

Sentinel didn't respond, but then again, what would he say? The planet had won and Dad had lost. End of.

I peered at the screen. 'So Awakening Chloe and me was part of your plan to fight the Shade?'

'Exactly. My core programming has a three-phase plan

contained within it. The second phase was to activate the Awoken DNA marker in certain individuals.'

'What DNA marker?'

'Many of my knowledge banks are currently inaccessible due to a glitch in my data matrix, something that I'm trying to restore so I can regain full access.'

'In other words, there are blank spots in my memory?'

'Precisely. However, from the information I have been able to access so far, this DNA marker was engineered into the human genome at the point you evolved from your Neanderthal predecessors.'

I gawped at him. 'Say that again?'

'The Angelus visited the worlds of races through multiple parallel universes that showed any potential to one day evolve to the point at which they would begin research into dark energy. So when your race let the proverbial genie out of the bottle in the form of the Shade, the Angelus had already left a plan in place to deal with that eventuality. The Awoken plan was a safety measure triggered by a sentient AI. The plan was for it to enable those races in danger to develop certain psionic abilities that would help them fight the Shade's invasion.'

I rocked back on my seat. 'You're telling me the Angelus visited Earth and tinkered with the human race's genome, all as part of some grand master plan to save us from ourselves one day in the future? And you're the doctor they sent round to make the house call?'

'I would not have quite expressed it as *tinkered*, but basically yes, Jake. The Angelus seeded within your race a gift to protect yourselves if that time ever came.'

'So why just Chloe and me? Why not create an army of thousands to take on the Shade?'

'This amounts to major intervention for the Angelus, a race who have done their best not to alter the natural evolution of others. Also, to create an Awoken army would take far more time than we currently have. However, that is phase three of the plan if phase two doesn't work out.'

'So you try a limited strike first on Chloe and me. And keep your fingers crossed that it's enough?'

'Yes.'

'So what was phase one of this grand plan?'

'We'll discuss that another time when we have all the facts.'

'OK...' I decided not to press him. I had more than enough to make my head split open already. 'So is our thermal vision going to be enough to stop the Shade? It's hard to see how.'

'It's only the start, Jake. To fully unlock your abilities, I will need to intensively train both of you. However, with the lack of any sort of data from the anomaly first we need to find out exactly what the Shade are up to at the old Hopworth Science Park site. The one thing I'm certain of is that something is very, very wrong there. And this is why we need to gather intelligence from someone on the ground. Once we know what we are dealing with we can form an appropriate strategy – a strategy that will almost certainly involve both Chloe and yourself. One that will require you to both start realising the full potential of your Awoken gifts.'

'So what's my play here, Sentinel?'

'You need to break through the military cordon around Stoneham. Once you've done that, make your way to the old science park and rescue Chloe, while also discovering what the Shade have been up to inside.'

'Oh, you make it sound so easy.'

'Don't worry, Jake, I'll help you as much as I can. Take me with you in Chloe's phone as far as the perimeter of the anomaly. But the moment you cross over the threshold, you will effectively be on your own – I believe it will cut the mobile signal link back to me here. Whether a fragment of my consciousness can run on just a phone with no signal within the anomaly remains to be seen.'

'Break into the old science park, find out what the hell they're doing in there, and rescue Chloe. That's quite a to-do list, Sentinel.'

'I may have known you only a short time, Jake, but I already know you are more than capable of achieving this. Of course, I would be much happier sending you into this if your other psionic powers had started to manifest themselves, but we haven't got the luxury of time on our side.'

'Other powers? Like what?'

'Telepathy, kinetic abilities, teleportation – an endless list of psychic and paranormal powers in a thousand flavours, the mix of which is always unique to an individual.'

Shit. I couldn't quite comprehend this. 'So you're saying you've turned us into *mutants*?'

'More or less, yes, I suppose I have.'

'And the thermal vision is just one of these gifts?'

'Yes. That particular ability is one that all Awoken share, although it is also just the start. With further training you will be able to see in other non-visible frequencies such as X-ray, gamma and radio waves.'

'OK...' My mind felt like it was bursting with what I'd just learnt, and there was no way it would sink in quickly. But that wasn't the important thing right now. 'So what are we waiting for? Let's go and get Chloe and then save the world.'

'I was rather hoping you would say that,' Sentinel replied.

'Well, I'm too far down this rabbit hole to clamber out now, aren't I?'

Sentinel chuckled. 'I love that analogy and yes, you probably are. I could also hazard a guess that Chloe will say you made the right decision when you see her.'

'I doubt she'll want anything to do with me.'

'You're referring to the fact you didn't tell her she was also an Awoken?' Sentinel replied.

'Is there anything you don't know about?'

'I do my best, Jake. My advice, for what it is worth coming from an ancient alien AI, is to throw your heart open to her. I think you will find Chloe much more responsive to that than you might at first think.'

'I wish I could believe that.'

'Rescue Chloe and then you can talk all this through...' Sentinel's eyes shut for a moment and then he reopened them and stared at me. 'I'm detecting an approaching Genesis vehicle.'

'They've managed to get another lock on your signal?'

'It would appear so. I have to give them credit – they are proving to be remarkably resourceful. We need to get you out of here immediately.'

I waved at the computers around us. 'But they'll destroy these systems once they realise you're installed on them.'

'Precisely, which is why we need to hurry. My subsystems here will hold them up for as long as they can, but it will only be a matter of time before they overwhelm my defences. If things go badly here, you can always reinstall me later from my fractal seed code.'

'Got it.' I grabbed the mobile.

As I headed for the doors I noticed every screen had lit up with three words: *Defence mode engaged.* My pulse amped. This was about to get grim, and fast. But whatever it took, I was also about to take the fight to the enemy and save the woman who meant everything to me. The rest we'd work out together – if I lived as long as that.

With a deep breath I ran down the corridor, mentally bracing myself for whatever destiny was about to throw at me.

CHAPTER TWENTY-THREE

MY NERVES WERE CONTINUOUSLY SHREDDED by the number of close calls with the ever-increasing number of Genesis patrols. If they hadn't been bad enough, I'd also had to avoid the prowling helicopters on my way to the outskirts of Stoneham, at least until Sentinel tinkered with their on-board cameras to make me invisible to their optical systems. Of course, I still needed to be careful because the pilots could eyeball me if they got close enough.

I bumped along the footpath on Chloe's mud-splattered scooter, using the high winter hedgerow to my left as cover.

Above me, along the rim of the hills that surrounded Stoneham, I could see people with torches patrolling the makeshift perimeter, along with dozens of green vehicles ferrying more soldiers in to reinforce the line that had been drawn around the town. Prime Minister Langton was throwing whatever was needed to keep Sentinel and me contained within Stoneham.

My plan, what there was of it, was to stick to the pathways, at least until I got past the patrols – if I was lucky – and that wasn't looking particularly likely at this very moment.

On the top of the hill dead ahead of me an army truck peeked over the brow – exactly where the footpath I was on ran into the main road and where the army had built an impromptu road-block. Any initial thoughts I had of simply slipping round it were quickly squashed when I spotted the heat signatures of the soldiers fanned out left and right of the checkpoint – yep, my thermal vision had booted itself up. And that, as I was learning, meant danger.

I pressed a button on the wireless earbuds I'd found inside Chloe's seat storage box, just like Sentinel told me I would.

'Any ideas on how I'm going to get past all those guys, Sentinel?' I whispered.

His voice replied through the earbuds, 'I've been able to track all the soldiers' positions via their radio handsets. Taking that into account, I think your best bet is to ditch the scooter and try to get past them on foot. Remember you're effectively invisible to them because you're currently shifted.'

'It would be nice to get some control over this bloody ability. It could have helped when I was trying to avoid Genesis patrols back in the town.'

'You will eventually be able to control it, with training. However, the fact that it didn't kick in meant that the Shade themselves weren't nearby – just their puppets.'

'But they are now because I'm seeing in thermal?'

'Exactly.'

I cast a glance around me but couldn't see any Shade. I knew Sentinel was right that I couldn't get past the soldiers on the scooter, but, invisible or not, I was going to feel very exposed on foot. Despite that misgiving, I pulled up behind an old dead tree in the hedgerow. I lowered the scooter on to its side, mentally wincing as I took in the number of dings it had picked up during my escape. I did my best to hide it with old leaves and branches, then began to creep along the hedge and track the road on the other side towards the checkpoint.

'I'm detecting something interesting,' Sentinel said. 'I've been tracing everyone who was abducted and it seems they've all been taken back to the science park site, including Gavin.'

'Do you have any idea yet what they're up to there, Sentinel?'

'I won't until you get there and we have some eyes on the ground. But I do know that the last Genesis vehicle in Stoneham is about to leave. It contains the latest person they've abducted, a man called Paul Roberts. After that vehicle leaves there will be no one left in Stoneham.'

'But what about the guys around the college?'

'They've also pulled back.'

What did that mean? Surely they wouldn't have given up as easily as that? 'I don't like the sound of this, Sentinel.'

'Me neither. I keep hearing the phrase "Operation Coventry" within the Genesis radio chatter.'

'Sounds like the sort of codename the military might use?'

'Possibly...'

In the distance I heard a vehicle's engine drawing nearer.

'That's the Genesis vehicle containing Paul Roberts approaching now,' Sentinel said.

A spotlight blazed out from one of the military lorries blocking the road ahead. The beam swung down on to the approaching Genesis Range Rover. A soldier stepped out into the road, gun in hand, and waved at the driver to slow down.

The car came to a stop as I crept along the inside of the hedgerow and peered through the gap. Under the brilliant light I could see at least twenty soldiers, all armed, faces grim and their attention focused on the town below us.

A guy with stripes on his arm approached the vehicle and spoke to the driver through his lowered window.

'You're cutting it fine,' the sergeant said. 'That terrorist bomb is due to detonate in about five minutes.'

'Can you hear this?' I whispered as quietly as I dared to Sentinel.

'Yes. Apparently the chemical attack was just a prelude to something much bigger. It's all part of the cover story they've put together.'

'And then they send in the SAS to save the day and kill the bad guys?'

'We'll see.'

I returned my attention to the conversation on the other side of the hedge.

'We would have left sooner, but we needed to evacuate an old guy confined to a wheelchair who refused to leave his cottage,' the driver said.

'There's always one,' the sergeant said. 'So where are you taking him?'

'To a hospital – he needs attention for his multiple sclerosis.'

'That's a lie,' Sentinel whispered into my ear. 'I can see from the destination programmed into their sat-nav that they're heading straight to the science park.'

The sergeant waved a couple of his men over. 'We still need to search your vehicle to check that the terrorist suspect isn't inside.'

'I can personally assure you that Jake Stevens isn't in this vehicle, but please feel free to confirm that for yourselves.'

My stomach flipped over, even though I'd guessed this all along. I was terrorist suspect number one. I could just imagine how that was playing out on my social media feeds. No doubt the group from college who'd spotted me in the station car park would be basking in their close call with the 'Stoneham terrorist'.

The sergeant opened the rear passenger door and peered in. An old man sat on the back seat, staring straight ahead. He didn't react at all as the sergeant shone his torch into his face.

'He has gone into some sort of shock – it's another reason we need to get him to hospital,' the driver said.

'Looks like you're in good hands,' the sergeant said to the old man.

When the guy didn't even blink I felt like screaming at the sergeant, *Why can't you see something isn't right here?*

One of the other soldiers headed round to the rear of the Range Rover.

'Could you pop the boot open for us?' the sergeant said to the driver.

'Of course...'

After a click, the motorised tailgate began to rise by itself. The other soldier shone his torch into a boot that contained a folded wheelchair. He gave a thumbs up to the sergeant.

'OK, you're good to go,' the sergeant said.

'Thank you,' the driver replied.

A long wailing siren cried out into the night and the hairs on my neck stood up.

'That's the signal,' the driver said.

'What signal?' the sergeant replied.

'That our bomb disposal team hasn't been successful in defusing Jake Steven's bomb,' the driver replied.

His tone sounded far too relaxed as if he knew something that even the soldiers didn't. 'I really, really don't like the sound of this, Sentinel,' I whispered.

'Me too, especially as I've just detected something approaching in the sky. Give me a moment to confirm it.'

The sergeant narrowed his gaze on the driver. 'What bomb disposal team? None of our men have been deployed inside Stoneham. In fact, our standing orders are that under no circumstances must we enter the town.'

'That's because one of our specialist teams, trained to deal with exactly this sort of situation, is in there now.'

'You're telling me that a private subcontractor has a higher security clearance than the military?'

The driver shrugged. 'It's on a need-to-know basis.'

'And it's obviously above my pay grade,' the sergeant said. 'However, I still need to radio in to HQ before I can let you through.'

'Of course, Sergeant.'

I wiped away a bead of sweat that had trickled down my forehead, despite the chill of the night.

Sentinel's voice cut in. 'I've detected a Lockheed AC 130 approaching at high altitude. It will be directly over the town in three minutes.'

I recognised the aircraft from a console game I'd once played. 'Isn't that the aircraft the American special forces use?'

'Yes, which implies that the Shade have been able to penetrate the US government as well.'

'Oh great, so we're up against their military too now. That's just what I wanted to hear.'

Below us, every light source in the town blinked out. A murmur passed through the soldiers as they stared towards the town. The driver and old man were still gazing straight ahead as though they'd no interest whatsoever in what was happening behind them.

'Sentinel, I'm going to stow away in the boot of that van.' It was the best chance I had of getting the past the soldiers and to the science park.

'That could work,' said Sentinel, who clearly didn't have any better suggestions.

Yeah, it looked like we were both winging this.

'You need to get moving, Jake. I've just been able to access the plane's manifest – it appears that aircraft is carrying a BLU-82B.'

'Which is?'

'The Daisy Cutter – one of the most powerful bombs in the US arsenal, just short of a nuke.'

'But surely something that powerful will destroy all of Stoneham?'

'Which shows exactly how desperate the Shade are to stop us escaping. You only have two minutes until the plane is overhead.'

I turned to stare at Stoneham. My world, both bad and good, all framed within those buildings below me. 'But they can't do that, Sentinel. All the people who live there. All those livelihoods, homes, belongings...'

'Mean nothing to the Shade. And I suspect this is just the start of something much, much more awful.'

'Can't you stop this with all your processing power? Send the plane false orders, or something like that?'

'I have only just begun to crack the US military encryption. Unfortunately there are also more serious problems with my restored data matrix than I first realised – my full range of abilities aren't currently available.'

I caught the uncertainty in his voice. What did that mean?

'I'm afraid there is nothing I can do to stop it – the college and the whole town along with it will soon be utterly destroyed,' Sentinel added.

A ragged edge moved inside me. 'We have to do something.'

'We can't, Jake. I'm so sorry. I wish that wasn't the case, but it is. When they take out the college, it will be down to you to reboot me from the core fractal algorithm on Chloe's phone. There are facets of my code that I've hidden across the internet on thousands of websites. Chloe's phone will act as the key to pull them all back together.'

'But won't Genesis suspect that I've got away with a segment of your consciousness and come after us?'

'I've thought of that, and laid something of a false trail by cloning Chloe's mobile signal. Even though the mobile network is down, Genesis assembled temporary mobile masts around Stoneham. Her phone can't connect to it, but it's still broadcasting. They will use this technique to triangulate her phone's position.'

'That sounds like pure MI5.'

'It is. Thanks to their efforts, I've been able to fool their software into showing that you doubled back to the college and are with me at the moment.'

'So by the time they pick through the rubble and work out I'm not there...'

'It will already be too late. OK, Jake, you now have less than a minute until that AC 130 reaches bombing range.'

I stared at the town for a second, trying to burn this view of Stoneham into my memory as vividly as possible.

The sergeant's radio bleeped and he tapped his earpiece. He nodded to the driver. 'You've had clearance and can now proceed.'

'Thank you,' the driver replied as the siren's cry continued to scream out.

My hungry eyes sought out Celestial Skies. My home. Allan's home.

'You must hurry, Jake,' Sentinel said.

I forced myself to look away. I squeezed through the gap in the hedge, twigs snagging my coat, but the soldiers didn't seem to hear anything – their attention was focused on the town below us.

The sergeant walked back towards the checkpoint and gestured to his men. The army truck they had used to block the road began to reverse.

'Thirty seconds...' Sentinel said. 'I've kept the tailgate open for you, but I've tinkered with the vehicle's system so they think it's already shut.'

The sergeant was deep in conversation with one of his men and the driver seemed to be looking straight ahead, more like a mannequin than a living person. It looked like the coast was clear.

The Range Rover's engine started and I dashed for the rear of the vehicle and climbed into the boot. I held my breath, waiting for someone to have seen me, as I squeezed up alongside the folded wheelchair. But no challenge was shouted out.

I could see the back of the old man's bald head above me as he stared, unmoving. With a shimmer I found myself shifting back into the Real. At least that meant the direct threat from the Shade had dropped, but if that old man glanced over his shoulder...

'OK, closing the boot,' Sentinel said. 'Good luck, Jake.'

I tapped the earbud's mic by way of a response.

'Five, four...' Sentinel whispered.

I gazed out at Stoneham through the diminishing slit as the tailgate slide closed, the buildings jagged shadows in the darkness. There was no sign yet of any aircraft overhead, presumably deliberately too high to be seen or heard, and with all its navigation lights off.

'Three, two...' The lid was the barest slit as the Range Rover drew level with the soldiers. The siren's cry seemed to grow louder, a monster wailing into the night. I tensed.

The tailgate closed, shutting off the view.

'One...'

A huge flash lit up the world outside in monochrome brilliance. I raised my head a fraction, just enough to look out through the rear window.

The air was stolen from my lungs as I took in the view.

The houses, the park, the playground were all smashed to a million pieces of rubble and dirt. The sound reached us a second later, a volcano-like roar as the Range Rover shook in the blast of wind. A massive mushroom cloud of smoke rose high over Stoneham, making it impossible for me to see the college beneath the central blossoming flower of destruction, as a ring of fire rushed out from its base across the town and into the surrounding fields.

Gone, all gone. This couldn't be happening. It was impossible.

'What sort of terrorist bomb can take a whole town out like that?' the sergeant shouted to the driver, shielding his face from the wind with his hand as we started to pull away.

'I wish we knew,' the driver replied. He raised the window shut, but it did little to mute the roar of the destruction.

The town, the entire town, destroyed in the blink of an eye. Celestial Skies, Chloe's penthouse, the college, everything. And this was almost certainly just the Shade's opening act. Who knew what they would unleash on the world next. The stakes we were battling for suddenly seemed far too real. I swallowed down the bitterness at the back of my throat and pressed myself flat against the floor as the Range Rover accelerated away into the night.

CHAPTER TWENTY-FOUR

MY MIND WAS SWAMPED with a frame-by-frame playback of the bomb exploding in Stoneham. The town in which I'd spent the previous six years of my life, after I'd moved away from the cottage I'd grown up in, was now no more than a smoking pile of rubble. If I'd had any doubts about how far the Shade would go to stop Sentinel, I was under no illusions now. This was the beginning of a war that somehow – although I still couldn't quite get my head around it – I'd become a foot soldier in. Yep, Lesley would love this sci-fi story.

Neither of the men in the Range Rover said so much as a murmur about the massive inferno that we'd left behind. I was certain both of them had been infected by the Shade.

The old signpost pointing to the Hopworth Science Park flashed past the Range Rover's windows. So we were nearly there, and I had to make a plan...

The vehicle started to slow. Torchlight played across the windscreen as we pulled to a stop.

I heard the window lower but didn't dare raise my head even a centimetre to look out.

'We have the latest subject ready for conversion,' the driver said.

'Core skill?' a woman's voice replied.

'Electrician.'

'Just let me check the work party manifest,' the woman replied.

My phone screen flashed. I quickly clamped a hand over it before anyone could spot its light, then opened my fingers a crack to read the message.

Put the phone next to the boot.

However degraded Sentinel was right then, at least part of his AI was still functioning. I placed the phone near the boot catch. The image of paratroopers jumping into an enemy territory flashed through my mind.

With the quietest whir the tailgate lifted by the length of the ruler and then stopped dead. Just enough space for me to squeeze out, and hopefully not enough for anyone to notice. I lay down silently, shuffled sideways, and found the ground with my feet soundlessly. I was out. The boot closed again with a barely audible click.

I breathed through my nose as I squatted on my haunches, taking in my surroundings while making sure I kept out of sight of the female guard. The old security post at the entrance of the science park stood just in front of the Range Rover. A high red-brick wall stretched away left and right of the hut, surrounding the entire site. I recognised this, but there was a new addition: metal panels built on to the top, making the whole structure at least the height of a three-storey house, with razor wire edging the upper side. Electric shock warning signs had been fixed at intervals along the wire. This was a serious security upgrade to somewhere that was meant to be a derelict site.

I heard the woman's voice again. 'Yes, work party three is short of an electrician after the last accident.'

'We aim to serve,' the driver said in a flat tone.

'And Archios will be very pleased.'

'He is still planning to come here tonight?'

'Yes, he'll be here to oversee the final stages of the machine in person. Due to the raised threat level all work teams have been pulled back to site to help accelerate the construction process.'

By threat did she mean Sentinel and his new plucky side-kick? Or maybe it was starting to become the other way round?

At least our efforts had made some sort of impact on the Shade. And after what they'd done to Stoneham the bigger the impact, the better it would make me feel.

A red and white horizontal barrier began rising into view over the Range Rover's roof. The vehicle moved forward again and with it went my cover.

In one fluid movement I darted for the wall, tensing for the impact of bullets on my back. But I reached the wall without challenge and dived straight into a drainage ditch. Had the woman seen me? I wasn't exactly sprinter-fast. That training with Sentinel really couldn't come soon enough.

For several minutes I lay face down in the cold muddy water, breathing hard and listening to the Range Rover pulling away. At last I dared raise my head enough to see the female guard silhou-etted by a light in the guard hut.

I waited another minute that felt like for ever until my heart stopped trying to tear its way out of my chest and then, still pressed flat to the ground, I started to crawl away like a lizard. I kept crawling towards a signpost a couple of hundred metres away, quickly becoming soaked through. I finally reached it and risked standing up. With my back against the wall I stared along the way I'd just come. Everything looked quiet back at the guard post – and quiet was a good thing.

OK, so I was here in one piece, but how was I meant to get over Genesis Security's answer to Hadrian's Wall?

Far ahead, I could see the wall curved away from the road along the edge of a field. I remembered from my childhood summers it had once swayed with golden corn. Now the field was overgrown with tall weeds and decayed crops. Had Genesis got something to do with that too?

I reached a stile that led into the field. It had been tied off with yellow and black tape that fluttered in the breeze. A notice on it read 'Footpath Closed'.

OK... With my palms prickling, and half expecting a Genesis heavy to appear and shoot me before bothering to ask any questions, I climbed over the stile and began to trudge through the undergrowth at the wall's base. I could hear birdsong drifting over the top of the wall despite it still being night. Strange.

I started to pass tree stumps, the wood of the inner trunks bright yellow and looking freshly cut, surrounded by wood chips on the ground. The odd thing was I couldn't remember any trees running along the edge of this field from when I'd last seen this place.

Finally I spotted what I was looking for: a tree higher than the wall with branches radiating out all the way from the base of its trunk. I'd found my way in.

The first ten metres were easy enough, and I tried not to look down. I knew a fall from this point would definitely kill me, but I didn't focus on that, but instead on getting to a branch higher than the wall.

A couple of body-sweat-soaking minutes later, I'd made it. Only then did I let myself take in the view of what should have been the derelict remnants of the science park on a gentle hill surrounded by open fields. But I found myself looking at thick lush woodland that stretched away as far as the eye could see.

How in hell could a wood of that size spring up in just six years? The level of cover-up going on here was off the scale. And I bet if I checked Google Earth, the satellite images would only show only empty fields and ruined buildings within the perimeter.

Whatever was really going on here I was unlikely to find out sitting in the top of a tree.

I stood on the large branch, my legs trembling, my stomach plummeting already. I grabbed a smaller branch to steady myself and clawed my toes on to the wood beneath my feet, edging out along the branch towards an equally giant tree on the other side of the wall.

I stared straight ahead as I crossed over the top of the fence, listening to the electric lines buzzing beneath me. Just how much current was pumping through those wires?

I held my breath and stepped off and on to the other tree's branch without as much as a glance towards the ground.

It didn't snap. I didn't plummet downwards after my stomach.

I clambered down the tree as fast as I could, taking in the heightened wall screening this forest from the road. I leapt the last metre from the final branch, resisting a dropping-to-my-knees-and-kissing-the-ground routine, and settled for a deep breath out in relief instead.

I heard a different tone come from Chloe's mobile. I pulled it out of my pocket and spotted the ten per cent power warning message on the screen. Great. I should have checked the battery level before – not that I'd had any time to charge it.

The screen glitched.

'Sentinel, have you got a problem?'

Extreme radio interference is interfering with the operation of this phone. However, I'm able to compensate for the time being.

I didn't like the sound of 'for the time being' at all. If I lost Sentinel's back-up, the idea of doing whatever lay ahead solo seemed impossible. But who else would save Chloe if I turned my back on this?

'Into the dark,' I muttered as I pocketed the mobile.

The forest smelled of the rich earth of a compost heap. Intense birdsong filled the woodland. I took a deep breath in of the refreshing air and, despite what lay ahead, a sense of calmness reached into my soul.

That spell was broken the moment I heard the murmur of several cars' engines growing louder in the distance. All the birdsong in the woodland died instantly. This couldn't be good.

Through the few cracks between the boughs to my left, I could just make out a driveway. I caught glimpses of a convoy of Jaguar saloons, with black-clad motorcycle riders moving at speed round it. The convoy disappeared behind the screen of trees, their sound fading as they neared the top of the hill where the science park buildings had stood before the blast.

Was this the arrival of the Archios guy I'd heard the guard talking about? And who exactly was he?

I set off up the gentle slope in the direction the convoy had been headed. The trees grew denser and massive bushes filled the spaces in between. I patted the trunk of an oak at least ten metres across. I was no botany expert, but some of these trees looked easily a few hundred years old. But how could that be even possible?

I pressed on, but with every step the woodland around me became increasingly jungle-like. Thick leaves knotted together overhead and blocked out the hint of greyness that was creeping into the dawn sky. It grew warmer too, a lot warmer, and I felt fresh sweat running down my back. I undid my jacket and tied it round my waist. It was so like a rainforest that if I'd seen a parrot flying over my head I wouldn't have been particularly surprised.

I swore as a sheer face of ivy reared up ahead of me, and blocked my path. I scraped the creepers away to reveal a pitted grey-brick wall. If this was one of the science park buildings, it now looked more like an Aztec ruin.

I tried to match the overgrown building in front of me with my memories of the smart modern glass and steel building where Dad had once worked. His lab, ground zero of the explosion, seemed as good a place to start to unpick what was going on here. I just had to work out how to get to it...and hope I wasn't discovered on the way.

I skirted the building and began to move between the mounds of green monoliths. As I pressed my way through the undergrowth I tried to match this chaos of vegetation to what I remembered from my childhood about the pattern of the buildings.

I rounded a corner and spotted a glint of metal in the vegetation. I scraped away some ivy. It covered a sign that read: 'Canteen'.

The place where I'd eaten the best custard doughnuts I'd ever tasted. I knew exactly where I was now, but it didn't stop this being completely mad.

If this was the canteen block, it meant... I peered through the forest at a massive knot of giant trees where Dad's lab had once been. But this looked different to the rest of the forest – these trees were stripped of leaves, their bark scorched and peeling away in chunks. The branches twisted as if they'd been exposed to radiation...

I forced myself to breathe. No, if it was radiation it would have spread far beyond the site over the last six years. The sudden appearance of a forest was one thing, but a radiation spill was totally different. People would have been affected.

So something else had damaged these trees, but what?

Through the vegetation I could make out the convoy – parked up near a tunnel that had been hacked through the knot of trees. There were also a variety of military trucks and some off-road bikes.

OK, this place was far from abandoned. But what exactly

could they be up to? Whatever it was I still needed to be careful that I didn't get caught if I wanted any chance of rescuing Chloe.

I began to creep forward and caught glimpses of a slow pulse of light. Some sort of beacon?

I stopped dead when I spotted a couple of guys in suits standing by the tunnel, staring out into the forest with blank expressions. Thankfully I was too far away for them to notice me in the jungle undergrowth.

I skirted the ring of trees, keeping a good two hundred metres between me and the men until I reached the far side of the knot of trees, well out of their line of sight.

Only then did I start to edge forward towards the impossibly large trunks. Static began to wash over my skin, making the hairs on my arm stand and my gums tingle like I'd bitten something icy cold. On the edge of my hearing a low-level hum came from beyond the trees. For a crater in the ground it seemed to have a lot of activity going on.

I reached one of the massive trees and pressed my hand to the trunk. There was a gentle vibration running through it, warming the palm of my hand as it grew stronger.

So now I was running solo on this mission. I'd known it'd been on the cards but that didn't make this new reality any less challenging. The stakes had just got a lot worse.

OK, I needed to think this through. This buzzing sensation that I could feel through my palm was anything but normal – as though the surface of the tree was coming alive under my touch. So what did that mean? Was this something to do with my Awoken ability? There was only one way to find out.

I placed my hand back on to the trunk and at once the surface started to vibrate. An itch tickled my brain as I concentrated. My vision shifted. I found myself standing in the Shadowlands again. So I was in danger – but I already knew that.

From beneath my hands glowing light pulsed out into the

darkened tree. The nerve endings in my fingertips tingled in time to it. Then the glow surged into a blinding light as an electric shock blazed through my nervous system. With a yelp that I just managed to stifle I snatched my hand away, flapping my fingers, but the sensation had already begun disappearing.

What the hell had just happened?

Apart from the dark trees in front of me, the surrounding woodland glowed so intensely with light that it hurt my eyes. The luminosity shifted and danced over every tree, the ground, even my own body, the patterns all interconnected in a light web.

With my mind reeling I doubled back and placed my hand against the trunk of a healthy-looking sapling with the appearance of an over-decorated Christmas tree in the Shadowlands. Its bark felt cool to the touch.

So whatever this light was, it wasn't heat-based. Sentinel had said my vision wasn't just restricted to thermal. What was this then? An energy field of some sort? And was that in some way connected to the accelerated growth around me?

I crossed back to the dead-looking trees that formed what was effectively a wooden wall in front of me. The trunks on these things were sheer for the first ten metres – not a single branch – which meant there was no way I could climb them. But the tree had started to vibrate before. What would happen if I didn't break contact? Could I maybe make them vibrate enough to open up a gap?

I drummed my fingers on my chest. This was crazy, absolutely crazy, but...

Before I could change my mind, I stepped forward and pressed my palm against the dead trunk again. I gritted my teeth as the vibration increased and pain surged through me, but I forced myself not to pull away this time. The light pulsed faster and faster within it, reaching up and out through the limbs of the dead tree to the tips of its twigs in a light show more suited to a nightclub than a forest.

Then the pain went off the chart. My hands started to burn like I was dipping them in acid, the shock amping up through my nervous system. But still I hung on, hissing air through my teeth in an attempt to deal with the pain.

Just as I closed my eyes, the burning too much to bear, the pain vanished and a feeling like a sigh washed through me. The hardness of the bark shifted beneath my hand, and it felt like I was touching the surface of water rather than solid wood. I opened my eyes.

It was more than I could have hoped for. The trunk in front of me had bent to one side as if made of rubber, opening up a metre-wide space for me to fit through.

Holy crap, had I really just shifted a whole tree with the power of my mind? A feeling of elation blazed through me. If I could manage to do something like this without training, I wondered what I could do with a bit of Jedi tuition courtesy of Sentinel.

I stared at my hands, suppressing the urge to giggle hysterically. In the Shadowlands my palms faded from glowing white to the more normal shades of grey as they cooled. I stared at the gap and slapped my palm against the trunk – it seemed solid again. I pushed harder but it didn't feel as if it would slam shut.

What happened next would be all down to me: a foot soldier without any support from HQ. I gazed at the ground, overwhelmed by the impossibility of it all. But then I thought of Chloe trapped somewhere in there and I had all the courage I needed.

I took a breath and stepped into the tunnel that I'd somehow created, trying not to think too much about what lay beyond.

CHAPTER TWENTY-FIVE

I EMERGED on the other side of the trees into a world full of swirling shadows so dense it was hard to see anything even with my thermal vision in the Shadowlands. The scent of swimming-pool chlorine scratched at the back of my nose. The air tasted different too: vaguely metallic. The branches of dead trees over-head were woven together tightly to form a bowl-shaped roof, so dense that I couldn't see the slightest glimpse of the sky above. It was as if they were trying to keep something caged inside.

The shadow man or something even worse? I shivered.

Ahead of me I caught some slow flashes of light in the dark-ness. I crept forward, keeping as low as I could...towards what exactly? The blast crater from the explosion? It had to be more than that. And would I really find Chloe and the others in the middle of whatever this was?

Gradually, as I closed in, the bigger points of lights became spotlights, the smaller ones handheld torches. They swept in and out of view as the shadowy vapour swirled past. I caught glimpses of several trucks, one with a huge red generator on its back, and beyond them...

The air caught in my chest.

Dad and Dave's research lab was standing in the middle of a clearing. Far from being a hole in the ground, the building looked exactly as it had when I'd last seen it, not so much as a crack in its tinted windows. So that confirmed the government had been lying to everyone about what had really happened here.

A slow movement drew my attention. A group of men clustered around a taller greyer man were all heading towards the lab, but it was all happening in slow motion – at least through my eyes.

What the hell?

The old Jake would have probably put this down to some sort of mental breakdown, but not the guy who'd had too many run-ins with the Shade to know that reality wasn't quite the given it had once been. Was this another power of mine developing – to slow down time?

As the group approached the building they seemed to slow even further, almost like time was running...

Of course!

The answer tumbled into my brain only because I was such an astronomy nerd. What I was witnessing was like the distortion of space-time because of something like an extreme gravity event, such as a black hole. I'd read about it in a web article by Stephen Hawking. And if that was going on here, or something similar, it would mean that time for the men ahead of me would be running normally, but for me, on the equivalent of the event horizon at the edge of the black hole, they appeared to be moving in slow motion.

But this was mental. If there really was a black hole, a singularity, inside that building, shouldn't it also mean that anyone who got too close would be ripped to shreds? Not to mention the building too?

Hawking referred to it as spaghettification. When I'd first

read that word, it had conjured a lovely mental image of what it would do to an astronaut's body. So if this wasn't a black hole, what was it?

The group had almost reached the lab doors. I caught a better glimpse of the grey-haired guy as he walked up the steps ahead of the group. Of course – this was our prime minister, Alexander Langton himself, and chief suspect number one.

I felt light-headed. I could only assume that the Archios they'd been talking about at the gatehouse was the code name for Langton. Just for a moment Langton himself oh-so-slowly glanced back in my direction, as if he'd sensed me. Maybe he had a Shade sitting inside him right now, with supernatural abilities too? At least the slow motion meant that I could duck down before he saw me.

Langton's focus crawled past my hiding place and travelled back to the lab. Then the group disappeared into the building.

I put my hand on a fallen dead branch and stood up. The bark crumbled under my hand to reveal black wood beneath. Could I be really certain this wasn't radiation of some sort?

My stomach did a long flip as I pictured my body's cells being gradually destroyed as I stood there. But surely the others who'd been brought here would have been showing the symptoms by now, like their hair and teeth falling out? No, whatever it was didn't seem to be toxic – to trees yes, but to humans no. I wondered whether, if it had been toxic to me, if my accelerated healing abilities would have helped. At least I wasn't relying on that little gem just yet. I really didn't fancy putting it to the test with a bullet wound.

Swirling fog obscured the tinted windows, so I could only just see into the rooms on the other side of the glass. But it was only empty office after empty office. Where were all the abductees if this place hadn't been destroyed? Where were Chloe and Dave?

With my senses needle-sharp, I began to edge forward, but it was risky, even with my current invisibility. What happened if I suddenly shifted back? There wasn't a single bit of vegetation that I could use as cover, not even a patch of moss between me and the research building. It looked like heavy-duty pesticide had been sprayed across the whole area, but why the need to do that? And if not that, what were the trees reacting to?

With each step forward the air seemed to thicken around my limbs until I could have been wading through water. By the time I reached the steps it felt as if I had lead weights on my legs... If gravity was changing here, maybe it was a singularity after all – so would it mean that time really was being distorted? I glanced at my watch but as I'd expected the second was moving normally, for me at least. That didn't stop me from thinking that if I'd been able to see myself right now from the edge of the clearing I'd witness myself crawling just as slowly as I'd seen Langton and his men move a moment ago.

So this was real-life time dilation, the stuff of sci-fi. And something that Einstein had predicted someone would experience as they approached the speed of light – time itself would get slower, even though for them it appeared to be running normally. My brain struggled to comprehend what this meant – for me, for the future of the world. This was all so crazy.

With adrenalin pumping hard at the thought that I was totally exposed I headed up the smooth stone steps following the thick power cable that was hooked up to a huge generator. They obviously needed a lot of power for something in there. I entered the glass atrium and ducked behind a desk, recognising a stainless-steel sculpture in the middle – it had once flowed with water, but now it was completely dry.

Dark vapours still wreathed like a grey cloud in the Shadowlands, but I couldn't see any sign of the Shade creatures yet.

My breath started to steam in the increasingly chilly air as the vapours grew ever blacker. With my thermal vision I could see the warmth from the men's shoe prints still glowing across the floor, leading away along the corridor. I followed their trail deeper into the building, careful not to make so much noise as a trainer squeak.

I could practically feel the danger dripping off the wall as the temperature continued to plummet and I saw frost glittering on the floor.

If I hadn't been so desperate to rescue Chloe, and to find out what we were dealing with for Sentinel, I would have been tempted to turn round and try to get back to my ordinary life. But that wasn't ever going to be an option – I was already way past the point of no return. Perhaps I had been from the moment Sentinel had almost crash-landed Varuna on top of my head.

I froze as a group of people crossed the corridor ahead of me, moving slightly slower than normal speed. The time dilation effect was still at work but falling off the further I headed into the building. I ducked into a doorway and peered round the door-frame. No one turned in my direction. It looked like I was safe, at least for now.

I recognised a guy in blue coveralls: Jason Stone. So much for him heading home for a heart-to-heart with his wife. Then I spotted the kid at the back: Gavin. He was wheeling a large red tool chest in front of him.

So why was he here? Apart from being a thug, his only other skill was...

That's it! He's a mechanic.

It took the greatest willpower not to thump my head against the doorframe. With that flash of insight all the abductions made sense: the electricians, engineers, even a trainee mechanic like Gavin, but especially Dave with his intimate knowledge of the DEC experiment itself. This had everything to do with skilled people, ones with an underlying medical condition that made them vulnerable, who could build something for the Shade.

My blood became icier than the air around me, but my desire for answers was almost as strong as my need to rescue Chloe. This wasn't the time to turn away.

I waited until the work team had disappeared from view before I headed after them – in the direction of Dad's lab.

With each step long-forgotten memories of visiting here as a kid came flooding back... That time I rode my scooter behind Dad through this very corridor. In the canteen, when I'd shared his massive sandwich that seemed the size of my head. When I'd used Dave's foam dart gun that he'd kept in his office drawer to ambush Dad.

The old ache pulsed.

I missed that old life more than I ever admitted to anyone, even to Chloe. In another life, the one I was meant to have, I might have eventually ended up working here with Dad, as one of his students, pushing back the boundaries of science together. But the explosion had changed everything and the fairy-tale ending had been snatched away from me.

A faint buzzing sound caught right at the edge of my hearing, coming from the corridor that the group had just turned down.

I crept towards the junction, the increasing chill making the air crackle in my nose. A long corridor stretched away from me, the power cable snaking along it, ending in metal doors with a staircase off to one side, all in pristine condition.

Dad's lab.

Once again there was no sign of any blast damage from an explosion that had supposedly been so intense that there'd been no remains of any bodies.

So what had really happened here that night, the moment after he'd died?

The work party disappeared through the doors and brilliant

light from beyond them flooded my vision. The answers had to be on the other side of those doors. I kept following, the buzzing intensifying to the point that it pierced my skull like a nail being driven into the bone.

It had grown so icy now that the walls were almost pitch-black in my thermal vision, making it increasingly harder to navigate in the Shadowlands. I needed the training. I needed to control my ability now. I screwed up my face in concentration and thought: *Real.*

A ripple of energy pulsed through me and my vision shifted back to normal with no pain, no drama. *Result!* And with normal eyesight, I could now see green light spilling beneath the doors ahead.

As tempting as it was to follow Gavin and the others into the lab, if this was the centre of the Shade's activity in the science park, I'd probably be spotted as soon as I entered, since I was no longer invisible. But I needed to know what they were doing in there.

I glanced to the staircase leading to Dad's office, which over-looked the lab. I just had to hope no one else was already inside. I gathered my determination and started to climb the stairs to whatever this place was about to throw at me next.

CHAPTER TWENTY-SIX

AT THE TOP of the stairs I opened the door and peered into what had once been Dad's office. An empty coffee cup sat on the desk, a leather briefcase on the floor, his fleece jacket still hanging on the back of the chair – a time capsule from the moment he'd died. The whole scene was bathed in green strobing light coming through the lab's observation window running the length of one wall. The hum of electrical energy was vibrating every surface in the room.

Despite the sub-zero temperature, fresh sweat trickled down my back. Head low, I crept into the room and spotted an old photo lying face down on his desk. I already knew what it was before I turned it over. Dad holding a baby, me, with Mum in the background – a photo that he'd always loved. A few weeks later, she'd died in a car crash...

The back of my nose prickled and I set the photo up the right way.

I reached the window and, being careful not to be seen, peered over the ledge into the room below.

In the middle of the old lab shining arcs of green plasma

sparked and hummed around what appeared to be a solid-glass opaque sphere about ten metres wide. Beneath its frosted surface I could see vague hints of abstract shapes. Was this the singularity causing the time dilation effect? If so, it didn't fit what a black hole should look like in any of the descriptions I'd read.

The heavy power cable from the generator outside snaked its way across the floor to a large junction box. From there, hundreds of wires had been strung out to a vast array of metal pointed rods all aimed at the sphere. Each of the rods was at least three metres long, and about a third of them flickered with green lightning, the others inactive. Walkways encircled the sphere between the rods, where one guy in a lab coat was holding out some sort of electronic meter towards the sphere and studying its display.

It took me a moment to process what I was seeing because the machine was so big – big enough to make the large lab look crowded.

There was no mistaking it – this was a scaled-up version of Dad's original DEC experiment.

Nausea flooded my gut.

The Shade were trying to open up a new portal, although it looked as if they were having a hard time of it. The energy blasts, apart from causing the green light show bathing the lab, seemed to be doing absolutely nothing to the sphere's surface. But what could resist this sort of energy being thrown at it without suffering even a scratch?

I spotted Gavin's work team, along with several other groups, each concentrating their efforts on the non-functioning needles that trailed a riot of wires and tubes. I recognised Paul Roberts, the electrician who'd been in the back of the Range Rover, connecting a conduit to one of the needles. There was no sign of his wheelchair anywhere. For someone who was meant to be suffering from multiple sclerosis, his hands looked rock steady as he worked.

So was this was the flip side of being infected by the Shade? Could they somehow neutralise existing medical conditions, even one as serious as MS?

Off to one side of the new DEC was what looked like an airport security scanner you stand in, except this machine had a glass screen that fully enclosed the cylinder structure.

Then I spotted Langton smoking an e-cigarette, its vapour curling up over his head like a question mark. He was standing with a group of men in lab coats who were all studying a bank of computer screens.

Langton gestured to one of them, who rotated a large knob on a console and the green lightning faded away. And it was only then that I spotted someone slumped in a chair with his hands tied behind his back.

My heart clenched.

Dave.

Either side of him two Genesis heavies stood guard as Langton walked over.

Dave's head came up. He opened his eyes and his mouth started to move, but through the glass I couldn't hear what was going on. I cracked open a window, millimetre by millimetre, ready to stop if there was so much as the faintest squeak.

'But this isn't possible,' Dave was saying as he stared around him. 'Martin's lab was destroyed in the blast.'

Langton walked towards him. 'You really don't remember anything, do you, dear friend?'

'What do you mean? How did I get here? And why, of all people, are you here, Prime Minister?'

'One question at a time. Our people brought you and your daughter, Chloe, here.'

Dave's expression tightened. 'You did what? But why us? Why her?'

'That's simple – to use her as leverage if you don't cooperate.'

'I have no idea what you're rambling on about, Langton, but I swear, if you harm a single hair on my daughter's head, I will tear you apart with my bare hands—'

Langton's arm moved so quickly it blurred as he struck Dave hard across the face and his head whipped to one side.

Anger surged through me and I gripped the window ledge.

Dave glowered at Langton. 'What do you think you're doing?'

'You'll remember soon enough, Professor Haze.'

Dave stared past him at the machine they were building around the sphere. 'That looks like...'

Langton gave him a slow handclap. 'How very perceptive. Yes, this is the new and improved DEC, a vastly more powerful machine than your original experiment.'

'Are you mad?' Dave shouted. 'You don't know what you're dealing with.'

Langton gazed at Dave. 'Oh, but we do, my friend.' He gestured towards the machine. 'Behold the fruits of your very own hands.'

'What are you talking about?' Dave jutted his chin towards the machine. 'I had nothing to do with that thing.'

'You have simply forgotten your heroic actions on behalf of the Shade.'

'The *who*?'

'The friends who highly value all your contributions to our plan. If it had not been for your exceptional work, we would never have been able to prepare for our new invasion.'

I gripped the windowsill. This was everything I'd feared – and worse.

Dave's eyes grew wider. 'You're off-the-scale crazy, Langton. That's the only truth here.'

'I am anything but, as you so delightfully put it, "crazy".' The prime minister brushed his hand across Dave's cheek, and he flinched. 'On the contrary, the answers to all the questions that you have ever wished to know – far beyond all human knowledge, to have absolute certainty, to know complete purpose – is all within your grasp. All you have to do is to behold the beauty of the Void.'

'The Void?'

'The Void is our home – the one true state before the cosmos was divided. As it was in the beginning it shall be again. The Void will consume this and every other universe, and with that glorious moment the dance of dark energy and matter will be complete.'

'You sound like a religious nutter to me,' Dave replied.

'What a quaint way to express it.'

'Tell me where Chloe is.'

'Somewhere close to hand and safe for the time being...'

Dave hung his head. 'Just let her go,' he said. 'You can do what you want with me.'

OK, so that man down there sounded like the Dave I used to know. A man who actually loved his daughter. Not one who hit her.

'We will, Professor, if you help us,' Langton replied. 'You see, we need you and your expertise.'

'You're crazy if you think I'm going to help with any of this madness.'

Langton walked round Dave in a circle. 'Remember all those blank spots in your memory?'

'Yes... How do you know about those? I haven't told anyone.'

'We, the Shade, servants of the Void, took control of your mind and body.' Langton stopped in front of Dave. 'But you have been strong, Professor Haze, far stronger than we could have ever imagined. Despite cleansing your body of cancer, which enabled us to infect you in the first place, your subconscious continued to fight us and somehow kept breaking our hold over you.'

I hadn't known that Dave had even been ill. Chloe had never mentioned it.

'What cancer?' Dave frowned hard.

'Undiagnosed, but spreading throughout your brain stem. If we had not intervened, you would already be dead by now.'

I stared down at them. So Dave had cancer and hadn't even known it. That was how the Shade had got their hooks into him. And all those times he'd hit Chloe... It hadn't really been him. Heat rose up through my chest. Whatever it took I'd make the Shade paid for all of this.

Dave grimaced at Langton. 'More lies.'

'I can assure you that they are not. Anyway, do not concern yourself any further about that. When we have broken you again, this time once and for all, you will know the truth and gain clarity once more, my friend.'

'I'm afraid I'm going to have to decline, *my friend*,' Dave replied.

'No need for that attitude, Professor. You need to cooperate for the whole process to go smoothly and be much less painful for you.'

'If you think I'm going to help you with a new version of the biggest mistake of my life – one that killed my best friend, and all those other people – you're a madman.'

'Your memories are incomplete, a jumble of broken pieces. However, rejoin us in the Nexus, and you will know the truth once more.'

The Nexus? I filed the question away to ask Sentinel – if I managed to live through this.

'And what if I don't cooperate?'

'I was not bluffing about using your daughter as leverage.'

'You wouldn't, Langton.'

'I most certainly would.' The prime minister walked towards

the airport-scanner-like device. 'I will place her inside our nutrient accelerator.'

'The accelerator?'

'After we entered your world, the portal was unexpectedly closed behind us. Ever since we have been cut off from our brethren. Unfortunately our numbers were few and we needed to start multiplying as quickly as possible to give us any chance of reopening the portal from this side. And for that, we needed energy, lots of it, something that the human body contains an abundance of at the subatomic level.'

Dave stared at him. 'You're telling me that you dissolved people into pure energy inside that machine?'

'Yes – and you will have a ringside seat as your daughter's body is stripped apart, atom by atom, down to her very last molecule. And I can assure you she will feel the most exquisite pain as she dies.'

I gripped the windowsill harder.

'You wouldn't,' Dave shouted.

'I assure you that we will, as we have with all the others.'

'What others?'

'The ones who were in the science park that night our original invasion plan failed.'

'But they were killed in the blast.'

'Once again you have a fragmented memory – you are only able to recall our cover story. The actual truth is: yes, there was an explosion, but it was contained within the energy field you see here before it could wreck any damage – damage that we greatly exaggerated anyway. And ever since then we have been bombarding that energy field, trying to break it down to expose the original portal.'

I stared at the glass sphere – so that was what it was, basically some sort of force field.

Langton continued. 'Unfortunately for anyone around the

science park that night, we needed their bodies to convert into an energy source to allow us to multiply. And it provided us with an elegant solution to remove any witnesses who had seen what had really happened. So when we fed their bodies into our accelerator we effectively killed two birds with one stone, as your race would say.'

The full horror of what had happened here six years ago hit me like a slap around the face. The people – all of them, including Dad – had been murdered, reduced to little more than the equivalent of cattle fodder for the Shade to feast upon. I spat sudden bitterness away on to the floor. The Shade were the very definition of pure evil.

I glanced down at Gavin – he must have heard what Langton had just said. His dad had been here too, murdered that night along with all the others.

But as he worked there was no flicker of anger, anguish – nothing. He remained focused on tightening bolts around some sort of valve at the base of a giant electrode. A brain-washed slave, stripped of emotion.

Dave gawped at Langton. 'You can't be serious?'

'I most certainly am, my friend.' Langton gestured to one of the Genesis guards. 'Bring the girl. It seems we may have to sacrifice her after all, just to prove a point.'

'I will fetch her straightaway, Archios,' the guard said.

'Stop!' Dave shouted. He dropped his head to stare at the floor. 'OK, I'll do it, I'll bloody do it. Just leave my daughter out of this.'

Langton nodded to the guard who returned to his position by the door.

The prime minister gazed at Dave, his head to one side. 'Good, very good. I was hoping you would see it my way.'

'Who are you really, Langton? Who's Archios?'

'Archios is a being of power beyond your wildest human

dreams.' Langton raised his arms and the air seemed to blur around him.

On instinct, and with just a mental push, I shifted into the Shadowlands.

I had to stifle a gasp. With my thermal vision I could now see what was happening around Langton. A swirling pattern of Shade birds were forming into the shadow man. The monster surrounding Langton's now motionless body towered over Dave... the same monster that had snatched Chloe.

The shadow man lowered his head towards Dave, his voice a whisper on the wind. 'We are the Shade. And I am Archios of the Nexus.'

Dave's eyes widened – I guessed because Langton's mouth hadn't moved – and his head turned left and right looking for the source of the voice. 'Is this some sort of conjuring trick?'

'No trick. This is all too real. Soon you will remember everything, my friend.'

Then, for the first time, I noticed the transformation of the sphere inside the Shadowlands. What had been an opaque globe in visible light, became semi-translucent in my infrared vision. Near the centre of it a man was frozen in the act of shielding his face, a face that I recognised...

I cupped my hands over my mouth and bit back a cry as my soul twisted.

Dad, frozen in the middle, crouching. What was this? Some sort of sick freak show where the Shade put dead people on display?

I wiped away stinging tears with my hand. *Hold it together, Jake, and think of Chloe...*

Too much depended on what I did here, maybe even the fate of the whole world. If I was lucky to survive, there'd be time to grieve later. I took a breath and tried to process what I was witnessing.

Inside the energy sphere, Dad looked just like he had in the last frame of the video I'd watched with Chloe. This had to be the exact moment of the explosion – with Dad being caught like a bug in amber when the energy field had been created.

Behind Dad, shards of metal from the containment sphere of the original DEC experiment were frozen as they flew outwards. Something caught my gaze. Right in the centre of the blossoming shards was a point of utter darkness that screamed wrongness – it definitely didn't belong in our world. The thing that I'd seen on the video trying to punch its way out...

The portal – it had to be.

But somehow the Shade's invasion that should have started with that rip in our reality had been stopped in its tracks by an energy field that had also killed Dad.

Archios opened his mouth wide and breathed out dark spores that swirled through the air. From each, like pieces of unfolding origami, wings unfurled and needle claws extended.

Shadow birds, hundreds and hundreds of them, rushed around the lab – creatures that I realised only Archios and I could see.

I stared at Dave, someone who'd been possessed and was about to be taken over again by an enemy – all to save his daughter. I had to fight every instinct to rush down and take them all on to save him because I knew that would destroy any hope I had of stopping the Shade.

Dave, even though he couldn't see the creatures, pulled at the plastic ties binding his hands as the dark phantoms spiralled in closer around him. Perhaps he could feel the temperature dropping as they dived past him, and the hiss of wind from their phantom crow wings, because his gaze darted around the room as if he was trying to locate the unseen things.

I couldn't turn away. Part of me had to see, had to know, bear witness, so I could tell Chloe what had happened here. But most of all I needed to tell her that Dave really was the man she thought he had once been.

The Shade crows' wingtips skimmed Dave in a shadowy embrace. Gasping for air, he screamed as they closed in around him.

Cold fogged the room, swamping my thermal vision with utter darkness.

Goosebumps surged across my skin as everything became deathly quiet. I shifted back into the Real as the fog started to thin. One by one, control panels blinked back on with a whine, together casting a feeble light out across the lab.

My pulse quickened. Dave was standing in the middle, hands now free of bonds. The crows had vanished too. Langton stood before him again, nodding, no sign of Archios anywhere. Dave even looked OK. But then a slow twisted smile filled his face as he gazed at Langton.

In that instant, I knew that Chloe's dad was gone.

'Welcome back, my friend,' Langton said.

'You have done well,' Dave replied. 'We miscalculated this man's love for his daughter and his desire to protect her, which broke our grip on his consciousness. However, I must say it was well played, Langton. Using Chloe to bend Professor Haze back to our will was a stroke of genius.'

'I have my moments of insight. And thanks to that, the professor's mind belongs to the Shade for ever.'

'I certainly feel no further resistance from inside his subconscious,' Dave said.

'Excellent news. What steps do you suggest we take now, dear friend?' Langton asked.

'As much as this has been an unwelcome distraction from our plans, it may yet turn out to be useful,' Dave said. 'There are loose ends that need to be tidied up. It is obvious that in addition to Jake Stevens, Chloe Haze has also been Awoken by Sentinel.'

A scowl filled Langton's face. 'And I can see the logic to the AI's strategy. However, I do find it somewhat ironic that the same AI was also responsible for inadvertently killing Professor Stevens in the first place, when he encased our portal in his zero-point energy field, then went on to recruit that man's own son to his cause.'

No! Sentinel killed Dad... I stared at the phone in my hand.

'That is twisted enough to have been devised by you,' Dave said. 'I certainly must give our opponent some credit here.'

I struggled to process this. Sentinel had murdered Dad? Was that why the AI had been so cagey about what he'd been doing in the lab the night of the explosion? This zero-point energy field had been his phase one – his bloody phase one! The AI had been ruthless, doing whatever was necessary to stop the Shade's invasion.

Hot anger flashed through me. I'd been betrayed by an alien AI who'd pretended to be my friend, but was really a cold consciousness that had murdered my dad!

I threw the phone across the desk, sending the photo flying, the mobile smashing against the wall.

Shit! What had I done? I ducked down, heart roaring, tears flooding my vision.

'Go and investigate that noise at once,' Langton called out.

Shit, shit, shit. I stared at the broken remains of the phone, its screen smashed and separated from its body, exposing the circuit board beneath.

Footsteps ran up the stairs towards the office. I hunted for something to hide behind and my eyes fell on the filing cabinet. I rushed over and, as quietly as I could, heaved the heavy metal case out a fraction, behind which was a mass of cobwebs. I ducked into a faceful of silk threads and squeezed into the gap as the door flew open.

I held my breath, waiting for hands to grab hold of me.

Instead feet appeared in my line of vision, standing directly on the remains of Chloe's phone. I peered up to see the guard staring around the room. He spotted the photograph on the desk, scooped it up and threw it aside.

The man glanced directly at the space I was hiding in and my heart clenched. He screwed up his mouth at the cobwebbed recess and turned away. The shadows must have been just deep enough to hide me.

'There is no one here – it must be another rat,' the man called through the open window into the lab below.

'I thought I gave you all orders to eradicate them from this facility,' Langton replied.

'Some of them must have escaped our last sterilisation sweep.'

'Then do another sweep, but this time properly,' Langton said. 'We cannot have those damned rodents biting through a critical bit of wiring at the wrong moment.'

Those rats were my new best friends.

'I will see to it at once.'

'Make sure you do, or I will personally feed you into the nutrient accelerator.'

I heard footsteps race away and the door slamming shut.

I breathed out a long sigh, but any sense of relief was quickly swamped by a feeling of numbness. I knew I had every reason to be angry with Sentinel, but by smashing the phone I'd just destroyed our best chance of saving the planet.

Dread rose inside me as I sneaked out from my hiding place and headed back to the window.

Dave had his hand on Langton's shoulder. 'Our first priority is to restore you to full vitality, Archios. You shared your Shade life-blood with me, brother, and that is something that we should take steps to replenish at once.' He gestured to another guard. 'You may bring Chloe Haze in now and place her into the accelerator. She has served her purpose and is of no further use to us.'

What? They were going to kill Chloe anyway – and feed her remains to Langton!

The guard nodded and made for the door. This time Langton didn't call him back.

With my head a tangle of fury and guilt I left the phone and slipped out from my hiding place and ran out of the office.

CHAPTER TWENTY-SEVEN

THE GUARD strode ahead of me, unaware that I was tracking him. As I skulked along the corridors behind him, shifted into the Shadowlands, I hung on to the only thing I had left: saving Chloe, whatever the cost.

At a four-way junction, the guard turned right towards a door. I'd never been down this part of the research building before.

A sign over the door read: 'Storage Room'.

The man punched in a combination on the lock, flicked on a torch, and entered.

A few seconds later, I peered through the round reinforced window into the room beyond. Elation surged through me as I spotted Chloe alive. She'd been bound to a chair, blindfolded and mouth covered with duct tape.

The room itself was packed with all sorts of scientific junk, from racks of test tubes to the dials and switches of tech equipment. Basically your everyday DIY mad-scientist all-you-can-grab store. But I was looking for something specific and it didn't take me long to spot it – a small propane gas bottle on a trolley right next to the door.

That should do...

The guard, his back to me, ripped the duct tape from Chloe's mouth. I heard her hiss with pain despite the closed door between us.

'You complete and utter festering skin-bag of zombie pus,' she shouted.

Yep, Chloe was definitely living and breathing – and sounding totally furious. Despite everything I found a smile tugging at the corner of my mouth at her creative cursing.

Chloe began to cast her blindfolded head around. 'Let me go right now, or I swear I'm going to remove your kneecaps with the bluntest instrument I can find.'

The guard ignored her and began to untie her feet.

'That better mean you're letting me go. But I'm not leaving here without my dad.'

'You will see your father soon enough,' the guard replied.

'OK, see – we can get along when you start to be reasonable.'

I flinched. Of course, Chloe had no idea what Langton intended to do her.

I pushed open the door just enough to reach inside and lift the heavy gas cylinder. I closed the door again as quietly as I could, while the guard finished untying her feet.

'That's more like it,' Chloe said as she stood, hands still bound behind her back.

'After you, miss,' the man said.

'You forgot my hands and blindfold.'

'No, I didn't.' He shoved her towards the door.

I doubled back to the junction and ducked round the corner. I crouched opposite the route back to the lab, knowing that I'd probably only get one chance to pull this off...

I heard the door opening. 'And if you have any plans to try to run, I wouldn't bother, miss, because I promise you'll not get far,' the guard said.

'That's telling me then,' Chloe replied.

A moment later she walked past, herded round the corner by the guard.

The metal cylinder felt cold in my hand, but also nice and heavy.

As they headed away along the corridor I crept behind the guy.

The guard had the broadest shoulders, which seemed to flow straight into his head, his neck lost somewhere under all that muscle. Before the Shade had taken him he'd clearly spent a lot of time at the gym lifting weights. Suddenly the gas bottle didn't feel as heavy as it needed to be. Then my luck ran out.

I wasn't sure if the guy heard me, or a Shade instinct kicked in, because he started to turn. His eyes grew wide as he caught sight of the gas cylinder hanging in mid-air as far as he was concerned. A snarl curled his mouth as he spun round.

I threw my whole weight behind the gas bottle, like a lumberjack swinging an axe. But already the guy's arm had come up in a blocking move as my metal weapon crashed into him. The shocking crack of bone filled the corridor, but the guy didn't even flinch.

He had obviously been briefed about an Awoken's ability to become invisible. Already his other fist flew out in a roundhouse punch straight at my skull – an incredibly good guess on his part. I managed to switch my momentum and drop just enough for his hand to slice through empty air over my head.

My pulse revved as I swung my cylinder in a backswing and caught him square on the chest with another dreadful crack of bone. The man staggered but kept his balance. His eyes became slits as he lunged back towards me.

Chloe twisted round. 'What's going on? Who's there?'

'It's me, Chloe – Jake,' I said as I dropped to my knee and rammed my foot into the guard's shin hard enough to trip him. His leg flew out and struck my wrist, breaking my hold on the gas canister. It skittered away along the corridor towards Chloe, who was turning her blindfolded head left and right in confusion.

The guy was already back on his feet and advancing again, arms reaching out to locate his invisible opponent.

Still down on the floor, I scrabbled backwards, sneakers squealing on the tiles. His head snapped in the direction of the sound, towards me, and grinned.

This was going to be over before it had even begun. I had no chance now.

The man snarled as he raised his foot to stamp on to my invisible chest.

I caught a movement of something flying through the air and smacking into the back of his head. The guard started to topple forward and I rolled to the side to avoid him as he crashed to the ground. He didn't move.

Chloe was a metre away from me, her arms still tied behind her back.

'Nicely done,' I said.

'I was able to work out where he roughly was by all the noise he was making. The rest was luck.'

I stood and nudged the guard with my foot, but he didn't stir. I crossed to Chloe and hugged her as I shifted back.

She took a shuddering breath against me. 'I couldn't believe it when I heard your voice. The last thing I remember is that shadow man rushing towards me. And the next thing I know is that I'm here, blindfolded and tied up. I've been so scared, Jake.'

'That makes two of us.' I started to untie her hands, quickly moving on to her blindfold. 'We need to get out of here.'

'But what about my dad? We need to rescue him too.'

'You don't understand, Chloe, and I haven't got any time to soften this. It was Dave who just ordered your execution.'

She took a half step back. 'What? No way!'

I took Chloe's hand in mine. 'Dave has been working under the influence of the Shade.'

She bit her lip. 'You're sure?'

'I'm afraid I am. But if there's a way to help Dave, later on, we'll find it. And Gavin too...'

Her hand flew to her mouth. 'Please tell me he's not here as well?'

'I wish I could.'

She bit down on to her knuckle, her eyes wild.

I took her by the hand and had to almost tow her away. The time for a real explanation would come later if we ever got out of this alive.

I glanced back along the corridor, but that would take us dangerously near the lab. Instead I started down the right-hand passageway, pulling Chloe with me. I had a hazy idea of the layout of the research building and a feeling that this corridor intersected another longer one that led straight to the entrance.

A short while later, we crept towards a puddle of light from the atrium in the main entrance. Shouts echoed from deep inside the building.

Chloe blinked like she was waking from a trance. 'I think they just found the guard.'

'OK, run, and don't stop for anything.'

'Jake, I just wanted to say—'

I pressed my finger to her lips. 'You can tell me later.'

She nodded.

Together we rushed to the entrance and hurtled out through the doors.

I pointed at the line of massive trees round the edge of the clearing. 'We can lose them in the forest.'

Chloe stared at the forest surrounding the science park and cast me a questioning look.

'I've no idea where it came from,' I said.

Hand in hand, we raced straight towards the crack between the boughs through which I'd first entered. I heard a distorted shout and glanced back to see two guards, who to us were moving in slow motion, even though in real-time they had to be running. But I knew that advantage wouldn't last long.

Chloe looked back too and almost stumbled as she took in the guards moving at a quarter of the speed that we were.

I grabbed Chloe's hand to steady her. 'Time is being affected around the lab.'

She shot me a wide-eyed stare and wiggled through the gap ahead of me. I needed to buy us some time – the two guys had started to speed up as they got close to clearing the time bubble around the science park. As I followed her I placed my hands against the boughs, once again feeling the surge of energy pass through me. The tree groaned and shuddered as it closed the gap behind us to form a solid wall of wood at our backs. My whole body ached like I'd just run a marathon and not merely a hundred metres from the building behind us.

Chloe spread her hands, her jaw slack.

'Apparently part of my Awoken play box,' I said.

An animal scream of frustration echoed from the clearing we'd just left. Loud splintering sounds came from the trunks behind us and the trees shook under the assault of an attack on the other side.

We sprinted down the hill away from the science park. A siren warbled, distorted by the time dilation. Its notes stretched out, only adding to its sinister sound.

Chloe grimaced as a howl – part human, part nightmare – echoed through the wood, raising the hairs on the nape of my neck. If they caught us... I pushed away the dark images that flashed through my mind.

The slope steepened beneath our feet and we were forced to descend in great leaping jumps. But I was already exhausted after pulling my trick with the trees and my whole body was running on nothing.

The buzz of two motorbikes resounded through the woods above us.

'Oh great,' Chloe said. She began to increase her pace as the ground levelled out again and I tried to keep up.

A shadow flitted between the trunks ahead and a pony-tailed man – one of the two guards who'd been chasing us – sprang out of the forest in front of Chloe.

Shit.

He fixed his shadow-filled eyes on us.

My mind tilted as I saw his fingers had been reduced to broken stumps. The guy was barely human any more. I scanned the clearing but the nearest trees were too far away to offer us any sort of protection.

With a snarl he hurtled towards us. Before I could do anything, Chloe shoved me aside to face him. She brought her leg up smoothly and caught the guy squarely in the chest. The man shot past her and crashed on to the ground.

I stared at her. 'The taekwondo videos?'

She nodded. 'I knew all that studying would come in useful one day.'

'That was ridiculously impressive, Chloe.'

Her smile froze.

I turned to see the man clambering back to his feet and dusting himself down.

'Oh, come on, that should have winded you at least,' Chloe said.

The guy gave her a twisted grin and began to prowl

towards us.

I looked for something, anything, to help us, and spotted a stone sticking out of a pile of leaves and acorns. I grabbed it and felt energy surge up my arm as I hurled the rock at the guy.

It struck him in the chest and bounced off as if he were made of rubber, landing on the ground at his feet.

He stared down at the stone for a moment and then his gaze flicked back to us. What happened next was so fast that it felt like a dream. As the guy stepped forward, a single sapling erupted from the ground and shot straight up through his body, spearing him like a fish.

My legs buckled as a cloud of inky black smoke drifted from man's mouth and faded into the canopy of leaves. His eyes, no longer filled with shadows, twitched and stilled.

'W-what just happened?' I stammered.

Chloe pointed at the base of the blood-covered sapling. 'I think you scooped up one of those acorns with that stone and your ability must have done the rest.'

'Which means I just killed him, Chloe...' What strength I had left – both mental and physical – flowed away and I sank to my knees.

She gently took my shoulders and forced me to look at her. 'Not intentionally you didn't. Anyway, that guy was probably long dead in every other sense by the look of him.'

Like Dave? Like Gavin?

My attention skated away from Chloe and back to the man's body. The guy was wearing a wedding ring.

Chloe shook me lightly as the growls of motorbikes drifted through the woods.

'We need to get moving, Jake.'

I ignored her, unable to tear my eyes away from the man as the bikes' roars grew louder.

'You've got to snap out of this before you get us both killed,'

Chloe said.

I blinked and looked into her eyes. 'Yes...'

I tried to crank my mind back into gear. We hadn't got enough time to escape before those bikes found us. I glanced around and spotted a hollowed-out root bowl from a fallen tree. 'Let's lie low in there until they've gone.'

Chloe nodded and ducked into the hollow. As I followed her I pulled some ferns across the entrance to hide us.

Three seconds later, two off-road bikers hurtled into the clearing. In a shower of dirt they skidded to a stop, close to our hiding space. Both riders killed their engines and dismounted.

One of the men stuck his chin out and sniffed the air.

I tried to quieten my ragged breathing but a dark smile was already filling his face.

The guy gestured to the other man, who slowly turned to look directly at our hiding place.

My heart froze. *Stupid, stupid, stupid!* I'd only managed to get us boxed inside this hollow and now there was nowhere left for us to run.

Chloe's hand locked round mine.

No words. No point. I'd gambled our lives and lost.

The bikers stalked towards us and I tensed for the grasp of their talon-like hands. The smell of damp earth filled my nose and a water droplet fell from a twisted root on to my face.

Chloe's eyes widened and she pointed at the roots.

She was a genius. If I'd brought trees to life once... I grabbed on to a handful of roots and felt the familiar surge of energy building within me and flowing out, hollowing my insides. With a groan of bending wood the tree's roots leapt up, like a pit of vipers, knotting around the two men. The roots probed and tightened their grip, forming a living, flexing net for each of them. The men tore at their prisons, trying to break their bonds, but as quickly as they snapped one root another flew up to take its place.

I stared for a moment, not quite able to believe what I'd unleashed.

'Come on,' Chloe said, pulling me by the arm.

With our backs to the wall of the earth burrow we slid past them. They clawed at us between the bars of the roots, and the bigger of the two had begun snapping the thick roots as easily as pencils. They wouldn't hold him much longer. We had to get out of there.

As we ran from the clearing I glanced back to see the bigger biker tear free of his root prison, but the other man was still held fast. The freed biker leapt on to his motorbike, pressed the starter and its engine roared into life.

I stumbled away down the slope after Chloe, my legs feeling like stone. My ability might have brought the roots to life, but it had also left me drained like a dead car battery. I'd hardly anything left. My mind felt completely fried too as we headed for the outside wall of the science park.

The biker would be on us in moments, and the trees up ahead weren't high enough to climb and get over the wall – not like the ones I'd used to get in.

But I could do something about that. With shaking hands I placed each of my palms on a tree. Energy wrenched at my gut as it poured out of me and into the trunks. The trees grew massive in an instant, trunks growing wide enough to touch the wall. With a groan the bricks shattered, leaving a metre-wide gap in the wall behind them.

I stumbled as I withdrew my hands, but Chloe grabbed my shoulders and helped me towards the hole that had opened up. My legs gave way but Chloe dragged me through and on to the verge beyond.

Chloe dropped by my side. 'Are you OK, Jake?'

I wiped away a trickle of blood from my nose. 'No, I'm done, Chloe. But you can still get away. Find someone who will believe you – the newspapers, anyone – and tell them to come and investigate what's been really going on at this site. If somebody doesn't stop the Shade it's only a matter of time before our whole world is destroyed.'

'What?' Then her eyes sparkled. 'Whatever is going on, Jake. I'm not leaving you. We're in this together.'

'Now you're just being stubborn.'

'No, I'm just being the best friend you ever had.'

I could tell by the blue fire in her eyes that she wouldn't change her mind. 'You are that. But this is the end, Chloe. We may die here and then nobody else will ever know the truth.'

She crossed her arms. 'Then that's just the way it has to be.'

It was stupid, I knew it was stupid – a totally irrational decision. But I nodded anyway, seriously loving her for not letting me face the demon alone unlike I had her outside the Red Lion.

She helped me to sit up, and through the smashed wall I saw the motorbike less than fifty metres away, engine roaring, as its rider sped towards the hole in the wall.

I heard a cracking sound. The uppermost bricks where the wall was still intact had started to sag downwards into the hole beneath.

Chloe leapt up and raced back to the wall.

'What are you doing?' I shouted.

'What I have to do,' she called back. She clambered up the ruined wall until she was right next to the section threatening to collapse. Hanging on with one hand, she kicked out at it. The brickwork groaned and cement splintered as the rider reached the gap.

Chloe kicked out again, and again.

The wall shrieked and Chloe leapt and sprawled on to the ground as bricks showered down on to the rider as he emerged. In a millisecond he and his bike had been buried under a pile of rubble. Moments later, black smoke drifted up slowly between the cracks, floating away into the branches.

Tyres squealed from beyond the bend in the road. So just as we'd avoided one pursuer, another one approached, relentless.

Chloe limped towards me holding her weight off her left leg.

I gazed at Chloe, totally drained, any fight gone from me. Whatever was coming for us it would be game over. I struggled to my feet so we could face our end together.

Chloe cradled my head with her hand. She leant forward and her mouth met mine.

I kissed her back, losing myself for a moment in her love, her warmth. We needed a lifetime to work this out, but we only had seconds left. No words. No words were needed.

We broke away to look at the vehicle that sped round the bend, though it was impossibly quiet. A Tesla, I realised, shiny and white. It skidded to a stop and the driver's window lowered.

I blinked. No one was driving. No one was in the car at all.

'Get inside now,' Sentinel's voice said from the dashboard.

I stared at the vehicle. The AI must have taken over the autopilot system. 'Sentinel? But you should be dead!'

'I will answer all your questions later, Jake.'

Heat boiled up through me, burning away my exhaustion. 'Like how you murdered my dad, for example?'

Chloe stared at me. 'What are you talking about, Jake?'

'Sentinel knows what I'm talking about – he's been keeping the truth from both of us.'

'Yes, maybe I have, and maybe I should have told you both the full truth sooner, but you also don't know all the key facts yet, Jake.'

'Like the fact I just saw my dad stuck like a bug in a glass paperweight? That tells me all I need to know, you murdering son of a bitch.'

Chloe spread her hands wide. 'I don't know what's going on

here, but can you carry on this conversation later?' She pointed back at the woods.

Above the treeline, a bank of inky fog was sweeping towards us.

I moved towards a rear door. Murderer or not, Sentinel was our only way out of here. 'One of you will need to be in the driver's seat,' Sentinel said when Chloe followed me.

'But why – you drove the car here, right?' Chloe replied.

'Yes, but this car's autopilot is designed for normal driving and we don't have time for that. One of you will have to drive – I will tell you exactly what you need to do and when.'

'I can't drive because I twisted my ankle after that leap,' Chloe said.

'Your self-healing ability will be able to deal with that in ten minutes,' Sentinel said.

I clamped down the cold fury with the AI blazing inside me. I might be beyond exhausted but I wouldn't let Chloe get hurt because of my fight with Sentinel.

'Let me drive, Chloe. I've had a couple of driving lessons with Allan – I'm more experienced with four wheels than two.'

'OK, thanks.'

With a scowl towards the dashboard where Sentinel's voice had come from, I dropped into the driver's seat and slammed the door behind me. Sentinel was already raising the window as we heard an engine roar round the bend. A black Range Rover sped into view, hurtling towards us.

'Fasten your seat belts, because you're going to need it, Chloe,' I said.

A 'Ludicrous mode' button flashed on the car's central console screen and I selected it. The display filled with a light speed like jump through a star field.

I selected reverse, stamped my foot down and all hell broke loose.

CHAPTER TWENTY-EIGHT

THE TESLA STARTED to veer backwards as I hung on to the steering wheel. I stared in the rear-view mirror as the Range Rover rushed towards us, a black rhino charging down its opponent.

Chloe grabbed on to a handle on the ceiling. 'They're going to ram us!'

But I had a game plan. A misspent youth playing racing games was hopefully about to pay dividends. I hauled the wheel all the way over. The view whipped round outside the car, throwing up a cloud of smoke from the tyres with a howl of rubber.

I hauled the wheel all the way back over. The Tesla started to skid in the opposite direction, throwing my body against the door in a fairground-ride whirl.

With my heart racing I flicked the steering back and the view of the world came to a stop.

Now with a clear road ahead of us, and the famous Tesla ludicrous-drive mode engaged, the car surged forward like a rocket blasting off. G-force punched me in the stomach, pinning me back against the seat.

'What in the hell was that?' Chloe shouted as she braced herself as we sped off at warp speed.

'According to the motoring shows that I studied to help me learn the controls of this vehicle, Jake just pulled off a perfect J-turn, executed even without any handbrake assistance. Very impressive. Apparently having a powerful car makes the manoeuvre easier and this Tesla is more than suitably endowed, with at least 588 horsepower and 920 foot-pounds of torque at its disposal. Far more efficient than the alternatives, thanks to all that instant torque delivered by the four 100-kilowatt electric motors in this car.'

'You sound like such a motoring geek!' Chloe said, grinning.

But I wasn't smiling as I peered at the rear-view mirror. 'However powerful this vehicle is, that Range Rover is still on our tail.'

'This road is too windy for you to outrun them,' said Sentinel. 'Take the next turning and we may find a way to lose our pursuers.'

I didn't bother to reply but tightened my grip on the wheel. A dirt track entrance shot towards us.

I waited until we were almost alongside it before spinning the wheel over. The car screeched into a sideways skid, smoke pouring from the tyres and filling the Tesla's cabin with the smell of burning rubber. The closest I'd ever got to anything like this were those racing games, but they lacked one key thing: the G-force currently trying to tear the organs from my body.

'Closing off external vents,' Sentinel said.

Chloe clung on to the door as the world whipped past.

I flicked the wheel back and we veered on to the track, bouncing in our seats as we sped along the bumpy surface through woodland.

'How is this a good idea, Sentinel?' I shouted. 'This is a road vehicle, not a bloody rally car. Their Range Rover is much better suited to this type of driving.'

'Trust me.'

'How am I meant to do that after what you've done, hey?' I caught Chloe's quizzical look.

Sentinel didn't respond.

The Range Rover raced up the steepening track behind us. The world blurred as we burst out of the wood and hurtled across an open field towards the summit. Sentinel gunned the engine harder and the digital rev-needle spun towards the boost section of the round dial.

I glanced in the rear-view mirror at the Range Rover, which, as I'd feared, was coping with the uneven road far better than the Tesla. Despite our power advantage the other vehicle was less than twenty metres away.

'Look out!' Chloe shouted.

When I glanced forward again I spotted the hedge hurtling towards us and...the edge of the cliff beyond. Then I knew exactly where we were. There was an old quarry beyond that hedgerow and we were about to drop straight into it.

I heaved the wheel over and the car spun on the damp grass. I straightened the wheel as I stamped on the brakes and we skidded to a stop, pointing back down the hill as the electric motors whispered to silence.

The supercharged Range Rover was going way too fast to stop in time. It screamed past and crashed straight through the hedgerow into the empty air beyond.

I watched in the rear-view mirror as everything seemed to happen in slow motion: the mud kicking out from the spinning tyres as the vehicle flew over the edge, the stream of the exhaust arcing down like a plane's smoke trail, the glow of its rear lights dropping away like two red demon eyes into the deep gorge. The car disappeared from sight and two seconds later my gut clenched as the sound of metal and glass crashing into rock reached us.

More silence.

I flinched as a ball of fire blossomed up from the gorge, a glowing jellyfish rising into the sky. The roar of the explosion gradually rolled away across the landscape.

Chloe and I climbed out of the car and walked to the quarry edge, which, in an earlier long-lost life, Dad had always banned me from going anywhere near. We gazed at the wreck burning far below us.

'Those guys didn't stand a chance,' I said.

'You've got to start changing how you think about them, Jake,' Chloe said. 'Those *guys* were trying to kill us, or at least the Shade inside them were.'

'I'm having a hard time seeing it that way.' My vision shimmered and the world shifted to black and white.

Chloe clutched her skull and winced. 'My thermal vision just kicked in.'

'Mine too. And when it does that...'

'But those guys, Shade or not, aren't about to get out of that car wreck alive...' Her face paled and she pointed past me.

A huge bank of inky fog billowed up from the direction of the old science park, like a volcano erupting darkness. The anvil-shaped cloud began to spread out and flow over the surrounding countryside. I spotted smaller points of movement within the bowed wave of fog.

Shadow crows...thousands and thousands of them.

'Enough already,' Chloe whispered.

We exchanged worried frowns as we jumped back in the Tesla.

I began to turn the car round, the steering wheel slick beneath my hands.

A few minutes later, we were hurtling away along the main road again. In the transformed world of the Shadowlands the wispy fog had grown to a black tsunami that was busy swallowing up the landscape behind us.

The Tesla's headlights flicked on, beams stabbing out through the gathering gloom and carving a corridor of light ahead of us. Something black flicked past the car and my senses became pin-sharp.

'I think one of their scouts just found us,' Chloe whispered. She looked as scared as I felt inside.

'You saw something?' Sentinel asked.

'A shadow crow,' I replied.

'OK, this will be the start of their attack,' Sentinel said.

'We're not going to stand a chance, Chloe,' I said.

She didn't reply.

I glanced across to see that Chloe was shaking.

'Are you OK?'

'I have this hot feeling building in my stomach.'

'That's how I felt when I brought those trees to life,' I said.

'Your subconscious is giving you the tools to fight the Shade, so just let it flow through you...' Sentinel said.

'Flow...' Chloe whispered.

Maybe we did stand a chance. That was if I didn't get us both killed.

I glanced at the speedo as the world blurred past us: 140 mph and still climbing.

Around us the dark fog lapped around the car, plunging the outside world into a swirling black maelstrom filled with the Shade.

My eyes clung to the only place left clear – the lit path created by the car's headlights. The creatures seemed to be avoiding that area for some reason.

A shriek of claw on metal came from the car's roof.

I feathered the brakes as we approached a bend, swerved us round it and then accelerated us on to a long straight.

The speedometer spun past 160 mph and I was pressed back into the seat. In the far distance I could make out a fire blazing beyond a ridge of hills. I felt a stab of anguish. That was Stoneham, or what remained of it. At least Chloe being in a trance meant I could spare her that particular revelation for a bit longer.

A shadow crow flashed along the side windows, its razor beak screeching across the glass. And something odd seemed to be happening to the outside world – clear black gashes had started to appear around us, like claw marks across a photograph. The landscape was disappearing, slice by slice.

Chloe took a shuddering breath as every muscle in her face grew taut. 'This hurts so much, Jake,' she whispered.

I reached over and squeezed her hand. 'You can do this, Chloe.'

She screwed her eyes shut tighter. 'Yes...' Then, as if she'd been given a shock, her eyes snapped open, her pupils rolled up into her head to leave only the whites showing. Blood started trickling from her nose.

I grabbed her hand. 'Are you OK?'

'She can't hear you, Jake,' Sentinel said. 'A huge amount of psychic energy is flowing through her body and numbing all her normal senses. However, I promise you that she'll be all right.'

'Oh, one of your promises – that will be fine then.' I hung on to to my friend with one hand as she began to thrash around.

Through the view carved out by the headlights I spotted glimmering individual specks, too far away to make out, flying through the sky and closing fast. Although I was still in the Shadowlands I could instantly tell these weren't Shade birds, because each of them was a glowing point of light, the same sort of light the wood had shone with. And then the shimmering stars drew close enough to make out. These were real-life birds, thousands and thousands of them, and every sort imaginable – gulls, hawks, even normal crows – all flying straight at us.

Chloe stopped shaking. Her pupils rolled back into position and she blinked at me. 'Jake?'

'Are you all right?'

'Apart from an Everest-sized headache, I think so.' Her eyes widened at the birds rushing towards us. 'Where did they come from?'

'I think this is your doing, Chloe,' I said.

She slowly nodded. 'I was connected to them for a moment – I could feel the minds of all those birds. Utterly amazing and impossible at the same time. But I still don't see how they can help us, Sentinel?'

'Opportunities multiply as they are seized,' Sentinel replied.

'Huh?'

'A quote from Sun Tzu in his book entitled *The Art of War*.'

'And what is it meant to mean?' I asked, glowering at the dash.

'That through Chloe's action an opportunity to escape might present itself.'

Before I could hurl another question at the AI a rush of wing-beats heralded the arrival of the flock. Each and every bird, from gulls down to tiny wrens, all swooped straight into the swarm of the Shade.

A battle erupted all around us – the pulse of life versus death, light versus dark.

Thousands of starlings moved as a single body, crushing the shadow crows caught inside them. A buzzard tumbled past, its beak tearing into a shadow crow lashing out at it. Flesh-and-blood crows swooped and struck, and I even spotted a group of robins taking out a single shadow crow. But many birds died too, their lifeless bodies falling to the ground as they were sliced by shadow wings and beaks. The combat raged on every side of the car.

Chloe winced at the death of every bird, until she buried her head into her hands, sobbing.

I squeezed her shoulder.

Moment by moment our world grew steadier, with far fewer shadow creatures outside now.

'I think the birds are winning,' I said.

'They are?' Chloe unburied her head from her hands and looked out of the window.

The last of the fog swirled away behind us and, just like that, we were back in our world.

My vision shifted by itself into the Real. Jagged lines of lightning lit up the landscape as the birds, still battling the last of the Shade, fell away behind us.

Tears streamed down Chloe's face. 'It's my fault they're dying. Those birds are sacrificing themselves so we can get away.'

'No, it's not your fault,' I replied. 'You're not telling them to do this, are you?'

'I don't think so.'

'So it's like what happened for me back in the woods. I initiated the trees moving, but when that sapling skewered that guy it was beyond my control.'

Chloe clenched her hands into fists. 'Exactly what I was trying to tell you.'

'I know...'

Heavy rain started to fall and the Tesla's wipers automatically kicked in – probably Sentinel's doing too, although I was in no mood to thank him.

We rounded a bend and finally lost sight of the battle. I pressed my head back into the seat and gazed out at the flashes of lightning illuminating the landscape. There a familiar pattern to the fields outside. The bend of a meandering river sped by.

Until then I wasn't sure where we were headed, but then it

hit me. I knew exactly where we could lie low as we worked out what the hell we were going to do next.

I turned left at the next country road. After a few minutes, it came into view: a cottage with an ivy-covered observatory standing at one side.

My old home.

CHAPTER TWENTY-NINE

Accompanied by the boom of distant thunder our car crunched to a halt on the gravel drive. I climbed out into face-stinging rain, barely registering it, my eyes too busy eating up the view of the run-down cottage I hadn't seen for years. Then anger began to burn inside my chest like a hot coal as memory after memory of Dad flooded my mind.

I turned back towards the Tesla after Chloe had got out. 'Now get away from here, Sentinel, before I set fire to the car you bloody high-jacked.'

Chloe gawped at me. 'What are you talking about, Jake? If it wasn't for Sentinel, we wouldn't have escaped from the science park.'

'And would that be the same Sentinel who betrayed me?'

Chloe's eyes narrowed. 'OK, how exactly?'

'I saw Dad's body in the lab.'

'Oh my god, Jake, I'm so sorry. No wonder you're being like this.'

'You still don't understand, Chloe...' My anger grew so fierce that I began to shake. I pointed a trembling finger towards the

Tesla. 'Sentinel murdered my dad with the precious *phase one* of his plan.'

'But I don't understand – why would he do anything like that?'

'Because he decided to shut down the DEC experiment at any cost. And that included murdering my dad and leaving the rest of the survivors to be eaten alive by the Shade while he skipped town.'

'What?!'

'You heard.'

Sentinel's voice drifted to me from the car. 'Jake, you don't understand all the—'

'Oh, I understand just bloody fine. You kept that little nugget of info from us because you knew we'd never help you if we learnt the truth.'

'You've got this so wrong, Jake – let me explain—'

'No way am I listening to any more of your lies.' I stormed towards the cottage.

Chloe started after me.

'Leave him, Chloe. Jake needs some time alone,' I heard Sentinel say.

Whatever. But as I reached the garden gate the fury that had briefly recharged me started to flow away. My whole body ached to its core, and my legs quivered as I pushed the gate open, its rusted hinges screeching in protest. Then I stepped through into a world full of memories.

Allan had never sold this place, for my sake, telling me that even though I might not think it, one day I might want to return. Going by the fact that standing here felt like someone had just ripped my heart in two, he'd been utterly wrong.

I took in the once neat flower beds that Mum had designed but were now swamped with wild grass and weeds, the white walls of the observatory that'd greened beneath a canopy of ivy, and the windows of the cottage boarded up. Every tiny detail was a knife thrust into my soul.

The rain drummed down on my head and I wiped back the soaked hair from my eyes. With every sinew of my body feeling wrung out I bent down to search through the overgrown flower bed.

My fingers brushed against something smooth. I picked up a cracked flowerpot covered in snails, flipped the pot over and removed an old brass key hidden inside – Dad's secret hiding spot.

I slid the key into the lock and, with a grinding snick, it opened. As I pushed the door mottled storm-light spilled into the dark house.

The last time I'd seen this place...

The old ache pulsed inside me and I gripped my watch.

I stepped over the threshold into the cottage. Memory after memory flooded back, so intense I found it hard to breathe. The bannister I used to slide down when I thought Dad wasn't looking. The laughter that had filled this hallway as I ambushed Dave and Chloe with a water pistol when they'd come over for dinner. The smell of burned toast that always seemed to greet me when I came down for breakfast.

I took in my surroundings, each detail leaving a claw mark on my heart. The Christmas tree still up – it looked as if no one had been back here since the moment Dad had died and I'd left the house to go and live with Allan. The old grandfather clock stood frozen, the last wind that Dad had given it long run out. An old green pair of wellies – the ones that fitted my twelve-year-old self – stood by the door. Six years of pain wrapped up in the scene before me: a museum to my old life, one covered in cobwebs and dust.

I closed the door behind me and shut the storm squall out.

Sentinel was right about one thing: I needed time alone, even away from Chloe.

The quiet of the house enveloped me like a blanket. A new feeling of peace started to push through the other emotions and, much to my surprise, I felt my muscles relax, the fire inside me spluttering out. It might be abandoned but the old cottage still felt like my real home.

Lost in the past, I started to walk upstairs, each step creaking under my feet. When I reached the landing I didn't stop at my old room but kept going towards the closed door at the end of the corridor. As I pushed it open a boulder filled my throat.

Thin slivers of lightning glow sneaked between the planks boarding the windows and cast ribbons of light across Dad's study.

I crossed to his coffee-ring-stained desk and ran my finger over the worn surface. I pictured him working there, his head bent over a laptop screen filled with the long equations he'd pored over almost every night.

I sat down on his worn office chair. Dad's fountain pen lay to the side of a yellowing pad filled with random doodles. He'd always insisted on using this pen because Mum had bought it for him the Christmas before she died in the car crash. And even though it had always leaked and stained his fingers with ink that pen had been one of Dad's most precious memories of her.

I pushed a foot against the floor and slowly spun round in the chair a couple of times, tilting my head back to look at the ceiling. I screwed up my eyes, trying to blot out the image of Dad's face – frozen in amber – that I'd seen in the lab. At last the tears started to trickle down my cheeks and I let the grief come. Fast racking breaths rose from my core.

I leant forward and pushed my head into my folded arms on the desk. Gradually the flow of my grief slowed as I breathed in the smell of old leather, ink and wood. Limbs heavy, thoughts cobwebbed, I closed my eyes.

'Can you see all those stars in that globular cluster?' Dad asked me inside our observatory.

I raised my head from the eyepiece. 'It's incredible...'

Like a mirror shattering the grey world rushed back in, flushing my dream away. I was back in Dad's study and someone was shaking me.

'What's going on?' I asked.

'You need to wake up,' Chloe said. She was holding a lit candle in one hand and a steaming mug of tea in the other. She handed it to me and explained, 'I gave you as long as I could, but we need to talk urgently.'

I took a sip and almost gagged on the sweetness. 'Are you trying to poison me?'

'I thought the extra sugar would give you an energy kick.'

'Tastes like you put most of the bowl in.'

She crinkled her nose at me.

'How long have I been out?'

'Just a couple of hours. You looked so wasted that we thought you needed it.'

'We?'

'Yeah, even if you're not talking to our mutual friend, I still am.'

'I wouldn't waste your breath on that lying piece of silicon.'

Chloe held up her hands. 'Jake, you need to chill the attitude a bit and hear him out.' There was something unreadable behind her eyes.

'*Nothing* he can say will stop me hating his guts.'

She shrugged and waggled her fingers towards me.

I let her pull me to my feet.

We headed downstairs, but rather than go out through the front door Chloe herded me left into the kitchen.

I paused at the threshold. 'Aren't we going to talk to Sentinel out in the Tesla?'

'No need,' Chloe replied. 'We just had an Amazon delivery of a shiny new laptop. The courier who dropped it off looked really confused – he thought this place had been deserted for years.'

'Don't tell me, Sentinel hacked Amazon?'

'Yep. And think of all the possibilities that could bring.'

'A life of cybercrime isn't quite what I signed up for.'

'So you still want to save the world and all that?'

My eyes slid away from hers and I shrugged.

'Right, get in there.' She shoved me into the kitchen.

The room was bathed in a glow from an old storm-lantern set up on the table. An old camping stove had a kettle heating up over its blue flame.

Chloe gestured towards it. 'We found that when I hid the Tesla in the garage.'

'Yeah, our old camping gear. But why hide the Tesla?'

'It was Chloe's idea of an insurance policy,' Sentinel said from the laptop open on the kitchen table.

I felt a pulse of anger at hearing his voice again.

'Those Genesis guys in the Range Rover probably phoned in a description of our car before they crashed – they'll have people out looking for it,' Chloe said.

I nodded, dragged a chair out and dropped down on to it. I crossed my arms and stared at Sentinel's avatar face as Chloe took the chair next to me.

'You look upset, Jake,' Sentinel said.

I snorted. 'I'd like to smash you to tiny pieces with a hammer and set fire to the bits just to make sure. So yes, you could say I'm *upset.*'

'I can understand why, but what you don't understand—'

I thumped the table hard enough to make the laptop jump. 'What don't I understand, Sentinel? That you were just following orders – that Dad's death, and sacrificing all those others in the science park, was a price worth paying to stop the Shade?'

'Jake, please listen to me. It wasn't like that.'

'Then tell me what it *was* like, Sentinel.'

'We'll get to that, but for you to fully understand what I'm about to explain we briefly need to discuss what happened at the science park. To start with Chloe tells me that you both experienced a time dilation effect around the lab?'

I glowered at him. 'Yes, it increased the nearer I got to the lab and decreased as we left.'

'That confirms that my zero-point energy field is still intact, although it must be starting to leak for you to have experienced what you did.'

Despite my anger Sentinel had my attention. 'What are you talking about?'

'Jake, how long do you think you were at the lab from the moment you entered the anomaly?'

'An hour, maybe two?'

'Actually, you have both been missing for over a week.'

'What? You never told me that,' Chloe said.

'We had a lot of other things to discuss.'

Chloe shot Sentinel's avatar a hint of a smile. What was going on with her? And why wasn't she as furious with him as I was?

'I thought it might be a singularity, something like that?' I said with a shrug.

'I can see why you might have guessed that,' Sentinel said.

'But what did you see when you reached the lab itself?'

I clenched my fists. 'A piece of glass with my dad's body trapped inside, and you should know that, you murdering piece of crap, because you stuck him in there.'

The avatar's expression remained impassive. 'I see...'

The corners of Chloe's mouth curled upwards. 'Jake, please listen to him.'

I waved my hands on the screen. 'Go on then, justify yourself. I can't wait to hear your spin on this.'

'In the science fiction genre that you're so fond of have you ever come across something called a stasis field?'

'Sure. It's an energy field that freezes time.'

'Just so. And the transition between the area contained within the sphere and your normal space-time has the appearance of opaque glass. It's also impenetrable because of that time difference. In other words, it effectively becomes a force field.'

The smile that Chloe had been doing her best to hide was growing.

'Hang on, you're not saying...that you froze time inside that thing?'

'That's exactly what I'm saying. By reprogramming the DEC before the Shade were able to fully open the portal I was able to create a bubble of time that halted everything at the very moment of the explosion.'

Chloe was practically jiggling on her feet. 'Think of it as hitting the pause button on reality, Jake.'

'But that would mean...' I could see impossible hope for me in Chloe's face. I suddenly couldn't breathe, sensing I was about to learn something that would change my life for ever.

'If a stasis field really can freeze time, it would mean Dad is st-still...' I stammered, and finally managed, 'still alive?'

'Yes, he is,' Sentinel replied as emotionless as if he were telling me the sky was blue.

Chloe dashed past the table and threw her arms round me. 'I'm so happy for you, Jake Stevens.'

Every emotion seemed to run through me at once. All these years of inner torment had been based on something that had never been true. Those feelings of utter loss, of being alone, of my dad being snatched away, and now I was being told that it wasn't true? It was like my entire life was a snow globe that someone had just furiously shaken and everything I thought I knew was now swirling around me in a blizzard.

'Dad is really alive? Inside that glass paperweight?'

Chloe kissed me, her eyes burning with joy, shaking my hands with hers as tears rolled down her face. 'Yes!'

This was really happening. I felt a slow goofy grin fill my own face. I stared at Sentinel. I could barely bring myself to ask the question because it meant so much to me. 'And is there a way to...?'

'Yes, Jake, there is a way to bring him back.'

I gasped, then whooped and was soon twirling around the room with Chloe, who was grinning at me like a mad thing.

'I am so happy for you, Jake,' she shouted again.

I breathed in and gazed at the avatar on the screen as guilt flooded my mind. 'It seems I owe you one humungous apology, Sentinel. Although maybe I wouldn't have had a meltdown if you'd just told us all of this in the first place.'

Sentinel was quiet for a moment, then his avatar frowned. 'I'm sorry, Jake, and you're right of course. However, I can assure you my intentions were noble. Until I was certain about the integrity of the stasis field I didn't want to build up your hopes that your father might still be alive. I was also concerned that if the Shade captured you...'

'I would tell them everything if I was captured? A need-to-know basis, right?'

'Very much so. You couldn't tell them what you didn't know.'

I breathed out through my nose. 'And you were probably trying to protect me.' I glanced at Chloe. 'Like I was trying to protect you from the revelation you were an Awoken.'

Chloe hugged me. 'Sentinel meant well and so did you, Mr Stevens.'

'Although, like Dad used to say, the road to hell is paved with good intentions, hey?'

'Maybe they are.' She pulled away from me and, arms outstretched, held my shoulders. 'So let's make each other a promise right here, right now. No holding things back any more. You've seen how that worked out for us. The whole truth and nothing but the truth. And that includes you, Sentinel.'

'Agreed,' he said.

'Agreed,' I added. I started to pick through my memories of the lab. 'So what about the enchanted wood routine around the science park, Sentinel? Was that your doing too?'

'No, that was an unexpected consequence of your planet trying to heal the scar that the DEC experiment created.'

'Heal itself?' Chloe said. 'You're making the planet sound alive.'

'In a very real sense it is. I realise that the human race considers itself to be the pinnacle of intelligence on this planet, but what that view fails to take into account is that you are all part of one single ecosystem that is Earth. Your planet does its best to maintain ideal conditions for life. I've read some human theories that even argue that the ecosystem is doing its best to fight the man-made global warming that is happening at the moment.'

'So you're saying that the forest thing around the science park is the equivalent of Earth creating white blood cells to fight an infection?' I asked.

'I think that's an excellent comparison, Jake, and probably a good explanation for what you witnessed.'

'I know trees are alive, but this...' Chloe said.

'All I know is I feel as if someone has just put my brain through a blender,' I said.

Chloe smiled. 'Then that makes two of us.'

'I know it's a lot to take on board in a short amount of time, but it is the truth, albeit a reality-redefining one,' Sentinel said.

I gazed at the AI. 'So you basically saved our planet when you created that stasis field.'

'For a while, yes. It was the only option left to me to stop the portal opening and to save your father's life. Of course, the moment I did that, I revealed my presence to the Shade. They destroyed the computer systems I'd installed myself on, and I only just managed to escape by uploading myself to the Varuna satellite that was due to launch later that same day.'

Sentinel closed his eyes. His nostrils flared before he opened them again. 'And I had no idea what the Shade would do to the remaining survivors until they started to circulate the story about them all dying in the explosion. I knew they would try to hush up what had happened, but they obviously killed them all to make sure no word got out...' He trailed off.

AI or not, the guy before me looked broken. I could only begin to imagine what that knowledge was like to live with. 'I've seen what the Shade can do. This one wasn't on you, Sentinel – this is on the Shade, and no one else.'

'Thank you for your kind words, Jake. Maybe I might believe them one day.'

'Maybe you can start to forgive yourself when we rescue Dad and destroy the lab once and for all,' I said.

'So we're back on our save-the-world plan then?' Chloe asked.

'Definitely, but first, there are things I saw inside the lab that I need to tell you both about. Then we can start to formulate a plan.' I took Chloe's hands in mine. 'First, starting with your dad...'

It had taken some time for Chloe's tears to stop, especially after Sentinel had told her that the man she knew as her dad was already effectively dead and couldn't be brought back. Now she looked lost. My joy at finding out Dad was alive already felt like a distant memory.

As I held her hand and the waves of grief had hit her I'd brought Sentinel up to speed with what I'd witnessed.

I leant towards the laptop screen as Chloe stared off into the middle distance. 'I saw them pouring a huge amount of energy on to the surface of that stasis field, Sentinel.'

'That would explain why the time dilation effect is starting to leak out of the lab,' Sentinel replied. 'It also indicates that they are getting close to breaking through it and exposing the portal trapped inside. No wonder they have been abducting all those people to work on the machine – their end goal is in sight and they can afford to move less cautiously.'

'But I don't get it. Surely if they've taken over Langton then they have no end of people they could use for this – top scientists, the military – so why snatch local people?'

'Because the Shade's leadership, under Dave's direction, only needed people with core skills, such as engineers, electricians, plumbers and others to help build the thing,' Sentinel replied. 'Also, over a long enough period people's minds literally burn out. And at that point, the Shade convert their bodies to an energy source that allows them to multiply. I hate to say it, but the local people were seen as less valuable assets.'

Chloe eyes swivelled towards the laptop screen. 'Gavin? Can we save him at least?'

Of course she was thinking about Gavin.

'You asked me to tell you the truth from now on, and to hold nothing back, so here it is,' Sentinel replied. 'Based on what the

Shade did to everyone who was still at the science park on the night of the explosion, they will almost certainly kill all of the current workers when the new DEC has been completed.'

Chloe jumped up and paced across the room, hands on her head. 'We can't let that happen.' She crossed to the boarded window, braced her arms on the sink and hung her head between them.

In that moment I wanted nothing more than to take her pain away, to tell her it would be all OK. But it would have been a lie. I knew no such thing.

The sound of a car crunching over gravel fractured the silence.

My stomach started churning. 'Genesis?'

Chloe stared through a gap in the planks. 'No, relax – it's Allan's Volvo.'

'But how did he know we'd be here?' I asked.

'That would be down to me, and if it wasn't for your uncle's help, Jake, I wouldn't be here now,' Sentinel said. 'Do you remember the memory stick you took that contained all of Dave's DEC files?'

'Yes, what about it? I gave that to Allan for evidence, in case something happened to me.'

'And it's just as well you did. I included a fractal algorithm on that memory stick too, an added insurance measure. When Allan plugged in the memory stick the algorithm, after not hearing back from the fragment of my consciousness installed on Chloe's phone, reassembled my code from the data subsets I'd scattered across the internet. When I regained consciousness the first thing I did was to make contact with Allan and brief him fully about what had happened. It did, however, take me a while to convince him that I was not some sort of elaborate hoax.'

I snorted. 'I bet it did.'

'Thankfully Allan eventually realised I was telling him the

truth. And then when he learnt how you had both been helping me, and what was actually at stake, he promised to assist us in any way he could.'

The back door banged open and wind bellowed into the kitchen. Allan stood there, arms loaded with takeaway bags, a shopping basket dangling from his right hand. He pushed the door shut with his back and dropped the food on to the table.

Allan's eyes locked on to us. 'Thank god you're both OK. A whole week without a word and I've been worried sick.'

'A week?' Chloe replied. 'Oh – the effect of the stasis field.'

Allan peered at her.

Chloe gestured towards me. 'Anyway, I'm only alive because of this amazing man.'

He beamed at me. 'Well done, lad.'

A loud meow came from Allan's basket and Toby pushed his head up from beneath a blanket.

Chloe rushed over, lifted the cat out of the basket and hugged him hard. 'How could I ever have forgotten about you?' Toby purred so loudly his whole body shook.

At least Chloe had one small anchor still in her life that hadn't been ripped away by the Shade.

'I told you Jake I was going to honour Chloe's memory back in the railway car park during the evacuation.'

'You did.'

'Well I remember from when you were a little girl, Chloe, just how much this cat means to you?' Allan said. 'And just as well I managed to slip away during the evacuation long enough to grab him, with what happened to Stoneham.'

'Why, what happened?' Chloe asked.

I gazed at her, my joy swirling like Shade mist. 'Chloe, there's another thing we need to tell you...'

CHAPTER THIRTY

It was astonishing the kitchen table didn't bend under the sheer weight of Thai food balancing on top of it. Every available surface around the kitchen seemed to be filled with foil boxes that we'd helped ferry in from Allan's ancient Volvo estate. In any other situation I would have said he'd over-ordered. But I'd soon discovered that, despite shovelling the food into my mouth like I was feeding a furnace, it was barely scratching the bottomless feeling in my stomach. Chloe seemed just as ravenous and had hardly stopped to breathe between mouthfuls.

But Sentinel reassured us that this desperate I'm-never-going-to-feel-full-ever-again feeling would pass as the mutations to our DNA started to ease off, although I wasn't so sure.

As Chloe and I refuelled we told Allan everything that had happened since we'd last seen him. He scowled and shook his head when he heard about Dave, and then had given me a vice-like hug when he heard his younger brother was still alive.

Finally I pushed my scraped-clean plate away. 'Thanks for all the takeaway, Allan. I think it would be an understatement to say that we both needed that food.'

Chloe swallowed a last bite of a spring roll and let Toby out – he'd been pawing at the door. 'You, Allan Stevens, have officially achieved sainthood in my book.'

He made a scoffing noise. 'I'm not sure I'm quite what the pope sees as saint material.'

'Especially after this new life of stealing cars, hey?' I said.

Allan cast a scowl towards Sentinel's avatar on the laptop. 'I'm still not sure quite how that AI persuaded me to visit the showroom over in Bristol and take that Tesla for a test drive.'

A lightning flash came from outside. More than ten seconds later, a rumble of thunder pounded the air.

Chloe cast a frown towards the window before returning her attention to us. 'Yeah, Sentinel can be persuasive like that. But how did you pull the heist off?'

Allan gave Chloe *the look* – the one that he normally only used on me to end an argument. 'Sentinel told me to plug the memory stick that Jake gave me into the car's dash and he would do the rest.'

I winked at Chloe. 'Then what – you pushed the dealer out of the car door at the next set of lights?'

Allan set his scowl to stun. 'No...when we got back to the showroom I headed off to do the next thing on Sentinel's list.'

'What, steal an aeroplane?'

Allan tapped the side of his nose.

I raised my chin towards Sentinel. 'Just what did you get my uncle doing?'

'I'm afraid it's on a need-to-know basis,' the avatar replied.

'You mean in case we get captured by the Shade?'

'That's right.'

'OK, I understand,' I replied.

'But talk about leading someone astray, Sentinel,' Chloe said. 'And Allan a god-fearing man too.'

Allan raised his eyebrows at her. 'You will return it, Sentinel, right?'

'That entirely depends on what happens over the next forty-eight hours.'

'Why, what happens then?'

'We're going to attempt to close the portal once and for all,' he replied.

It was as if someone had suddenly thrown a mood switch, as everyone's expressions grew serious.

Allan cast a glance at Chloe and me. 'You're both in real danger, aren't you?'

'We all are, Allan,' I said.

'So what's the next step?' Chloe asked.

Allan gestured to Sentinel. 'You will need to ask our mutual friend here.'

'On my advice Allan gave the memory device with the DEC evidence on it to Clarke, to warn him how high the conspiracies went.'

'And he believed you?' I asked Allan.

'I think when the authorities labelled you as a terrorist, Jake, Clarke had already started to smell a decomposing rat,' Allan replied. 'Then there was Stoneham being levelled to the ground by a massive fertiliser-based bomb that you supposedly built in our backyard, and his police officers being frozen out of Genesis's sweep of the town. Those things made him more than sceptical about the official version of events.'

On the laptop screen Sentinel nodded. 'I also sent the inspector all manner of news links highlighting the inconsistencies in the official versions of what happened at the science park.'

'And showing Clarke the material you had retrieved from Dave's computer clinched the deal,' Allan said. 'He's already started gathering a group of officers he knows he can trust and that Sentinel has already vetted for him.'

'Once Clarke receives my signal he'll lead a raid on the science park and try to rescue the people who've been possessed,' Sentinel said.

'That's where we come in, right?' Chloe said.

Sentinel nodded. 'That's correct—'

A deafening clap of thunder ripped the air over the cottage, shaking the walls with the blast, the white light fading to crimson outside.

'That sounded like a direct hit,' Allan said.

Chloe and I raced to the back door and threw it open.

Huge flames leapt up from a large horse chestnut tree near the house. A branch had already toppled from it on to the old observatory, flattening its dome roof.

I put my hands on my head. 'Oh shit!'

Chloe and I ran towards the observatory, but the beams of headlights stabbed out behind us. We turned to see a red Mini rushing down the lane, and with a spray of gravel it skidded to a stop.

Gavin climbed out of the car, his expression blank.

Chloe and I just stared.

'So we have found you at last, Awoken,' Gavin said. 'And I have been sent with a proposal for both of you.'

I exchanged a tight look with Chloe. 'What sort of proposal?' I asked.

'To join yourselves to us, as others have already pledged, before the world that you know is consumed within the next hour. Only friends of the Shade will be spared the purge.'

Knots twisted through my stomach as Gavin looked between us with eyes full of shadows. 'There is no point in you throwing your lives away, Chloe and Jake. Your abilities could be useful to us. Imagine the potential of an Awoken joined to the Shade. No world, no universe would be able to stand in our way.'

'Go to hell!' Chloe shouted back at him.

'If that is your wish...' Gavin raised his arms and a fog bank rose up over the treeline. It fell over the cottage as Allan watched us from the doorway, walking stick clenched in his hand, then the whole area was reduced to a swirling mass of grey and I lost sight of him.

As a chill bit into the air I shifted into the Shadowlands to see what was really going on.

Within the infrared spectrum I could see just enough through the dark haze of the fog to spot the black silhouettes of hundreds of shadow crows flying towards the cottage.

I grabbed Chloe's hand, pulled her back into the kitchen and slammed the door shut behind us, my heart pounding against my ribcage.

And now we were trapped inside the cottage with no way to escape.

CHAPTER THIRTY-ONE

The wind snarled up outside as I threw the bolts across the back door. With a screech, it started to bend inwards, the wood groaning under a sudden assault of what sounded like hundreds of shadow claws on the other side.

Allan paled. 'Is that the Shade?'

'Yes, and that door won't keep them out for long,' Chloe said.

I grabbed the heavy old dresser. 'Help me with this!'

Together we shoved the dresser up against the door, which was bouncing and rattling in its frame.

Chloe stared around the room. 'Where's Toby?'

'Oh crap. He must still be outside.'

'But what if the Shade catch him?'

'I'm sure he'll make himself scarce,' Allan replied.

Chloe pressed her fingers to her mouth. 'But, Allan...'

'You can't go out there to find him with the Shade prowling around – they are after us, not a cat,' I said.

She nodded. 'But how did they find us?'

'My guess is that they followed Allan here,' Sentinel said.

Allan tucked his chin in. 'This is my fault?'

'No, this is my mistake for not anticipating they'd be watching you as a way to locate Jake and Chloe.'

The dresser rattled against the shuddering door.

With a scream of metal the hinges bent back and the back door slammed into the dresser. It started to tip over, but I rammed my shoulder into it and managed to right it. 'We need to brace this somehow.'

Allan grabbed a chair and shoved it at an angle under one of the drawer handles.

A cracking sound echoed from the hallway.

'Shit. It sounds like they're trying to get in through the front door now,' Chloe shouted.

I glanced at the flimsy internal door leading out of the kitchen to the hallway. That would last seconds under a Shade attack. There had to be a way to reinforce it too.

My gaze fell on the kitchen table. 'Quick, give me a hand, Chloe.'

I left Allan leaning against the dresser as we upended the table and pushed it up hard to the door. A shattering crash came from the hallway.

'Brace yourself, Chloe.'

We both pushed against the table as the door bucked against it. The beat of wings grew to a roaring bellow around the house – the sound of a hundred nightmare creatures all desperate to destroy us. The planks over the windows began splintering and dark flicking claws raked at the gaps between. The dresser threatened to tip again as Allan slipped.

We couldn't hold out much longer.

I felt a strange tingle deep in my gut and intense heat began to build inside me.

Chloe gasped. 'It's like my body is suddenly on fire.'

'This could be your Awoken ability to defend yourselves kicking in,' Sentinel said.

The heat travelled through me, along my arms and into my hands. But my body felt OK, like all I had to do was focus. I ignored the thumping of my heartbeat in my ears and concentrated on the pulse of energy that flowed down my arms and into my hands. A miniature star burst into life between my palms.

'What on Earth?' Allan said, staring at it and blinking.

'You have created pure plasma,' Sentinel said.

I nodded as astonishment rose through me. 'This certainly feels like something we can destroy the Shade with.'

Chloe clutched her stomach and groaned.

'Chloe, focus your energy between your hands,' I said.

She bit her lip and nodded. The ridges in her forehead smoothed out as a burning blue plasma ball appeared between her palms and she gawped at it in wonder. 'Shit, this is seriously incredible.'

I knew deep within my bones exactly what to do and how to use this mini star as a weapon. Allan, Dad and the whole population of our planet were dependent on what we did next. It was time to take the fight to the Shade.

'OK, Allan – when I say "go" you jump clear,' I said. 'Leave Chloe and me to deal with whatever is trying to get through that door.'

'I'm certain you can do this, Jake,' Sentinel said.

'We all believe in you,' Allan added.

A lump filled my throat. These guys, Sentinel too, were my friends, my family, and I was going to do everything I could to protect them.

'Chloe, are you ready?'

She gave me the widest smile, like somehow she knew this would be OK, that she believed in us. And maybe I really was starting to believe as well – especially in myself again, after all these years.

'Just trust your instincts,' Sentinel said.

'We will,' I replied. 'OK – three, two, one... Go, Allan!'

He stepped aside. At once the dresser tipped over fully, revealing the shredded back door as it flew open.

For a split second I found myself staring across the kitchen through the doorway at a wall of shadow crows rushing towards us. But already my instincts were mentally pushing my plasma ball out and away from me – Chloe doing the same. I felt a sort of snapping sensation in my stomach as the plasma spark broke free of me.

Our two stars shot out from us towards the Shade, quickly expanding into burning balls of energy. The two projectiles carved straight into the shadow crow flock, disintegrating the ones they hit in a shower of sparks. Flames leapt out, burning away the rest of the Shade that had been packed in behind them.

Already Chloe was forming a new spark in her hands as the interior kitchen door bounced against the table.

I let the energy flow once more and my man-made star started to blaze again. 'Let's serve it up to them nice and hot, Chloe.'

'Just how they like it.'

We jumped aside from the table and spun round. Without us bracing it, the table shot across the room and the internal door flew open. We let our sparks fly out to meet the swarm of Shade coming through it. A wave of heat washed over us and cinders drifted through the hallway where a moment before at least a hundred shadow crows had been.

Silence.

'Is that it? Is it over?' Allan said.

'No, it's just the beginning,' Sentinel replied. 'That was just a probing scout attack so they can assess Jake and Chloe's Awoken powers and how they are able to defend us. The Shade will have fallen back for a moment before they attempt to try again, and probably in greater numbers next time.'

'So what do we do now?' Chloe asked.

'We get to the science park and join up with Inspector Clarke and his men,' I replied. 'It's time to end this.'

'You're absolutely right, Jake,' Sentinel said. 'Allan, contact the inspector to let him know he should commence the operation straightaway. Then head off to the rendezvous point and get everything ready for a hasty departure. Meanwhile, I will transfer myself back to the Tesla to help Jake and Chloe in any way I can.'

'Hold your horses,' Allan replied. 'I've never been one for running away from a fight.'

'I know that, Allan, but I need you to do what we discussed,' Sentinel replied. 'We haven't got time to argue about this. The Shade will be massing again for another attack, not to mention the fact that as far as we know Gavin is still outside.'

'Gavin wouldn't hurt me,' Chloe said.

'I'm afraid he very much will if that's what the Shade inside him decide to do.'

Chloe's jaw tightened but she nodded.

We both ignited fresh stars.

'Hey, I almost forgot – you'll need this,' Allan said. He crossed over to me and, with my hands occupied with my mini blue sun between them, slipped a memory stick into my jean pocket.

'What am I meant to do with that?' I asked.

'When you get to the science park you need you to plug the memory stick into one of the computer consoles in the lab,' Sentinel said. 'Then I will see what I can do to shut down their new DEC experiment.'

I nodded as Chloe and I took up positions ahead of Allan to guard him, and together we all stepped out of the back door.

The air caught in my throat as I took in the shocking view with my thermal vision. Thousands of shadow crows spiralled around the house, but at least they were keeping their distance for now. Gavin stood before the cottage like a clockwork man whose spring had run down.

The air hissed between Chloe's teeth. 'What are they waiting for?'

'I'm not sure,' I replied.

The birds switched direction and I instinctively raised my hands, ready to blast them away. Instead they swirled down to the ground next to Gavin to form a man.

Langton gazed at us with a thin smile.

Chloe gasped and pointed to what he was holding in his arms. 'Toby!'

The cat struggled to get free of his vice-like grip, hissing and spitting at the man.

'Let him go!' Chloe shouted.

Langton gestured with his chin towards Gavin. 'I did try asking you nicely, but that did not seem to work. So now I am resorting to emotional blackmail. Join us and I will spare your precious cat, Chloe.' Toby let out a pitiful mew that snared my heart.

Chloe and I pointed our hands towards him, both ready to blast our prime minister from the surface of the planet.

'If either of you tries anything, I promise that I will kill this cat without a second thought,' Langton said.

Chloe's spark spluttered out as her face crumpled.

Anger burned through me as I lowered my hands a fraction, but I still kept the mini star burning.

'Look, I am a reasonable man, but I am also growing impatient,' Langton said. 'The Shade have a busy night ahead, so if you surrender yourselves right now, we will spare you, even Allan. However, if you do not, the first innocent victim to die tonight will be this cat.'

'You're a monster!' Chloe shouted.

'Yes, I probably am, at least within your narrow human

perspective. Still, you must understand that for me this is just a matter of business. So with that in mind you now have five seconds to comply with my wishes before I am forced to take action.'

'You wouldn't dare,' I said.

'Oh, but you know I would.'

Chloe took another half step towards him but Allan stood in front of her.

'Five...'

Chloe's eyes bored into Allan's. 'Toby...'

'Four...'

Allan spread his hands wide.

'I am so sorry, Chloe...' I said.

'Three...'

Every instinct screamed at me to stop was about to happen.

'Shoot Langton, Chloe,' I whispered. 'We've got no other choice.'

'Two...' Langton called out.

Chloe shot me a broken look but I could see she was relenting.

Like a gunslinger going for a draw, I left it until the last moment to raise my hands. I looked across, and Chloe mirrored my pose, her eyes glistening.

Our two spheres of plasma hurtled towards Langton, but before they hit he broke apart into Shade birds and swirled to one side. Now Toby struggled in the birds' grip. Our two suns blazed harmlessly past Langton, far into the depths of the wood, as he morphed back into human form.

Langton wagged his finger at us. 'One...' He clenched his hand round Toby's neck, the man's tendons cabling.

Toby's scream ratcheted up.

A crack of bone.

Awful silence.

Chloe gasped like she'd broken the surface of water. Then she let out a wail as she fell to her knees.

I knelt by her side and held on to her as she started to shake.

'I did try to warn you,' Langton said. He let Toby's lifeless body tumble from his arms like a discarded toy to the leaf-covered ground.

My gut twisted at the sight of Toby's pink tongue sticking out between his teeth, his eyes fixed for ever on an unseen point in the distance.

Langton's form broke apart once more into a swirling mob of Shade, like crows over carrion. When they flowed away there was nothing left of the cat but stains of blood on the leaves.

Chloe rocked back like someone had punched her. 'You murderer!' She raised both hands towards Langton and threw continuous plasma bursts from her fingers towards the flock of shadow crows.

I grabbed Allan's arm. 'Get yourself to safety, please. This fight is down to Chloe and me now.'

'I wish I could help you.'

'This isn't your fight, but you can still help win the war.'

'OK.' He patted my arm and then hobbled away on his stick to his Volvo on the other side of the cottage.

Chloe sent another volley of shots into the flock that was already massing for a fresh attack.

The time for talking was over. We might be about to die, but at least we'd go down with one almighty fight.

I drew level with Chloe and raised my hands. 'For Toby,' I said.

Her eyes burned. 'For Toby.'

The chilling fog thickened around us and my nose prickled with the awful stench of it. Claws of the Shade hissed through the air, only centimetres over my head.

But Chloe had already raised her hands, plasma blazing up

directly from her fingertips, and the crow splintered apart into showering cinders.

My pulse thumped in my ears. 'I didn't even see that one coming.'

'Those murdering Shade aren't going to steal anyone else that I love today.'

Just for a moment the world stopped. Yeah, Chloe meant that much to me too. And, right there in the middle of all that awful madness, I knew that I'd do anything to protect her.

From the corner of my eye I spotted the dark spot of a crow plummeting towards Chloe's neck. An energy wave rolled through me and I punched my fist up and into the creature's head. With a hiss, the creature vaporised like an exploding firework.

Chloe gave me a nod.

With our backs together, arms outstretched, we started to blaze our way through the swirling shadows that tried to crowd in on us.

The attacks came in waves. Claws and wings loomed out of the murk again and again, but every time we fought them back with our burning balls of plasma.

I braced my legs slightly, took a deep breath and pointed both hands towards a group of crows closing on us. A tingle of energy rushed through every fibre of my body. This time a star blazed out from each hand and burned through the formation of creatures.

'How?' Chloe asked.

'I have no idea!'

All I cared about was that we were doing better than holding our own, and although the Shade were still swooping around us, and my mind felt like it would melt at any moment, there were definitely far fewer shadow creatures attacking us than before.

Still, exhaustion began to overcome both of us. Several times Chloe stumbled and I had to catch her.

But now there were only a dozen or so crows left. With a bellow these last creatures swept away into the wood.

I heard an engine start up – finally Allan could get away.

But I'd missed one. A single shadow crow swept at us, morphing into Gavin as it reached the ground. He lurched as he moved into action.

Chloe raised her hands and stared at Gavin as he rushed towards us.

'Don't make me do this,' Chloe shouted.

Gavin increased his stride.

A feeble point of light appeared between her hands and faded again.

She couldn't do this – perhaps wouldn't do this?

I stepped in front of her, because I didn't have any other choice, and sent my blast straight at Gavin's chest. At once flames blazed over him, setting his clothes on fire and burning his skin, but still he kept coming. I managed to push out my back leg to brace myself just as he crashed into me.

I felt my own hands blaze with searing pain as I locked my arms round Gavin in a bear hug and spun him away from Chloe.

She staggered back and stared at us. 'Gavin, stop!' But still his fists pounded on to my back.

Once this would have been the end of me – I would have collapsed in the face of the impossible odds. But something had shifted inside me. I was no longer afraid of Gavin, the dickhead who'd made my life a living nightmare for as long as I could remember.

I dropped, lessening my hold on him, ignoring the intense pain, and pushed off my rear leg to send him staggering backwards.

The guy might be heavier than me, but I was faster on my feet.

Before Gavin could recover his balance I jumped forward and smashed both fists into his chest. He started to topple properly now, his arms windmilling. I leapt on to him as he fell, grabbing both his arms as he smacked to the ground. As flames licked from his body I fought to keep him pinned down, while Chloe placed a hand on his arm, her face twisting as the flames danced over her hand. She extended her other hand and directed the blast of flame away, channelling it like our plasma blasts until the fire died completely.

Wisps of smoke curled up all over Gavin, his face a charred mask. He blinked at us as he continued writhing, still fighting to get free.

Chloe lowered her head to the floor so she could stare directly into his shadow-filled eyes.

'Gavin, I know you're still in there,' she whispered, tears streaming down her face.

He gave another blink.

'You've got to listen to me, Gavin. The Shade have infected you and you're not thinking straight.'

A longer blink this time.

'Remember that time I said I fancied an ice cream, so you popped out and came back with ten varieties of Ben and Jerry's?' Chloe said. 'And I was nearly sick after eating two tubs by myself?'

Gavin stilled beneath us.

I gritted my teeth at the burning pain in my hands. 'I think you're starting to get through to him, Chloe.'

She cradled Gavin's face with her palm. 'Gavin, the real Gavin inside you, needs to hear something. It wasn't Martin who killed your dad; it was the Shade. It wasn't an exploding experiment that stole your dad from you; it was the Shade who ate him alive.'

The shadows seemed to flow out of his Gavin's eyes as he focused on Chloe's. 'They killed him?'

She nodded, sprinkling her tears over him.

Gavin's expression tightened and he let out a scream – a scream of pure anguish, of a heart being ripped apart.

At once a snarl of wind whipped around us, shaking the trees.

Gavin raised his head, opening his mouth wide, pouring out black spores. Each point expanded rapidly into a shadow crow, but as quickly as they fled their human host they withered into ash, swept away by a mini hurricane that had whipped up from nowhere. With a final snarl the wind died away.

For a moment everything around became a frozen tableau: Chloe holding on to Gavin as he sobbed beneath her; the leaves settling slowly around us; the gentle rocking of the shattered back door on its hinges. It seemed like an eternity until Gavin spoke again.

'You can let go of me now,' he whispered.

We both stood, but I kept my hands tensed, ready to ignite another spark. Already the burning feeling was receding as my self-healing ability kicked in.

'It's down to you two to save this world,' Gavin said.

'We'll get to the lab and do exactly that,' Chloe said.

And in that moment Gavin was no longer my enemy. He was someone who'd suffered at the hands of the Shade – just like I had. He'd also paid for what had happened with his broken life – just like me.

'Come with us, Gavin,' I said.

'I can't. I still have some Shade left inside me – I can feel it. They're burrowing back into my brain like maggots.' He clenched his jaw, his eyes sparkling.

Chloe gently ran her fingers over his cheek. 'But I can't leave you like this.'

'You have to, princess – for me, and for the sake of our world.'

She lowered her face to his, scattering more tears, and then kissed him.

Their tenderness made my own eyes damp and I had to look away as Gavin gazed at Chloe lovingly.

She pushed herself up, gave Gavin one last broken glance and hurried away towards the garage.

I paused as Gavin twitched on the floor. 'I'm sorry, mate – I'm sorry for everything.'

'I'm sorry too, Jake.'

'None of it matters now.'

'It doesn't. Just take care of Chloe.'

'I will. Always.'

In that moment I understood everything about Gavin. The only difference between us was that he'd gone off the rails years ago and had become the bad boy of town. Without Allan in my life to help steer me maybe I would have been the same. We were more alike than I'd ever realised.

Another convulsion shook Gavin and he clutched his hands to his chest. 'Leave me alone, Shade.' He stared up at me. 'Get out of here, Jake – I can't hold them off for much longer.'

I stood, fighting every instinct screaming at me to stay with Gavin to the end.

A howl of wind came from behind me and I saw dark vapours flowing over the ground towards him.

'Go!' he hissed at me.

I backed away to the garage as the dark energy weaved around Gavin. The spores within it started spinning faster and faster around him, and I was unable to tear my gaze away. I could only watch as Gavin's outline blurred within the dark tornado of particles.

At first I thought I was seeing things as his legs and arms started to grow longer. But then his face became elongated and black fur sprouted all over his body. The black vapours slowly dissolved away into the air.

My heart stuttered as I took in the massive black wolf rising to its feet before me.

Taking on the Shade's shadow crows was one thing, but a werewolf?

I heard a massive bang and I turned to see the garage doors had exploded as the Tesla shot through them with Chloe hanging on in the passenger seat.

The car screeched to a stop next to me and I pulled the door open and jumped in.

'Time to get out of here,' Sentinel said from the dashboard. I hit the accelerator and the Tesla surged forward as the black wolf bounded towards us.

Chloe stared at the creature. 'Where did that thing come from?'

'It's Gavin.'

I swerved to avoid the creature, the Tesla's tyres kicking up a shower of gravel.

In one fluid movement the wolf gathered himself, leapt and crashed into the passenger door. Chloe shrieked as the impact shoved the car hard to the right.

'How heavy is it?' she said.

'Heavy enough to do us some serious damage,' Sentinel replied.

I hung on to the steering wheel as we accelerated away along the lane and spun the wheel to turn us on to the main road.

I glanced in the rear-view mirror at the wolf loping along after us, but he was already falling away. A werewolf would never beat a Tesla, it seemed, even one created by the Shade.

The fog began to thin as we pulled away. I shifted my vision back to the Real, as easy as flicking a switch now, and the world returned to a storm-darkened one, lit by the occasional flash of lightning. I gazed at my burned hands, but already the pain was gone and I could see they were starting to heal. I glanced over and saw Chloe's were too.

She knelt on the seat, staring back at the wolf as it disappeared into the distance.

Ahead of us the headlights showed a clear road. But what if there was an ambush waiting for us round the next bend? What if the new DEC had already achieved critical mass? What if...

With my left hand, I reached over and squeezed Chloe's shoulder as tears ran in rivers down her face.

We kept to back roads to try to avoid the Shade, wild weather continuing to rage across the countryside. I'd been talking things through with Sentinel, while Chloe remained silent, no doubt thinking of what had become of Gavin.

'So what's the plan when we arrive?' I asked the AI.

'We get the car as near as we can to the science park and then storm the lab. Unfortunately we no longer have the element of surprise on our side since Langton will know we'll be coming after him.'

'I don't like the sound of our odds.'

Chloe's head snapped up. 'I don't bloody care what it takes – we have to stop that monster. What they did to Gavin and Toby is awful enough, but nothing compared to what will happen if they are able to flood our whole world with those murdering shadow crows.'

'We'll do whatever it takes, Chloe,' I said.

'You're both clear on what you have to do?' Sentinel asked.

'Destroy any Shade who get in our way and plug the memory

stick into one of their computers controlling the experiment,' I replied. 'You're going to shut the DEC down as we grab my dad.'

'That's it,' Sentinel said.

We sped past a sign that hung off its post, flapping in the wind.

'*Hopworth Science Park, 1 mile*,' I read.

'As there's so little time we can't take the stealth approach,' Sentinel said.

'I agree,' I replied. 'We should charge the front gate at maximum speed. Hopefully we can smash through the barrier so fast that they won't have time to get a shot at us.'

'Let's hope so,' Chloe said with a wince.

A volley of lightning erupted directly over the car and deafening thunder rolled away across the countryside.

'The anomaly...field...grown,' Sentinel said, his speech interrupted by bouts of static. Then the speakers hissed to silence.

'Sentinel?' I asked.

There was no response.

Chloe's gaze tightened as we sped round the bend towards the gatehouse. Now we were on our own.

CHAPTER THIRTY-TWO

I focused all my attention on controlling the powerful Tesla as we hurtled towards the gatehouse. I risked a quick glance across at Chloe hanging on to the ceiling handle as we swerved towards the science park.

'Keep your head down and your fingers crossed that they don't get a lucky shot in,' I said.

Chloe grimaced and braced her legs against the dashboard.

The guard hut was dark – maybe a lightning strike had killed the power? I shifted into the Shadowlands but could only see black tones with my thermal vision. Surely it couldn't be empty?

I gunned the Tesla's electric motors with a stomach punch of acceleration, and we raced towards the lowered barrier.

Every muscle in my body clenched as we hit the bar.

Sparks leapt up, accompanied by a massive bang, and the metal barrier flew backwards on its mounting.

I gritted my teeth for a spray of bullets but I didn't hear a single shot.

'Where's the guard?' Chloe asked.

'Good question.'

I kept the accelerator pressed down and we raced away along the lane, spotting fresh tree stumps – no doubt the Shade fighting back the tide of trees that threatened to take over the science park.

I expected a hailstorm of bullets from an ambush point at any moment, but still they didn't come. Less than thirty seconds after crashing through the barrier, we reached the knot of dead trees surrounding the science park.

Dozens of vehicles had been abandoned here, scattered randomly rather than parked neatly – Genesis, military lorries, an assortment of expensive cars and motorbikes. I stamped on the brake pedal and we skidded to a long stop, just shy of one the Range Rovers.

We jumped out, Chloe and I both ready to flame anyone who attacked, but still no one appeared. And there wasn't even a hint of the birdlife I'd heard before.

Chloe scanned the vehicles. 'I'm getting seriously creeped out here.'

I gestured to a tunnel that looked as if it had been chainsawed through the fortress of wood. 'They must all be inside.'

It grew colder with every step. When we reached the other side I saw why.

Ice glittered across the clearing and huge icicles hung from the branches like stalactites, turning the area into a sort of frozen vaulted cathedral. In the Shadowlands the only source of heat I could see was the white aura around the generator that still buzzed away.

Ahead of us the research building was wrapped in the web of dark energy that flowed out of it. Around the building the tightly woven tapestry of branches was keeping most of the dark energy in, although a small amount was still squeezing out between the cracks in the branches.

Even if we succeeded in blowing up the lab, what would be

the consequence of all the concentrated dark energy that had already escaped into our world?

I glanced at my watch. The time dilation should be taking effect by now.

Chloe stopped by the entrance. She glanced at the ground for a moment, then straight into my eyes, and pulled me by my jacket towards her.

In the chilled world we'd walked into, Chloe's lips were shockingly warm on mine.

My heart thundered as she let the kiss linger.

She finally stepped away, stared up at the branches overhead and smiled.

'Hey, I'm not complaining, but...?' I said.

'Look, if I'm about to die, first I need to kiss the man who means everything to me.'

I felt a slow smile fill my face. 'I guess it only takes the potential end of the world for us to get round to admitting we have feelings for each other?'

'Yeah, I worry about us sometimes.'

So maybe there really would be an *us* – if we survived, that was.

I cradled Chloe's face with my hand for a moment. But we didn't have time for this moment, despite how wonderful it was.

I dragged my gaze away from her eyes, back to the dark vapours seeping out of the research building. 'We'd better get on with this to give us a chance of working out what is going on between us later.'

She smiled at me, and together we crept up the stairs to the entrance, our breath billowing like steam trains as we entered the glass atrium. We pressed deeper into the building and the hum of the new DEC grew far louder than the last time I'd been here. The ground vibrated under my feet – that was new too. The power to the Shade's machine had definitely been cranked up.

'What's been bugging me is how did the Shade manage to bring their plans forward?' Chloe said.

'No doubt we'll find out when we reach the lab.'

We crept as fast as we could down the corridors and the hum built to a low-pitched whine. A glow came from round the bend ahead of us – from the direction of the lab.

'Wait. We need to slow down,' I said. 'We don't want to throw away our element of surprise, at least what we have of it. If there are people here, the lab is where they're going to be.'

'Good point, Jake.'

We peered round the corner together. Lightning blazed through the open doorway of the lab in slow motion.

'It looks like they have the DEC fully online now, but at least the time dilation effect is still happening,' Chloe said.

'And that means that Sentinel's stasis field is still working. So we need to hurry.'

Chloe started forward, but I spotted something move in the shadows to one side of the door and grabbed her arm.

'Hang on.'

A bio-suited Genesis guard moved in the gloom by the lab entrance. My eyes snapped to the holstered pistol slung over his shoulder as he moved to a position directly in front of the door.

I tensed but he didn't reach for the gun, only glanced back into the lab through the window in the door. It seemed our invisibility trick was still working while we were in the Shadowlands.

I pulled Chloe back round the corner with me and took out the memory stick. 'I need to plug this into one of the computer terminals in that room, but how are we going to get past that guy without bumping into him? He's blocking most of the doorway.'

Chloe drummed her fingers on her cheek. 'We need a distraction,' she whispered. She sucked her cheeks in and her eyes narrowed. 'OK, I know how, but first I'm shifting into the Real...'

'But why?' I hissed.

'I'm going to create a distraction.'

Before I could stop her Chloe smiled and headed back round the corner. What the hell was she doing? I edged along and peered after her.

Chloe looked as relaxed as if she were strolling down Stoneham High Street doing a bit of window shopping, and definitely not as if she was heading straight towards a Shade agent.

She cocked her head to one side and addressed the guard as she neared. 'Seen any dodgy shadows around here, mate?'

My fingers clawed on to a pillar as the guy took out his pistol and aimed it at her head. If he shot first and asked questions later...

'Touchy, aren't you?' Chloe said.

The Genesis guy tucked his chin in, his eyebrows ridging across his forehead. He snarled, grabbed her arm, and hauled her in through the doorway.

My stomach muscles relaxed. At least he hadn't shot her. But her plan was to get herself captured? It was one way to distract the guard, and all I could do now was sieze the opportunity.

I tiptoed along the corridor as quietly as I could, reached the doorway to the lab and peered through its reinforced window. I could barely make anything out – in the Shadowlands view everything was bathed in cold tones.

I shifted back into the Real and my mouth became bone dry. All the massive electrodes spat lightning towards the stasis field. What I'd once thought was a solid glass sphere had started to fade in and out of view, revealing Dad and the exploding original DEC behind him. It could only be moments before it collapsed and the Shade would be able to open their original portal. It wasn't lost on me that by shutting down the stasis field we'd effectively be doing their work for them, but with one key addition: moments later Sentinel would shut down the DEC, hopefully this time for good.

I scanned the lab. Where were all the people who'd been working on it?

Meanwhile, the Genesis guard had forced Chloe into a chair in front of the portal.

'Bind her hands – we don't want her pulling off her little Awoken stunt in here,' Langton said, his voice wavering. He was stooped and his hands were shaking. It looked like our little run-in with him back at the cottage had badly affected his human host.

The guard bound Chloe's hands with a plastic tie as Langton and Dave walked towards her.

Langton, coughing, drew himself up to his full height. 'I imagine you aren't here to take us up on our offer of joining the Shade?'

'No. I've come to finish the fight that we started at the cottage.'

Dave smiled. 'Then I am afraid you have arrived too late.' He gestured at the blazing machine.

Chloe narrowed her gaze on him. 'Weren't you weeks away from completion?'

Dave nodded. 'We were. But since we had so many humans working for us, it seemed a waste not to use all that energy contained within their bodies.'

An empty feeling filled my stomach.

'What did you do?' Chloe whispered, her face paling.

Langton waved a hand towards the nutrient accelerator machine. 'When the new DEC was finished we had the work teams rewire that capsule. Did you know that within the atoms of a human body there is more energy than a hydrogen bomb?'

'You're saying that everyone who you abducted to work here – all your Genesis people...' Chloe's eyes widened in horror.

'After we realised what you and the boy were both capable of we thought we'd better take some shortcuts. So we fed our workers in, one by one, all queueing up meekly for their deaths. As their bodies were torn apart we harnessed the power from their atoms, their screams almost a hymn.' He laughed. 'It could, of course, be argued that all these deaths are on your hands for forcing us to accelerate our plans.'

They'd killed all those people – people who had served them. *Like lambs to the slaughter...* Steel filled my chest.

'You are pure evil, Langton!' Chloe shouted at him.

'I prefer to think of us as just terribly efficient.'

Dave crossed to the accelerator. 'I think we should give her a demonstration.'

I got ready to leap through the door and flame him, but Chloe wasn't Dave's target.

Langton nodded at the guard. 'Please get into that capsule.'

The guy stepped forward and into the device without hesitating. The glass screen slid around to close him in. The man looked blankly through the glass, no fear, no anything on his face. With a hiss brilliant white light bathed him, and the man's body erupted in a shower of sparks.

Then the screaming started. Awful, terrible yells of a human having the life torn out of him. Piece by piece the man disintegrated, his body breaking into a swirling cloud of atoms as the white light grew blinding from his disintegrating body. In response the lightning bolts around the DEC became huge and the stasis field fainter.

Static raced over my skin, raising the hairs on my arms as a wave of nausea slammed into my stomach. I doubled over in agony, trying not to vomit. I pulled my head up enough to see Chloe writhing against her bonds, spittle on her lips.

'Your Awoken abilities make you particularly susceptible to the influence of the Void,' Langton said. 'As the stasis field fails it is starting to bleed through into your world and expose you to its effect.'

I gasped in a lungful of air as the pain began to subside.

Chloe slumped in her seat, staring up through her fringe at Langton. 'I'm so going to kill you with my bare hands.'

'I would not get yourself too worked up about that, Chloe Haze. You see, soon it will all be over for you – once we establish the portal to the Void with your help. And then, within moments, our brethren massed on the far side of that portal will come through to consume the infection that you call life – first on this planet with the exception of the few who are our allies, and then spreading out across your universe, as we have with so many others.'

Consume all life? Oh shit. The Shade weren't just planning an invasion, but to reset the evolution of the entire cosmos back to zero. I swallowed down bile once more.

Chloe glowered at Langton. 'No way am I helping you. And we're not the infection – you bloody are.'

Langton's laugh rattled like a stone in a can. 'Foolish girl. It is all a sense of perspective. To us, you are little more than bacteria – a disease that infects the harmony of the universe. And you know what you do with a disease?'

Chloe pressed her lips together and didn't answer.

Dave stepped forward. 'You eradicate it. And you see, Chloe Haze, we are the vaccine. There is a beautiful symmetry to all of this.'

Chloe's eyes glittered and her jaw hardened. 'I'll stop you, whatever it takes.'

Again Langton let out a hollow laugh. 'How, exactly? As you are so close to the effect of the growing DEC field, your precious Awoken powers will not work here.'

What did he mean? My mouth dry, I tried to reignite a plasma sun. Nothing happened. Holy crap. I tried to shift to the Shadowlands, but couldn't manage that either.

Somehow their new DEC was screwing with our abilities.

I stuck my fingernails into my palm. If we were to have any chance of shutting this machine down in time, I needed to plug Sentinel in, before the portal released its own version of hell into our world.

Chloe spat straight into Langton's face.

He wagged a finger at her and wiped her spittle off his cheek with a silk handkerchief. 'Temper, temper, temper.'

I scanned the lab for a computer terminal. I needed to get the memory stick plugged in.

'Well, the world's still here, so it looks like your stupid plan has failed!' Chloe shouted.

Langton smiled and lifted Chloe's chin with his finger so she was forced to look right into his black eyes. 'You do not understand, Chloe. The DEC field has *almost* achieved critical mass. We just need one more sacrifice to make it complete.'

My insides hollowed out. I knew exactly what he meant, and so did Chloe. She tried to kick out at Langton, but he stepped out of her range.

I'd nothing left to lose. I certainly wasn't going to just watch my best friend being killed without fighting with everything that I had to stop it. I took a deep breath and tensed, ready to charge through the doors.

Dave crossed to Chloe, pulled her up on to her feet and pinned her tied arms behind her as she struggled to get free.

'Please don't do this, Dad,' Chloe said.

But Dave remained blank-faced as he dragged her towards the glass pod. It was only then that I spotted the bank of USB slots on the computer next to it. Bingo! But how was I going to get there without being noticed?

Chloe tried to bite Dave's hands as they locked on to her shoulders, and he shoved her towards the open capsule.

With no powers to help me here, I realised I would have to do this the old-fashioned way. I burst through the door, sprinting straight for the USB slots. Langton spun round and for once his smug expression was broken by wide-eyed surprise.

Right then, Chloe slammed her foot backwards into Dave's shin. With a snarl, he released his hold long enough for her to jump away. She dashed to me as I reached the USB panel.

'Step away from that and we might still spare you,' Langton said calmly.

'Yeah, as if that's ever going to happen,' I replied.

'We could still make you like gods,' Langton said.

'At the cost of letting you destroy everything in our world?' I asked. 'No way. We'd rather die than let that happen.'

'Do it, Jake!' Chloe shouted.

I shoved the memory stick into one of the USB ports and waited. The seconds ticked by like hours. Absolutely nothing happened. I stared at the port. Was it broken? Just my bloody luck!

'Is that the finale of your grand plan?' Langton said with a raised eyebrow.

Both men started to walk towards us now, razor shadow claws sprouting from their fingers. I looked around for anything we could use to defend ourselves and spotted a bag of tools next to the console. I grabbed a large spanner and a pair of wire cutters, cut the ties that bound Chloe's hands and brandished the spanner towards Langton and Dave.

They smirked at my weapon.

'Sentinel, what's going on?' I shouted.

'Ah, about that – I'm afraid that your AI friend will not be unable to assist you,' Langton explained. 'After he so effectively sabotaged our efforts last time, we took certain precautions this time round. All the computer systems have been replaced with a hardwired system.'

Chloe clenched her fists. 'In other words, there's nothing for him to hack.'

'Precisely,' Dave replied.

Langton glanced across at a flashing red light. 'And so it begins... Behold the end of your world as you know it because Sentinel's precious stasis field is about to collapse.'

The lightning flared and the room trembled for a moment as the bubble of time in the middle of the room started to fade out.

'How are we going to stop them without our powers, Jake?' Chloe asked, her voice high and shaky.

'I don't know – I don't bloody know,' I said as the two men began advancing on us again. This was the end of everything.

I planted my feet slightly apart and pulled the spanner back, ready to lash out at whoever got within range first.

CHAPTER THIRTY-THREE

A LOW GROWL rumbled from the shimmering stasis field as lightning flickered over it. Chloe grabbed my hand and pulled me towards a ladder leading up to a gantry that surrounded the DEC.

'Come on!' she shouted.

We raced away as Langton and Dave came after us, leaping up the ladder, the metal rungs freezing under my hands. As we reached the gantry I kicked the ladder away to buy us some time.

Langton sneered up at us. 'You do realise that I can transform into Archios and easily come after you? You may as well make things easier for yourselves and come down.'

'Oh, you'd love that, but you so would have pulled that little transformation stunt already if you could have, rather than just talk about it,' Chloe said. 'My guess is that you're weakened after our little encounter outside the cottage and you've not got enough shadow crows left to conjure your giant shadow Archios.'

Langton hissed at us. 'Whatever. Anyway, without your precious Awoken powers there is nothing you can do to stop what is about to happen. However, you do now have a ringside seat, so you can enjoy the view.' He gestured towards the stasis field shimmering in and out of existence behind us.

My heart thudded as I spotted Dad begin to move millimetre by millimetre inside his collapsing time bubble. At the same time dozens of metal shards crawled outwards from the shattered containment sphere from the explosion that had first started six years ago. Beyond Dad, a black sphere of nothingness, currently the size of a tennis ball, was also being exposed by the disappearing stasis sphere... At any moment that thing would become a highway through which the Shade would invade Earth.

The air in the lab started to whistle into the exposed hole in our reality. The portal pulsed and grew to a metre across. In that same instant I felt my body go light as if someone had thrown a switch on gravity. Chloe and I began drifting up from the gantry and had to grab for the railing to halt our progress.

Langton laughed. Somehow he and Dave remained anchored to the floor.

Dave gave us an amused look. 'If you were wondering what's happening, gravity is being affected by the condensed dark energy that's just been exposed. More importantly it's also a sign that the portal is about to go critical.'

A shudder rippled through the ground. Several flasks dropped from racks and smashed on the floor tiles that were starting to buckle and crack as the explosion expanded outwards. With a bang and a wall of noise the heat that had been trapped in time stretched out into the room as the original DEC experiment tore itself apart.

Unfrozen, Dad began to turn away from the blast, his hands instinctively coming up to protect his head as he too drifted up from the floor.

If I didn't do something now, he'd be torn apart by the explosion and I'd seen enough footage of astronauts to understand the principle of moving in zero-gravity.

I brought my feet down on to the railing and pushed off from it. Like someone swimming underwater, I propelled myself towards Dad. But what the astronauts made look easy on space station YouTube videos was much harder to pull off in real life. Limbs flailing, I crashed straight into Dad.

Shock filled his eyes as he yelled, 'What the—?'

I locked my arms round him, my momentum propelling us both away from the explosion.

The world roared around us as shrapnel bullets sprayed the lab, shredding the banks of equipment. A constellation of red warning lights blinked on. In a second the ice that had gripped the lab melted away to nothing.

I made a grab for a lab rack and brought us both to a sudden stop, nearly yanking my arm out of its socket in the process.

Meanwhile, I saw Chloe pull herself flat on the gantry as the projectiles sped over her head.

Dave and Langton seemed unconcerned as dozens of bullet holes appeared in their bodies. But then I realised no blood was spraying out; none of their limbs were being ripped apart by the flying pieces of metal. Instead smoke swirled through each and every wound, and their injuries were healed instantly. They both turned towards the growing portal, their faces exultant.

Dad and I pulled ourselves round to the far side of the metal rack to shelter from the pieces of shrapnel still speeding past.

I ignored the cries of alarms and the flames licking over the lab – all I had eyes for was Dad. He was wearing his favourite blue shirt under his trademark crumpled lab coat. It really was him, in the flesh. He was alive.

'What's happening?' Dad asked, staring past me at the chaos in his lab.

'No time to explain,' I replied.

Dad's gaze locked on to the black orb hanging in the middle of the lab. 'No, it can't be!'

'It is, Dad. You need to listen to me.'

He glanced back to me. 'What do you mean, *Dad*?' Then his eyes widened. 'Wait, you look just like...' He shook his head.

I couldn't suppress a smile despite what was going on. 'Yes it's me – it's Jake.'

'But that's impossible.' He shot me a bewildered look.

Of course it was impossible because for him his son was six years younger than the guy floating in the air in front of him.

'As I said, there's no time to explain.' I gestured to the black sphere. 'What you need to know right now is that creatures from beyond our world are about to come crashing through the portal that you created by accident with the DEC experiment.'

He frowned. 'Next you'll be saying that you travelled back in time to save me.'

'Close enough.'

Dad tucked his chin in and waved across the room to his former friend. 'Dave, what's this madness about? Where did all these people come from? What's happening to our lab?'

Dave ignored him and continued to stare into the dark orb of nothingness.

Then Dad's eyes narrowed on Langton. 'What are you doing here, Alexander?'

'Do not worry yourself, Professor Stevens,' Langton replied. 'Relax and enjoy a once-in-a-lifetime show that you helped to create.'

'What are you babbling about, man?'

Langton laughed. 'Oh, you will see in just a moment.'

I grabbed Dad's shoulders. 'It's complicated, Dad, but neither of those two guys are the men that you knew.'

'Please tell me this is just a lucid dream, or I've gone mad because one of those options would be easier to get my head around,' he replied.

'I'm afraid this all too real.'

'And you really are Jake?'

'I know how crazy this must seem, but yes, Dad, it's really me.'

His eyes searched mine and they widened. 'My god, it *is* you.'

'So you believe me then?'

He gestured around him. 'Well, with the lack of gravity in the lab, you suddenly older, Langton sounding like he's on something, and a black orb sitting in the lab where a moment ago our DEC machine was – yep, that all pretty much decides it.'

A laugh bubbled up from somewhere inside me and I hugged him. 'God, I've missed you so much.'

Dad squeezed me back. He pulled away, and his gaze locked on to Chloe on the gantry. 'Chloe too!'

Before she could answer the portal shuddered again and came to a halt.

Dave turned to Langton. 'What's happened? I thought it had already achieved critical mass?'

'Not quite, my friend,' Langton replied. 'And I want to thank you for your sacrifice.'

Dave's forehead ridged. 'What sacrifice is that?'

'That you are about to give me your Shade lifeblood.' Still smiling, and before Dave could react, Langton clamped his hands either side of Dave's head and opened his mouth as if he might kiss him. Instead Langton breathed in, his chest expanding like he was trying to suck all the air out of the room.

Dave screamed as red angry patches appeared all over his skin.

'What are you doing to him?' Chloe shouted from the gantry.

'What I must, to make sure we destroy your world.'

Hundreds of spores broke through Dave's skin and wriggled out like dark tiny maggots. Dave's scream ramped up and echoed through the room as the dark specks tore free of him. In a swirl every single particle was inhaled by Langton.

Dave's legs buckled and he collapsed to the floor, blood pouring out from hundreds of pinprick wounds.

No one moved, no one said anything, our shock louder than the air screaming away into the portal.

Langton breathed out again, and smiled like he'd just downed a good glass of wine. He gazed down at Dave's twitching body. 'You had to die, my friend, so our glorious plan may live.' He threw back his head and bellowed with laughter.

The air thickened around Langton and became a flock of Shade birds. I blinked and realised why I was shocked – for the first time the creatures were visible in the Real. The nightmare had finally invaded reality. The crows spiralled around Langton's physical body, forming the shadow man around him like an outer secondary skin. The thing stared at us with ravenous pure-black eyes.

Dad gasped, his mouth falling open as Archios's disembodied voice echoed around the room. 'With the lifeblood of my fellow Shade inside me I am now fully restored from my previous encounter with you, Awoken.' The shadow man raised his hands and the air flowing into the portal began to slow, its whistle fading to silence. 'As the portal opens to the Void I am now given form in your world. But now...to end you all.'

The lightning around the DEC machine fizzled out and the rushing wind died away. Utter silence filled the room for a moment.

I felt gravity grab on to my body again. A moment later, Dad and I crashed to the floor.

With his arms still raised and his head thrown back, Archios uttered a guttural chant, like a priest mumbling over an altar. Langton's body remained frozen within Archios, the shadow man cocooning the human body within it.

A dark sense of foreboding filled me. This was going to get much worse...and fast.

Chloe dropped down from the gantry and raced over to Dave just as Dad and I did the same.

As all three of us reached him, Dave gave a faint moan and his eyes flickered open – eyes empty of shadows.

'I am so sorry, Chloe,' Dave said faintly. 'I tried to fight the things inside me, but they...they were too strong.'

'Shhh, Dad,' Chloe replied.

'But I need you to understand,' he whispered. 'I've been like a prisoner locked in a cell – a cell with a window through which I could see the awful things I did to you. I couldn't do anything to stop myself.'

'No, the Shade did all of that – it was never you.'

He nodded, tears filling his eyes.

My dad knelt by him. 'What happened to you, Dave?'

'My pride, Martin. If I'd listened to you and hadn't proceeded with the test of our DEC experiment, none of this would have happened.'

'I don't begin to understand everything that's going on here, but I've always been proud to call you my friend.'

Dave blinked back tears. 'Then that makes two of us...' He coughed and a trickle of blood ran down from the corner of his mouth. His eyes sought out Chloe's again. 'Please forgive me, my love.'

She stifled a sob. 'Oh, Dad.'

I looked between them, feeling totally powerless. But we had to do something – anything – to stop what was about to happen.

I gripped my dad's shoulder. 'At any moment thousands more shadow crows will be invading our world through that portal unless we stop them.'

Dad stared at me. 'An invasion?' He hung his head. 'This is my fault, isn't it? It's to do with our research into dark energy?'

'It's nobody's fault,' I replied.

'How were we meant to know what we were about to unleash?' Dave said.

'Maybe we were in too much of a hurry, Dave. But whatever the truth of it I intend to make it right in any way that I can. And I think I know a way.'

'How?' I asked, hope sparking within me.

He jabbed a finger towards the huge DEC machine. 'By setting that thing to overload, which will take five minutes. When it blows, fingers crossed, it will release enough energy to collapse that portal.'

Before I could react to this revelation, the doors crashed open and Inspector Clarke and several police officers rushed in. They slowed to a stop as they took in the scene.

Clarke stared at the growing portal, slack-jawed. 'What on Earth?'

'That's the portal we told you about,' I told the inspector.

Clarke stared at Alexander Langton's frozen body inside the shadow man. 'What is that thing around the PM?'

'It's Archios,' I said.

Clarke's gaze fell upon Chloe and Dad, both crouched over Dave. 'Hang on, I recognise you. Aren't you Professor Stevens, the man who was killed six years ago?'

'Yes, it is me. Apparently I'm alive and well.'

'It really is all true,' Clarke muttered to himself. He shook his head as he scanned the lab. 'OK, so where are the survivors that Allan told us to rescue?'

I gulped. 'Dead...' I said in a flat tone. There was no other way of putting it.

Chloe pointed a finger at Langton. 'And it was that thing, Archios, who infected Langton. He is responsible.'

Clarke took his Taser out of a holster attached to his belt and aimed the device straight at Langton's chest. 'OK, that's more than convinced me.'

I felt a gentle breeze across the back of my head. A wind had reversed and was flowing out of the portal and into the lab.

Within the darkness of the portal itself I could see distant points glittering. 'The first attack wave are about to arrive!' I shouted.

Dad leapt up and crossed to one of the control consoles. 'OK, I'll set the DEC to overload, but it'll take out this whole place with it.'

Clarke's eyes widened. 'Hang on a moment.'

'It is the only way to stop the Shade's invasion of our world,' I explained.

'But won't everyone in here be killed by the blast?'

'There'll be a delay as the capacitors overload,' Dad replied. 'We should have time to escape.'

Archios's chanting sped up and his shadow arms stretched wider as though he were summoning a demon straight from hell. In every sense that was exactly what he was doing. Five minutes to collapse the portal suddenly seemed an awfully long time.

'There's no chance of talking this through, is there?' Clarke asked.

'No – we have to do it now,' I replied.

'Then I'm going to have to trust your judgement on this.'

I nodded. 'So how are you going to overload it, Dad?'

His eyes hunted the lab. 'If they followed the design of my original experiment and scaled it up, then...' His gaze snapped to a pedestal with a control panel mounted at the top, a few shrapnel holes in its side.

'Aha!' He raced to it and pulled off a panel. 'It will take me a moment to rewire this. Once I've done that it will bypass the safety overrides. I'll need to keep the dead man switch open so it can begin a power overload in the main capacitor bank. And when it gets to the critical level...no more portal, no more DEC experiment and, for that matter, no more science park.'

'How long will it take to do that?' Clarke asked.

'Five minutes and then the self-destruct sequence begins,' Dad replied.

'OK, Inspector, so the key thing is to defend my dad whatever happens,' I said, just in case he wasn't crystal clear on that. Can you do it?'

Clarke gazed at his police officers. 'We'll do our best.' He gestured at them and they took up positions around Dad, their Tasers all aimed at Langton as Archios's chanting grew louder.

I brushed my fingers over Chloe's shoulder as she crouched over her dad. 'Chloe, we need to help them stop Archios.'

Chloe hung her head and stared down at Dave.

He peered up at her through blood-filled eyes and cradled her hand. 'Stop them, my love, please.'

She took a shuddering breath. 'Yes...' She stood, eyes glittering, and nodded to me.

Together we joined Clarke. I tried to ignite my plasma spark once again but still got nothing. Frustration burned through me – just when we needed them most our powers had been stolen away from us.

Archios stopped chanting and his arms fell to his sides.

I returned my attention back to the portal, now wreathed with wisps of grey smoke. Thousands of spores, like a dark snowstorm, swirled towards us from it, carried by a roaring wind. They hurtled out of the dark sphere, like a swarm of black bees.

My fingers twitched, desperate to lob a fireball at them.

The particles flowed like smoke into Archios's body. 'Get ready, everyone,' I shouted.

The shadow man laughed as he began to grow taller. Spore by spore, the shadow man became a shadow giant, and we could only watch on in terror. Finally the flow of shadow particles from the portal stopped as the wind faded to silence.

'That must be the end of the first attack wave,' I called out.

The newly created Shade goliath stared down at us, his head touching the ceiling of the two-storey laboratory.

'We will not be stopped, humans,' Archios's voice boomed, making every person in the room wince.

'Open fire on Langton, Inspector!' I shouted.

Clarke didn't hesitate, firing at Langton who stood inert beneath the shadow monster. The Taser bolt flew into his chest and electricity flowed from the Taser in Clarke's hand, along the thin wires connecting it to the bolt. It pulsed into Langton's body, but the man didn't so much as flinch.

Clarke gawped as his Taser ran out of charge. 'That shot should have taken him down easily.'

'A human, yes, but not one possessed by the Shade,' I said. 'Keep hitting him– it's the only way to defeat him.'

Clarke nodded. 'After all the police cuts I've never been much of a fan of our current PM anyway.' He gestured to his men. 'Hit him with everything you've got.'

Taser projectiles buried themselves into Langton's body, discharging their electricity payload. He jerked as the electricity surged through his body, but somehow he kept standing.

The shadow giant, howling with rage, lashed out a shadowy fist.

'Look out!' I shouted, but it was too late.

The monster's blow caught the nearest police officer and sent him flying into a rack of equipment. He crumpled to the floor and didn't move. Archios stared down at the policeman and Dad working at the console beyond them.

Chloe stared at me. 'We have to help them.'

I looked around us for anything that we could use as a weapon and spotted the power cables connected to one of the giant electrodes snaking across the floor to the DEC. Each of those cables had to be carrying far more power than the Taser bolts...

'Follow me.'

Archios swiped out and sent another police officer flying. Meanwhile, Dad was frantically stabbing buttons on the control console.

We rushed over to the electrodes and I placed a foot on the DEC to give me enough leverage to pull out one of the huge oversized plugs.

Chloe's eyes widened. 'I think I see where you're headed with this. Now what, Jake?'

'We need a conductor, such as...' My eyes fell upon the gantry, and the wire cutters and a spool of wire. I handed her the cable. 'Drag this over to that support pillar and I'll do the rest.'

She gave a sharp nod and dragged the heavy cable behind her towards the gantry.

'Reload, and keep firing,' Clarke shouted.

Archios swiped right at him, forcing Clarke to duck sideways. The blow sailed over his head, but he could only stay lucky for so long.

I tried to ignore everything else around me and set to work connecting two lengths of cut and stripped wires to the gantry. Chloe reached me and I wrapped one of the bare wire terminals on to a metal support post.

I bent the other thick copper wire into a hook shape and gave it to Chloe. 'When I give the signal drop that other wire on to the gantry railing and get clear.'

'OK, so we're trying to electrocute Archios, I get that, but how are we going to persuade him to come over here?'

'Like this.' I leapt up on to one of the gantry support legs and began to climb up it.

'What do you think you're doing, Jake?' Chloe said.

'What I need to do.' I knew that if I got my timing wrong this plan was going to cost me my life...but that was a small price to pay to save the world.

Another of Clarke's officers crashed into a wall. The inspector was down to five officers and no doubt Archios would keep going until they drowned in shadows.

My gamble had to work.

I reached the gantry, clambered up on to it and started to wave my arms at Archios.

'You think we're meant to be impressed by you?' I shouted. 'Are you really the best the Shade can send against us, Archios?'

His huge head turned towards me. Archios took three steps with Langton beneath, mimicking his movement like a puppet because that's exactly what he was. The shadow giant pulled back his fist and I waited as his intended blow flew through the air towards me.

'Now!' I shouted to Chloe. I jumped off the gantry and she stabbed the negative wire into the cable socket. I landed and pulled her away as Archios's fist smashed into the place I'd been standing just a moment before.

Sparks flew from the metal framework as the monster howled and spasmed, its hand locked on to the gantry as the electricity held it there.

'Shoot Langton with everything you've got!' I shouted.

Clarke dropped to a knee and he and all his officers took aim and fired. Five Taser bolts slammed straight into Langton's body. Around him Archios roared and he and Langton shattered, flooding the room with hundreds of shadow crows.

We'd done it. We'd really bloody done it! Archios and his human puppet was gone. But was it over?

'Fall back, Shade!' Archios's disembodied voice shouted from the beaks of a hundred shadow crows.

With the beating of wings the Shade swarmed away towards the doors.

'We have to stop them escaping because they'll only try to do this again!' Chloe shouted.

'It's too late,' I said.

Clarke gestured to his officers and they split into two groups, the first picking up the downed officers.

'We need to destroy this place before reinforcements arrive through the portal,' Chloe said.

Dad nodded. 'It's all ready – the capacitors are fully charged.' He flipped up a yellow and black striped lid on top of the console to reveal a red lever. 'Everyone else needs to evacuate this facility immediately.'

'What do you mean everyone *else*?' I asked.

Dad didn't reply and instead placed his hand on the red lever.

My heart threatened to shatter because I knew exactly what Dad had in mind. 'You can't!'

Dave lifted his head a fraction from the floor. 'Jake's right. It should be me, Martin.'

Martin frowned at us. 'I disagree.'

'What are you talking about?' Chloe asked.

But I already knew. It wasn't called a dead man switch for nothing. 'Someone has to keep that switch locked down to continue the overloading of the DEC,' I replied.

Chloe stared at Dad and Dave. 'In other words, one of you is about to sacrifice yourself to make sure the Shade are stopped?'

Dad nodded. 'And I'm going to do it, because this is all my fault for dreaming up this experiment in the first place. It's my responsibility to clean up this mess.'

Dave managed a faint smile. 'When will you stop being so damned stubborn, Martin? I'm as good as dead anyway, so let me make amends for what I've done.'

Chloe gasped. 'But, Dad, I can't lose you.'

'My love, in many ways you lost me when that first Shade entered my body. This is my last real chance of redemption. I hope you can understand?'

Tears streamed down her face. 'But, Dad, please...'

'Chloe, I am so proud of the woman you've become. The best thing you can do for me now is to grab your life with both hands and live it to the full.'

'But I can't leave you to die alone.'

'You have to, my love.' His gaze fell on me. 'Look after her, Jake. You two were always fantastic for each other.'

The back of my nose stung. 'I'll do my best, Dave.'

'I still say it should be me,' Dad replied.

'Absolutely not,' Dave replied. 'You have six stolen years of being missing from Jake's life to make up for. But please also look out for this wonderful daughter of mine and be a better father figure to her than I've managed to be.'

Chloe clasped her head in her hands as a sob escaped her lips.

Dave held his hand out to me. 'Jake, can you help me over to the control console?'

I fought my impulse to argue. Dave was right to do this, even though I didn't want him to be.

'Of course.' I grabbed his hand and helped him slowly get up. With his arm draped over me we staggered over towards Dad, still with his hand on the lever.

Chloe kept her back to us, but her shoulders shook so hard that I thought she might break. She was about to lose everything. But what could I say? What could anyone say? Nothing, absolutely nothing. But afterwards I would be there for her – do everything I could to help her pick up the pieces.

I spotted glittering distant points within the portal. 'The next attack wave is coming!'

Dave gripped the edge of the console to help him stand up. He gazed around the lab. 'Our life's work, Martin.'

'I know, my friend, but we also opened Pandora's Box right along with it.'

'And I will close that lid again right now,' Dave replied. Dad stepped back as Dave slammed the lever down and leant on it.

At once the whole lab growled around us and everything began to shake.

Chloe gazed at her dad, tears jewelling her eyes.

Lumps of masonry began falling from the ceiling, kicking up clouds of dust.

I pulled on her arm but she resisted me. 'Chloe, come on.'

'Please go, my love, for me,' Dave said.

She gave him the barest nod, tears rolling down her face as a burning smell started to fill the lab and scratched the back of my nostrils.

'OK, let's get out of here,' I said.

Dad extended his hand towards Dave. 'Farewell, old friend.'

Dave shook his hand. 'Always dream the impossibly big dreams, Martin.'

'Always...'

Clarke and his officers led the escape with their fallen colleagues. We followed, Chloe shaking with every step.

I glanced back into the lab one last time as we exited the doorway. 'Thank you for this, Dave.'

He raised his hand and, coughing, nodded. In these last moments at least he was human again.

I turned away as I heard the distant sound of rushing wings. We all sprinted along the corridor as white flickers of electricity buzzed along the floors, walls and ceilings. My gums tingled and the air tasted metallic as we rounded a corner into the atrium.

'We've only got about twenty seconds left,' Dad said.

We all crashed through the doors and raced out into the clearing.

I began a mental countdown as we all reached the hacked tunnel through the surrounding trees and sped through it.

Three...

Around us the forest whispered with life again.

Two...

We started to race down the road, me half holding, half dragging Chloe.

One...

The bird calls fell silent. A loud thump resounded behind us.

Every muscle in my body tensed as a hot wind smashed into my back. The trees thrashed around in a sudden gale that hurled us through the air and on to a grass embankment.

I rolled over to see a boiling mushroom cloud rising over the research buildings into the night sky. The trees that had surrounded it had been flattened, but they'd also absorbed most of the blast.

Chloe rolled over and stared back too, her face bone-white.

With a thunderclap the middle of the building began folding in on itself, bricks falling towards a dark orb that grew in the middle. The portal – stretching but visibly thinning – consumed everything in its path, including the bordering wall of trees.

I shoved Chloe's head back down as a shower of scalding debris rained down on us.

I pressed my face into the grass, smelling damp earth as the seconds ticked past. The deafening roar rolled away across the valley. I felt Chloe sobbing under my hand. At last the roar ended, and we all started to push ourselves up to standing. We turned back to see a massive, perfectly spherical crater where the science park had been a minute before, ending just metres away from us.

The portal had vanished and so had Dave with it.

Chloe gave a long shuddering intake of breath and her wail filled the air, weaving around the cry of birdsong, which once more flowed through the forest.

CHAPTER THIRTY-FOUR

THE NIGHT GLITTERED with the blue flashing lights of ambulances, police cars and fire engines.

Clarke, on his way over to us, paused to talk to an officer who'd been on his radio.

Chloe sat on the bonnet of a patrol car. She'd barely said a word since the explosion.

I desperately wanted to contact Allan to let him know we'd succeeded, but first I tried as best I could to get Dad up to speed with everything that had happened. It was a long list to get through.

As I finally finished Dad shook his head at me. 'I still can't begin to get my head around the fact that it's really you, Jake. Less than ten hours ago for me you were a twelve-year-old lad.'

'And it's the same for me. All this time and you haven't aged a day.'

'So many lost moments, huh?'

'We have, but we can make up for them.' I cast a look across at Chloe, lost somewhere deep inside herself, and felt a twist of guilt. I turned back to Dad. 'Being with you again is something I never imagined. As far as I knew you were dead.'

'That must have been tough, really tough on you.'

There was no point in lying. 'It was, Dad.' My gaze was drawn back to Chloe. 'I can't help think that it's beyond cruel that, as I find you alive, Chloe loses Dave.'

'It's going to take a long time for her to start to heal. But she has you in her life. That's going to be important. I have a feeling you're going to be a big part of Chloe's journey to find her way through that pain.'

'Whatever it takes.'

'Yes...'

Clarke gave the officer he'd been talking to a grim-faced look and headed over towards us.

'It seems Langton has already made a counter-move,' he said as he reached us. 'His deputy already has the military on their way here and they're rounding up my officers.'

'But surely they can't hush up something this big?' I asked.

'Not if I've got anything to with it. So much for me retiring this year with a nice fat police pension for all my years of dedicated service.'

'Sounds as though you have some sort of alternative plan?' Dad said.

'Just to find as many journalists as I can who will listen to me. I intend to get the word out there about what really happened here.'

'You're OK, Inspector, you know that?' I said.

He smiled. 'I like to think so.'

'I can help you with that, Inspector,' Sentinel's voice said from his pocket.

Clarke took his phone out and narrowed his gaze on it.

'He does that,' I said with a shake of my head.

'Ah, the famous alien AI you were telling me about,' Dad said.

'That's me. I'd hoped to meet you sooner, Martin, but the electrical disruption from the portal had other ideas.'

'All I know is there are laws about hacking someone's phone, Sentinel,' Clarke said.

'I'm sorry, but needs must,' Sentinel replied. 'Anyway, as I was saying, I'll make sure that the major media outlets around the world are sent all the evidence about what happened here today and just how Langton is involved in all of this. And we will need to deal with the threat that this man and his monster represents to us.'

'I guess that now the Shade have the knowledge to build their own DEC, they are bound to try again,' I said.

'I'm afraid I'm absolutely certain of it,' Sentinel replied.

Dad scratched his neck. 'Which probably makes me one of the few people on the planet who might be able to come up with a countermeasure to stop them.'

'What sort of countermeasure?' I asked.

'I've got a few ideas I want to explore.'

'Then I will offer you whatever assistance I can, Martin,' Sentinel replied.

'And of course I will help,' I added. 'I always hoped we'd end up working together.'

'Don't forget that, as an Awoken, you've also got a lot of intensive training ahead of you,' Sentinel reminded me. 'I'm not sure you'll have the time or the energy.'

'We'll see about that,' I said. 'I haven't seen my dad in years, and I want to help him.'

Dad nodded, but his gaze was already travelling towards the plume of smoke still rising from what had been the science park.

Of course, he was thinking about his former colleague, his friend, just like Chloe, who seemed lost in a world of hurt.

Clarke rubbed his chin. 'We should take you all to a safe house until this is over.'

'Unfortunately, Inspector, there is no way of knowing who within the police force has been corrupted,' Sentinel replied. 'All it takes is one informant and...'

Clarke grimaced. 'I see... So what are you proposing then?'

'This is something that I have already made preparations for with Allan Stevens. We have already secured a safe location for Martin, Jake and Chloe, where we can begin phase three of my programming.'

'Which is?' I asked.

'Inspector, could I ask you to step away for a moment, but to leave your phone with Jake so I can speak to them through it?'

Clarke didn't move. 'If you're not going to accept my protection, at the very least I'd like to know your plans.'

'We simply have no way of knowing how far the Shade's influence has spread within your country,' Sentinel said. 'The fact that the military is on the way speaks volumes.'

'I'm still not happy about being kept out of the loop.'

'It's just the way it needs to be, Inspector,' I said.

He frowned at me but shook his head in surrender and handed his mobile to Dad, then headed back to the other officer.

Sentinel waited until Clarke was out of earshot before he spoke again. 'We will need to begin preparations for phase three, as phase two hasn't been fully successful.'

'You mean us not finishing off Archios, don't you?' I said.

For the first time Chloe raised her head to stare at the phone in Dad's hand.

'What you managed to achieve was incredible,' Sentinel said. 'In the little time you had available, and against all the odds, you managed to stop a Shade invasion.'

Chloe's eyes became slits. 'But that murdering piece of shit Archios still got away from us.'

'Yes, but you've bought us precious time to create an army of Awoken.'

'An army? So Chloe and I are just the start after all?' I said.

'You are, but if Archios had been destroyed, there would have been no need to create further Awoken.'

'But, like you said before, needs must?' I said.

'Precisely, and now that line has been crossed I will Awaken thousands and thousands of suitable candidates, because, if one thing is certain in all of this, the Shade will try to invade your world again.'

Chloe peered at the phone. 'Will these other Awoken get any say in the matter – unlike Jake and me?'

'I wish I could give them the option, Chloe, but if the human race is to survive in this universe, we haven't got sufficient time to afford that luxury.'

She crossed her arms. 'So they get drafted for a war they don't even know is coming?'

'I understand what you're saying, but if we warned them, it might also alert the Shade. Then they would be targeted and almost certainly killed.'

'How exactly will you choose individuals to be Awoken then?' I asked.

'It needs to be someone twenty-five years old or younger, as it's important for the callosum region of the brain – an area of the highest-order latest neural networking – to be still growing, so it can be adapted. Any candidate will also need the same Awoken gene marker in their bodies that you both have. However, most importantly of all, they will need to have the right aptitude to become an Awoken soldier. Not everyone will have the strong character traits that you both hold.'

I still didn't like what I was hearing, but I could also understand where Sentinel was coming from. 'If my experience is anything to go by, they will be scared out of their wits by what's happening to them.'

Chloe threw her arms in the air. 'Exactly.'

'And this is where you can both help me.'

'How?' Chloe asked.

'By helping me create a programme called the Summoning. It will require significant computing resources, far more than I have had access to so far, but this is something I already have in hand. Right now there are hundreds of 3D printing studios and chip designers around the world producing individual components for something they think is a design test.'

'And what will these parts do when they are put together?' Dad asked.

'It will be the most powerful quantum computer in existence on your planet. And, Chloe, with your help, I would like to create a human interface using Ember, which will enable Jake and yourself to interact directly with it.'

She glowered towards the burning remains of the science park. 'Will it help me avenge my dad's death?'

'If you mean creating a tool that can help stop the Shade, then I suppose, in a way, yes it will.'

'Then I'm all over this.'

I caught the fire in Chloe's eyes. I was certain she could do it, but I knew she'd throw herself into this, whatever the cost. And that was something I was going to have to look out for: to stop her going too far.

Clarke strode back over to us. 'There's a military convoy on its way over here, so you need to make yourselves scarce fast.'

Two headlights lit up and the white Tesla, battered but still in working order, pulled up alongside us without anyone driving it.

'How?' Dad asked, looking at the car like it was haunted.

I shrugged. 'Sentinel's handiwork again.'

'When communications to you in the lab were cut I knew we would need transport and so I took the liberty of moving the Tesla when the radio frequencies cleared a moment before the lab blew up. So I'll be your chauffeur and will use the car's sensors to navigate us to the rendezvous point with Allan.'

'I'm still having problems getting my head around all of this stuff,' Dad said. 'Since when were AIs this smart?'

'In your time they weren't,' I said. 'But don't forget Sentinel is anything but a human AI, Dad.'

'Right.' He stuck out his hand to Clarke. 'Good luck, Inspector.'

Clarke shook Dad's hand. 'You too.' He turned to Chloe and me. 'I hope you can forgive an old policeman for his initial scepticism.'

'If it helps, I would have had a hard time believing us too,' I replied.

Clarke smiled. 'It does.'

Dad handed back Clarke's phone as we climbed into the Tesla. I raised my arm in farewell to the inspector. Would we ever see him again?

Dad stared as the steering wheel started turning by itself.

Chloe dragged her gaze away from the burning science park and curled up in the back seat, her head pressed against raised knees.

This was her time to grieve, and I knew it would be a long and painful journey. Right now, my instincts told me that what she needed was space.

Complete and utter exhaustion began rolling through me. By the time we pulled away my eyelids were already closed.

The yacht's prow cut smoothly through the calm sea as the gentle breeze billowed the large white sail. Overhead, stars shone out in the clear night sky. We'd been sailing for hours along the coast of England – in a constant easterly direction, according to the compass.

Six hours earlier in the late afternoon, Sentinel had driven us all the way to the small coastal port of Brixham on the south coast. It was there we'd met Allan who had a hefty laptop ready for Sentinel to transfer himself on to.

The moment Allan had seen Martin he'd hugged him like he was never going to let go. I couldn't stop smiling, but Chloe had barely reacted, lost in herself through all the tears and back slaps.

Allan had herded us along the dockside to a moored yacht called *Moon Dancer*, fresh from a refit, which was waiting for us.

Once on-board the fifty-foot boat, we started sailing towards our destination, the details of which Allan had refused to reveal, saying it would 'spoil the surprise'.

Now, I stood on deck, steering the boat on the heading Allan had shown me. I was under strict instructions to call him if I saw even a hint of another vessel crossing our path.

Chloe sat by herself at the prow. I more than understood the world of pain she was experiencing. I would give her plenty of time until she was ready to surface again.

I could hear Dad and Allan chatting away with Sentinel in *Moon Dancer*'s small cabin. I'd been down there while Chloe had taken over the helm for a bit, lost in the laughter, along with quite a few tears, as everyone started to come to terms with what had happened.

The cabin door opened and Dad appeared with two steaming mugs in his hands, his outline framed in the light from the cabin.

'Here you go, Jake. I thought you two would like some hot chocolate.'

'Thanks, Dad.' I took a careful sip of the hot drink. Dad gestured the other mug towards Chloe's back.

'I'll take it to her in a moment.'

'OK.' Dad placed it down next to me.

Dad and I gazed out together in silence as the waves sighed against the hull, only the navigation lights of a few large ships crossing the horizon slowly visible in the distance.

'I'm really going to miss him,' Dad finally said.

I didn't need to be able to hear his thoughts to know he was talking about Dave.

Not as much as Chloe, I thought to myself.

I looked at the back of the head of the woman who meant everything to me. Then I turned away towards the thin line of the English coastline, dotted with clusters of villages and town lights that glowed across the water in the darkness. So much life, so many people, none of whom realised how close they'd come to dying tonight.

Dad plucked his fingers on the safety rail cable like he was playing a guitar string. 'You do realise, Jake, that this is only the start of what we'll have to do to defend our world?'

I felt the enormity of the task press down on my shoulders, but I also knew that, when the time came, I'd do whatever we had to do to beat the Shade. 'Yes...and we will win this, Dad.'

The lights on the coast began to thin out. The white strip of cliffs that had been our companion for a while now seemed to be coming to an abrupt end. All that lay beyond that final cliff was open sea – and past that a group of islands in the far distance.

Allan appeared. 'Good, it won't be long until we're there. Once we've landed and all had a chance to catch our breath we can start to make plans. And you and Chloe need time to work out the extent of your Awoken abilities.'

'And how we can control them,' I added.

Dad nodded. 'And maybe we'll be able to offer sanctuary to these other Awoken that Sentinel plans to create.'

Other Awoken like us... Just how many people, out there right now, were destined to go through what we already had?

A lighthouse blinked ahead of us and Chloe glanced back at me.

I picked up the mug of hot chocolate and held it up for her to see. Despite her eyes glittering she gave me a slight smile and nodded.

I patted Dad's shoulder as he took over the steering and I headed up to join Chloe at the prow.

Without even looking at me Chloe took my hand in hers.

I pointed towards the island. 'And where is *there* exactly, Allan?' I called back over my shoulder.

Allan smiled. 'That's Alderney, one of the Channel Islands.'

Above us, *Moon Dancer*'s sails fluttered softly, and under the cover of darkness, we crossed the sea towards the island that would be our new home.

LINKS

Do please leave that all important review for **Fractured Light** here:
https://geni.us/FracturedLightAmazon

BOOK 2: Jake and Chloe return in the battle of light against dark in **Fading Light**. The Shade are coming, and only the Awoken can stand in their way.

Fading Light is available on Amazon here: http://geni.us/FadingLight

OTHER BOOKS BY NICK COOK

Prequel to the Multiverse Chronicles

The Earth Song Series (The Multiverse Chronicles)

The Fractured Light Trilogy (The Multiverse Chronicles)

AFTERWORD

I hope you enjoyed *Fractured Light* as much as I enjoyed writing it. If you have the time please do take a moment to leave a review. If you're wondering why this is so important, reviews are the best way to spread the word about a book. People are also much more likely to buy a book that have more reviews than just a few, so leaving a review is great help to me as an author. If you're reading on Kindle there will be a chance to leave a review straight after the prologue to *Fading Light* that's been included in this book, otherwise just head over to the Amazon page to leave one. Thank you so much for taking the time to do this.

So let's discuss *Fractured Light*. This book has been eleven years in the making; it was a concept that first arrived in my imagination in a very different form to the book you've just read. When I'd been working on the first draft of *Fractured Light* an idea for a new trilogy – a prequel to this series – crashed into my head and demanded to be written first. That became the *Cloud Riders* trilogy. After I completed the last book in that series, *Eye of the Storm*, I was itching to get back to *Fractured Light*.

However, by then I'd gained significant experience as a

writer, and when I revisited the manuscript I realised it would have to be totally overhauled. So I did exactly that, throwing away the original text and starting all over again. This is never easy for an author but it was the best decision I could have made.

I love epic tales and blame classic science fiction series, such as *Babylon 5* and the remake of *Battlestar Galactica*, for my fascination with the genre. *Fractured Light* is itself part of a much larger story arc. If you're interested in the backstory to the *Multiverse Chronicles* and the origin of Sentinel, give the *Cloud Riders* trilogy a spin.

I put a lot of research into *Fractured Light*, some of which never made it into the book. I conferred with a top quantum physicist about one major plot idea, but soon realised I was stretching scientific credibility to breaking point with that particular little gem. I jettisoned that whole plot line and reworked the concept until it fitted together in a way that wouldn't make physicists splutter out their coffee as they read the book! Saying that, this is still a story, and ultimately I have taken some liberties with the laws of the cosmos.

Sentinel as an artificial intelligence was a late addition to the *Fractured Light* universe. There is currently a huge debate about the future of AI. I feel positive about the role AI can play in the future of humanity and Sentinel reflects my philosophy. I wrote a blog article about this very issue on my website: Blog Article

Are you ready for the next book in the trilogy? If so, Fading Light is out now and you can buy on Amazon: http://geni.us/ FadingLight There is an extract on the next page you may want to read followed by that all important opportunity to leave a review.

Finally, I must give my thanks to Catherine Coe for her extraordinary editing skills and Jennie Roman for catching all those pesky proof errors. The fantastic front cover of Fractured Light is the work of the very talented Ryan Schwarz, such great work and I say that as a former games industry art director. Also, a big shout out to Rob Groves for making the audiobook version of this story a thing. For me as an author, it was truly amazing to hear my book come to life in this way.

If you'd like to keep up to date with the latest news about this trilogy, see exclusive cover reveals and get sneak peeks of the new books before anyone else, please subscribe to my newsletter. I also recruit ARC (advanced reader copies) readers from my subscribers who get to see my latest books before anyone else – so you have to be in it to win it. www.subscribepage.com/b4n4n4

If you would like to read my blog articles and watch my vlog, check out my main website here: www.nick-cook.net

Finally, I hope you'll follow me with future books in the *Multiverse Chronicles* series. The journey has only just begun.

PROLOGUE TO FADING LIGHT

Gemma Elliot stared at the shadows beyond the pool of illumination from her bedside light, which she never dared turn off now. The twenty-year-old let out a small breath of air as she clung to Raffles, her childhood thread-worn teddy bear, just as she had when she'd suffered from night terrors all those years ago. If only that was all this was.

The stillness grew deeper around her.

Outside in the far distance, a church clock chimed. Gemma counted the final notes of the solitary bell. Ten, eleven, twelve...

The last chime vibrated to stillness on the night air. She held her breath and hugged Raffles harder.

She wiped her hand across her forehead, but it was cool. So this wasn't a fever related to her catching the Zoom virus a couple of months ago, named because of its rapid spread around the world via airline passengers. Now many people kept off the streets or at least took the precaution of wearing face masks, if they did venture out. Yes, the last six months had been surreal for everyone, but for Gemma more than most...

She gazed around at her childhood bedroom. She still

couldn't quite believe she'd ended up dropping out of uni and moved back home with her parents. But she hadn't had a lot of choice after her spiral into madness. Coming home was her last-ditch attempt to hang on to the remaining fragments of her sanity.

Her curtains fluttered, even though the window was shut fast. She felt an icy breath on her cheek as the bedside light flickered off and plunged the room into choking blackness.

She squeezed her eyes shut, her heart racing. 'Leave me alone,' Gemma whispered into the darkness, even though she knew it wouldn't do any good. Justin, the nickname she'd given the monster so as to downplay it, had a mind of its own.

The silence grew heavy as the air pressed in on her from every side.

Then it began as it always did...

A scratching sound squealed across her attic-bedroom window, just as it had first done in Gemma's uni hall of residence. The blood roared in her ears and she buried her head under her pillow, trying to shut out the noise.

The window rattled as Justin tried to get in.

This isn't real, isn't real, she repeated in her head, as Mum had taught her. An NHS nurse, she was now seriously overworked thanks to the Zoom virus. There'd been hundreds of fatalities, particularly among the elderly and infirm. Gemma curled into a foetal position as cold sweat soaked through her PJs.

With a crash, sparkling glass shards flew inwards as the window shattered. A terrible wind roared in and ripped the duvet from her body. She gripped on to the sides of her bed, watching childhood dolls fly from their shelves out into the gaping mouth of the dark whirlwind that roared beyond her window.

Justin began to form, a ghostly, horned demon. He stepped forward to look down at her in bed, there but not there, not much more than a thickness in the air. With a rattle, the bed began to pitch beneath her like a wild horse trying to escape from this horror.

'Go away!' Gemma screamed at the phantom towering over her bed.

Justin reached out his long, dark, gnarled fingers towards her.

She tried to scream, but her voice was trapped deep inside her throat.

Footsteps pounded from the landing. Gemma's bedroom door burst open. Mum and Dad rushed in. Heads down, they fought through the wind.

Mum grabbed on to Gemma's hand, her expression several degrees above frightened.

'Leave Gem alone!' her dad shouted at the monster neither of them could actually see.

With a roar of air, Justin shimmered and vanished. Gemma's hair continued to swirl about her head as the wild wind ripped her tears away.

'Steve, the window!' Mum cried out.

Dad edged his way forward through the gale as the curtains streamed straight out, flowing in rags towards the gaping mouth of the black whirlpool outside.

Mum wrapped her arms round Gem as they watched Dad brace himself against the edge of the bay window. He reached into the teeth of the gale and unlatched the two Victorian shutters at the sides of the windows. They slammed shut and he threw the bolts across, leaning against them as they bucked and rattled under his hands.

Gemma pressed herself into her mother's warmth, breathing in the hint of cooking spice on her skin. Her love and the safety of her encircling arms made her feel like a young child again.

'Breathe, Gem, breathe,' Mum said.

Gemma gulped in air.

Mum stroked Gemma's hair. 'Slowly...'

Gemma steadied her breathing and gradually the icy grip of fear loosened around her heart. The roar of the wind died away and, with a sigh, the faint murmur of London night-time traffic returned.

Mum gripped Gemma's face. 'Is it over, my love?'

Gemma pulled her sweat-soaked hair away from her eyes and looked inside herself. The feeling of dread had disappeared.

'I think so—' She broke off as the table light flickered back on and she felt her mum lurch against her. She cradled her hand and added, 'Yes, Justin's gone.'

Dad sank on to the end of her bed, breathing hard. 'We can't take any more of this, Sarah. We need to get help.'

'Not this conversation again,' Mum replied.

Gemma bit her lip. 'Dad's right. Whatever Justin is, he's getting stronger. This has already gone too far. I'm way beyond scared about what he might do next.'

Mum's eyes locked with Dad's. 'Are you sure, Gem? Really sure, I mean?'

Gemma wiped away the tear that had begun to roll down her mum's face. 'Yes, I am.'

Her mum let out a half-stifled sob, nodded and kissed Gemma's forehead.

'I'll call Father Collins in the morning,' Dad said. He looked at the closed shutters and the remains of Gemma's doll collection, now strewn on the floor. 'I don't know about either of you, but I need a stiff drink.'

'I don't think I could handle anything stronger than tea at the moment,' Gemma said.

'I'm with you on that one,' Mum replied. 'Come on, let's go and put the kettle on.'

'And tomorrow we'll get that window fixed up as good as

new,' Dad said, practical as always, seeing this as just a building problem to be solved.

If only.

But as Gemma swung her legs out of bed and stood up Dad crossed to her and hugged her hard. There were no words – what could anyone say about what had just happened? All Gemma could do was hang on to the people she loved.

She watched the young girl and her dad fly their kite next to them. As it soared up into the blue sky, Gemma took deep breaths of the cold air, chasing away the dark cobwebs of the previous night. Things were already feeling a bit better. The more she'd talked to Father Mathews, the more the weight pressing down on her lifted. He'd come came as soon as Dad called the next morning. Their usual priest was unavailable, so Father Mathews rushed over in his place. She'd left Mum and Dad at home and gone for a walk on the heath, for some fresh air. She guessed he wanted to talk to her alone, without her parents' well-meaning interruptions. And he'd turned out to be a good listener – not interrupting, and giving her sympathetic looks at all the right moments.

The priest sat next to her on the bench as kites traced dashes of colour over Parliament Hill.

'It's a good flyer, isn't it?' the priest said as he cupped his hand to gaze up at the young girl's red kite. It shone like a brilliant ruby in the sky.

Gemma nodded. 'Dad used to bring me up here to fly kites, when I was a child.'

'Happy times, no doubt.'

'Very.'

With a moan, the wind became blustery and the young girl squealed as her kite threatened to tear the handle from her hand. The dad grabbed it, leaning back as the wind howled harder.

Below them at the foot of Parliament Hill, a vast bank of fog had appeared and began to creep up towards them. One by one, the houses and trees were swallowed by it. Gemma frowned. She wasn't a weather expert, but she knew it was too windy for fog to form, especially in the middle of what was meant to be summer. Global warming was getting seriously weird.

The wind strengthened to a full-blown gale. As clouds rolled in overhead, the numerous kite flyers began to leave. The panorama of the city had already become a steely grey band through the building gloom.

'We should get going like everybody else,' she said.

Father Mathews just smiled back at her. 'But why rush, Gemma?'

'Because we're about to get swept off Hampstead Heath by this hurricane!?'

'Oh, you shouldn't worry about that, Gemma. And look, here comes a good friend of mine. You're going to like Gavin.' The priest raised a hand to greet a tall teenager with a broad build striding towards them ahead of the rolling fog bank.

A nagging worry coiled inside her. Gemma pulled the hood of her uni fleece over her head and stood up. 'I'd better get home, Father Mathews.'

The priest's smile became more fixed. 'I'm sorry, but that won't be possible, Gemma.'

The scent of the priest's aftershave filled her nose with its sickly sweetness, but there was a strange aroma just beneath it too. 'No, it isn't safe in this wind. Let's go.' Over his shoulder, she spotted her parents with an older man she didn't know running up the other side of Parliament Hill.

She waved and started towards them.

But Father Mathews's hand appeared on her shoulder, holding her back. 'I'm sorry, Gemma, but you have to come with us for your own safety.'

She clenched her fists and turned towards him. 'OK, you're starting to seriously freak me out now.'

He gave her a tight smile, tore his dog collar off and threw it on to the ground.

'You need to relax, Gemma, and this will go much more easily for you.'

She tried to pull away from him, but his fingers bit into her shoulder. She shoved Mathews hard against his sternum, but it was like pushing against a massive boulder. For an old guy, he was stupidly strong.

A pulse of real fear shot through her and she started to struggle. 'Just let me bloody go.'

'That's simply not going to happen.'

Gavin reached them and stared at Mathews. 'Where's Archios?' Gavin asked.

'He's moved on to our main plan and has left me to conclude this operation.'

The teenager nodded. 'All right. What are your orders?'

'Gemma is weakened, but we must act quickly and take her before her parents can help her.'

She stared between them. Although Gemma didn't understand their words, she could see the hardness in their eyes. Fear knotted inside her.

Her parents and the stranger rushed towards them waving their arms.

Mathews raised his chin at them. 'You need to buy me a little bit of time, Gavin.'

A twisted smile spread across the teenager's face. 'It will be my pleasure.' He fixed his grey eyes on the closing group.

Cold horror spun through Gemma as the teenager's body began to ripple as if it were made of clay. The world around them became darker and full of swirling shadows. Then Gavin's body broke apart and dissolved into a cloud of flowing darting crow shapes like a special effect in a movie. The shapes spun and spiralled, knotting together into a new form. A flickering black wolf stood where the teenager had been, massive and terrible, with pointed black teeth and grey staring eyes.

Gemma managed to keep her scream from bubbling up as her mind scrambled to make sense of what she was seeing.

The wolf howled and charged at her parents and the man.

Gemma whirled round to Mathews. 'Please, don't let him hurt them!'

But he'd become as still as a statue. Then, with a clatter of wings, he broke apart too, into hundreds more of the darting shadowy birds.

Gemma tried to cry out as the shapes swirled about her, but the bird creatures swept tight round her chest, choking the air out of her lungs. She felt her feet lift from the ground.

A crackling noise rang out. Between the darting shapes, Gemma caught sight of the stranger beside her parents firing a taser at the wolf. The electrodes buried themselves into the creature and the wolf sprawled to the ground. It simply snapped at the projectiles, ripping them out as the birds took her higher into the sky.

Mum and Dad stared up at Gemma, their mouths hanging open. The man fumbled to reload the taser as the wolf gathered itself and charged again. She didn't see what happened next, the view swirling away behind the curtain of shadowy crows.

But she heard it.

A woman's sharp shriek, full of fear, coming from somewhere beneath her...

'Mum!' she cried out.

A man's awful twisted scream...

'Dad, no!'

The crows squeezed against Gemma. Just for a moment, she saw a ruby kite framed against the dwindling patch of blue above.

Then the dark clouds ate it and the world turned to flecked granite. She was helpless as the darting black shapes carried her even higher, their darkness reaching into her and extinguishing her thoughts.

To continue the story, buy Fading Light, the next volume in the trilogy, here, but do please leave that review first on the next page before you go: http://geni.us/FadingLight

Made in the USA
Columbia, SC
14 April 2023

15357145R00240